Sublime Subjects

Sublime Subjects explores two fundamental questions: what is the start of humanity? When and how does a newborn child become a subject? These are relevant to psychoanalysis not only theoretically, but also in clinical practice, where the issue at stake is how to help the analysand's mind to grow or, better, to increase the ability to give a meaning to experience.

Giuseppe Civitarese here argues that the psychoanalytic theory of sublimation and the aesthetic theory of the sublime are theories of subjectivation that can illuminate each other and give us a better understanding of the birth of the psyche. The aesthetic experience in art and in psychoanalytic practice are concerned with the social constitution of the individual, understood at its pre-reflective, non-verbal or inter-corporeal level. It is at this level that, thanks to the encounter with a receptive other, the turbulences of sensations and proto-emotions become soothing rhythms, proto-ideas or sensible ideas at first and, once words are added, concepts.

In Bionian terms, the *at-one-ment* between mother and baby is *a form of primordial abstraction* and occurs first in the dimension of the purely sensory and indistinct, and then in the affective space, which nonetheless is always a symbolic space if we take account that sociality is provided for the couple-system by the mother. It is exactly the intersubjective process of elevating towards conceptual thinking, but without ever detaching oneself from the thinking deposited in the body as procedural knowledge, that justifies the definition adopted here of human beings as *Sublime Subjects*.

This book explores these topics not only through the lens of the concept of sublimation or the theory of the sublime, but also through those of masochism, hypochondria, truth and two readings of classical Freudian papers such as the clinical case of Dora and 'Formulations on the two principles of mental functioning'. *Sublime Subjects* will appeal to psychoanalysts and psychoanalytic psychotherapists, as well as literature and philosophy scholars.

Giuseppe Civitarese, MD, PhD, is a training and supervising analyst of the Italian Psychoanalytic Society (SPI). Previous work includes, *The Intimate Room: Theory and Technique of the Analytic Field*, *The Violence of Emotions: Bion and post-Bionian Psychoanalysis*, *Truth and the Unconscious in Psychoanalysis* and, as editor, *Bion and Contemporary Psychoanalysis: Reading 'A Memoir of the Future'*.

The New Library of Psychoanalysis
'Beyond the Couch' Series
General Editor: Alessandra Lemma

The New Library of Psychoanalysis was launched in 1987 in association with the Institute of Psychoanalysis, London. It aims to promote a widespread appreciation of psychoanalysis by supporting interdisciplinary dialogues with those working in the social sciences, the arts, medicine, psychology, psychotherapy, philosophy and with the general book reading public.

The *Beyond the Couch* part of the series creates a forum dedicated to demonstrating this wider application of psychoanalytic ideas. These books, written primarily by psychoanalysts, specifically address the important contribution of psychoanalysis to contemporary intellectual, social and scientific debate.

For a full list of all the titles in the New Library of Psychoanalysis main series and also the New Library of Psychoanalysis teaching series, please visit the Routledge website.

TITLES IN THE 'BEYOND THE COUCH' SERIES:

Under the Skin: A Psychoanalytic Study of Body Modification *Alessandra Lemma*

Engaging with Climate Change: Psychoanalytic and Interdisciplinary Perspectives *Edited by Sally Weintrobe*

Research on the Couch: Single Case Studies, Subjectivity, and Psychoanalytic Knowledge *R.D. Hinshelwood*

Psychoanalysis in the Technoculture Era *Edited by Alessandra Lemma and Luigi Caparrotta*

Moving Images: Psychoanalytic Reflections on Film *Andrea Sabbadini*

Reflections on the Aesthetic Experience: Psychoanalysis and the Uncanny *Gregorio Kohon*

Psychoanalysis in the Age of Totalitarianism *Edited by Matt ffytche and Daniel Pick*

Sublime Subjects: Aesthetic Experience and Intersubjectivity in Psychoanalysis *Giuseppe Civitarese*

Sublime Subjects

Aesthetic Experience and Intersubjectivity in Psychoanalysis

Giuseppe Civitarese

Routledge
Taylor & Francis Group
LONDON AND NEW YORK

First published 2018
by Routledge
2 Park Square, Milton Park, Abingdon, Oxon OX14 4RN

and by Routledge
711 Third Avenue, New York 10017

Routledge is an imprint of the Taylor & Francis Group, an informa business

Translated into English by Adam Elgar

British Library Cataloguing in Publication Data
A catalogue record for this book is available from the British Library

Library of Congress Cataloging in Publication Data
A catalog record for this book has been requested

ISBN: 978-1-138-50524-7 (hbk)
ISBN: 978-1-138-50525-4 (pbk)
ISBN: 978-1-315-14646-1 (ebk)

Typeset in Times New Roman and Gill Sans
by Florence Production Ltd, Stoodleigh, Devon, UK

For my Father

Contents

Acknowledgements

I would like to thank the journals and publishers for permission to use the following papers in this volume:

Chapter 1 first published as 'Bion and the sublime: The origins of an aesthetic paradigm', *International Journal of Psychoanalysis*, 95, 1059–1086, 2014. Reprinted by permission of the journal and John Wiley & Sons, Inc.

Chapter 2 first published as 'On sublimation', *International Journal of Psychoanalysis*, 97, 1369–1392, 2016. Reprinted by permission of the journal and John Wiley & Sons, Inc.

Chapter 3 first published 'Masochism and its rhythm', *Journal of the American Psychoanalytic Association*, 64, 885–916, 2016. Reprinted by permission of Sage Publications Ltd.

Chapter 4 first published in Italian as 'Vortici, ritmi, idee: Esperienza estetica e costituzione intersoggettiva dell'individuo', *Rivista di Psicoanalisi*, 62, 987–984, 2016. Reprinted and translated by permission of the journal.

Chapter 5 first published as 'L'ipocondria e le politiche del narcisismo', in M Breccia (ed.), *Narciso e gli altri*, Alpes, Roma, 2014, pp. 73–82. Reprinted by permission of Alpes Italia SRL.

Chapter 6 first published as 'I poscritti di Dora', *Rivista di Psicoanalisi*, 61, 665–683, 2015. This chapter was translated by Philip Slotkin. Reprinted and translated by permission of the journal.

Chapter 7 first published as 'Where does the reality principle begin? The work of margins in Freud's *Formulations on the Two Principles of Mental Functioning*, in L Brown and G Legorreta (eds), *Formulations on the Two Principles of Mental Functioning*. IPA, Karnac, London, pp. 107–125, 2016. Reprinted by permission of Karnac Books, Ltd.

Chapter 8 first published as 'Truth as immediacy and unison: a new "common ground" in psychoanalysis? Commentary on essays addressing "Is truth relevant?"' *The Psychoanalytic Quarterly*, 85, 449–501, 2016. Reprinted by permission of John Wiley & Sons, Inc. This chapter was translated by Gina Atkinson.

Introduction

Psychoanalysis obtains its idea of therapeutic action from models that describe the birth and development of the psyche. The idea around which the various essays in this book revolve is the concept of the 'sublime', both in the field of aesthetics – beginning with the eponymous treatise of the Pseudo-Longinus, and moving all the way to Kant and Lyotard – and in psychoanalysis, where it becomes interwoven with the concept of sublimation, and may help to hone further the now broadly shared conception of the social or intersubjective constitution of the individual. My principal thesis is that both the aesthetic theory of the sublime and that of sublimation can be read as theories of subjectivation, or rather of how a mind is formed and how we become human. For this reason, we can say that human beings are 'sublime subjects'.

The adjective 'sublime' normally describes the aesthetic feeling (in the sense of *aísthesis*, or 'sensation') of elevating oneself in the presence of a spectacle which exceeds the common parameters of the beautiful. There is, in addition, the idea that the experience is in itself ineffable – that is, unsayable in words. From a psychoanalytic perspective it is easy to translate this experience in terms of a feeling of unison or *at-one-ment* with the object. This happy encounter is achieved, as can easily be seen in many paintings of the Romantic era, when an ideal distance is reached, sheltering us from the threat represented alternatively by the absence of the object, or by its excessive presence.

From a metapsychological viewpoint, the upward direction indicated by the term 'sublime' corresponds to the movement which leads from proto-sensations and proto-emotions, what Bion calls beta elements, to representations or alpha elements, and hence to concepts and thoughts, whether in dream or waking. And indeed in this author – perhaps of all authors the one who has, overall, the most intersubjective vision of the psyche's origins – several themes of the aesthetic of the sublime can be found, absorbed through the medium of literature from the Romantic period.

In fact, in constructing his theory Bion drew on a number of symbolic matrices: psychoanalysis, philosophy, mathematics, literature and aesthetics. The least investigated of these is the last. True, we know that he cites many authors of the Romantic period, such as Coleridge, Keats, Blake and Wordsworth, as well as others who were held in high esteem in the Romantic period, such as Milton. However, less is known about the influence exerted on him by the aesthetics of the sublime, which while chronologically preceding Romanticism is in fact one of its components. My working hypothesis is that tracing a number of Bion's concepts back to this secret model can serve several purposes: first, it contributes to the study of the sources, and, second, it makes these concepts appear much less occasional and idiosyncratic than we might believe, being as they are mostly those less immediately understandable but not less important (O, Negative Capability, nameless dread, the infinite, the language of achievement, unison, etc.). Finally, connecting these notions to a matrix, that is, disclosing the meaning of elements that are not simply juxtaposed but dynamically interrelated, in my view significantly increases not only their theoretical intelligibility but also their usefulness in clinical practice. In conclusion, one could legitimately argue that Bion gradually subsumed all the other paradigms he drew on within the aesthetic paradigm.

Having explored the theme of the sublime in Bion, I move on in Chapter 2 to revisit the Freudian and post-Freudian theory of sublimation in the light of the new paradigm which Bion inaugurates in psychoanalysis, and which can be called aesthetic in that he puts emotion at the centre of its theoretical elaboration. Although it encapsulates the Freudian theory of art, the theory of sublimation has become outmoded. What is more, since its inception there has always been something ill-defined about it. Does sublimation use sexualized or desexualized drive energy? Is it a defence or an alternative to defence? Does it serve Eros or Thanatos? Is it useful in clinical work or is it unusable? The only, albeit uncertain, aid to a definition relies on the extrinsic criterion of concrete artistic realization. My aim here to revisit and possibly 'reinvent' sublimation in the light of certain principles of the pre-Romantic aesthetics of the sublime. Both are theories of spiritual elevation, in other words, elevation that moves towards abstract thinking, and of man's 'moral' achievement; and both attempt to explain the mystery of aesthetic experience. On the one hand, the aesthetics of the sublime offers a modern myth that helps us articulate a series of factors occasionally referred to by various authors as constitutive of sublimation but which have not been incorporated into a single organic framework: loss and early mourning work; the earlier existence of a catastrophic factor – to be regarded, depending on the situation, as either traumatic or simply 'negative'; the correspondence of subjectivation with a process of somato-psychic categorization. On the other hand, it also helps us grasp the experience of negative pleasure empathically, living it 'from the inside'.

In Chapter 3, 'Masochism and its rhythm', I venture onto the terrain of pathology in order to try and make a reciprocally illuminating comparison between, on the one hand, the 'negative' pleasure inherent in aesthetic experience of the sublime and the process of sublimation, and on the other hand the 'pleasure of pain' which we encounter along the spectrum of masochistic disturbances. Over five years, from 1919 to 1924, Freud dealt with masochism in three texts written in close proximity: 'A child is being beaten', *Beyond the Pleasure Principle*, and 'The economic problem of masochism'. Initially Freud explains masochism as incestuous fixation on the father and regression to pre-genital, sadistic ways of loving. Subsequently he considers it primarily as subservient to the death drive. This chapter starts from an idea present in two of the three texts, but not developed by Freud, in which he refers to the role that the 'qualitative' element of rhythm could play in the occurrence of pleasure in masochism. In this element – this is my hypothesis – traumatic aspects of the primary relationship with the object could be stored as fantasies in the body. In any staged masochistic fantasies of being beaten or in masochistic perversion, the pleasure of pain would lie in the attempt to 'dream' the trauma not only in the imagination but also, 'aesthetically', in the body. What is manifested as pure repetition in perverse pathology would then be the failure of the process which forms a 'concept' of the traumatic experiences suffered in earlier stages of life.

Secondary masochism becomes the specific narrative of a trauma which has intervened in the primary relationship with the object. In its violence and exemplary character, it makes us realize how primary masochism is nevertheless nesting unseen in representation. The negative pleasure of representation is in effect not negative. It is a 'different' pleasure, the pleasure of representation, but we could also say of subjectivation or sublimatory emancipation implicit in becoming a person. The negative is only the prelude, or rather the simultaneous correlative. Indeed, we should not confuse the trauma with the *mise-en-scène* (although all the 'feelings of trauma' which have not yet arrived at a satisfaction that is rendered aesthetic can be seen as partial re-traumatizations). The pure negative connotes only the unrepresentable trauma.

The essential rhythm of masochism, which is that of a dramatic alteration of a healthy rhythm of the object's absence/presence, is the same intrinsically masochistic but normal rhythm of symbolization, representation and aesthetic experience. Every pleasure is negative because every pleasure – though at this point it is a pleasure that coincides with the pleasure of being – arises along the axis that runs from fear to anxiety. Even when it is beautiful and pleasurable it still carries the sign of absence. Names, representations, works of art are similar in this. They all celebrate this passage, which does not fill the emptiness of being but renders it tolerable. The pleasure therefore lies essentially in this passage, which is concerned above all with the aesthetic/rhythmic plane of experience. *Primary* masochism could consist in this.

Chapter 4 is concerned with the search for figures and metaphors that may be effective in helping us to represent the paradoxes of psychic birth. From Benjamin and Agamben, I take the figure of the *whirlpool* as the image which describes an early organizing of forms in the body, beginning with a primary sensoriality in a medium to which it continues to belong. I then introduce some suggestions which may help us to think about further transitions towards *rhythms* – there is an obvious link here with the subject of the previous chapter – and finally towards *ideas*. The point at issue is the passing from sensations, which are tied to reality, to concepts which allow us to detach ourselves from sensations as far as possible: in other words, the relationship between sensoriality and ideation (a classical theme of philosophy too), and ultimately between personalization and depersonalization. Indeed, as Bion often quotes Kant saying, thoughts without content are empty, while intuitions without concepts are blind.

Chapter 5 takes up and develops the subject of the previous one: that is, the intersubjective constitution of the individual, starting from the Freudian concept of narcissism and the very common pathology of hypochondria. The crisis of the lived-in body, to which we give the name hypochondria, lends itself well to illustrating how the body that engages with psychoanalysis is a body 'written' by society: that is, the depository of relational inscriptions – enigmatic sexual messages (Laplanche) or unconscious fantasies transmitted to the infant by the object (Gaddini) – which powerfully condition its functioning. The merciless and obsessive investigation undertaken by the hypochondriac into his body's illness is actually the symptom of a crisis in the intersubjective matrix or semiotic *chora* (Kristeva) or of contiguous–autistic relating (Ogden) which nourishes a sane narcissism and founds the Ego.

As far as writing in concerned, we can say that it has relevance for psychoanalysis not only as 'writing' in or on the body, but also in the literal sense. If we have a radically social, trans-individual or 'linguistic' vision of the unconscious and of subjectivity, it follows that the links between the two types of writing are even closer than we could have thought. Freud's case histories, as we know, can be read as novellas. Moreover, the understanding of the psychic which has been achieved by the great authors of psychoanalysis is also expressed in their pages 'aesthetically' and not only conceptually. This is what justifies the inclusion of a chapter (6) on the most classic of Freud's cases, *Dora*.

Re-reading *Dora* today is perhaps meaningful in creative terms, rather than as an aspiration to compete with Freud by adopting the approach of a detective with a view to deciphering what he is considered to have been unable to decipher. I take the view, on the other hand, that what is most important in this text is the unfolding of indications that anticipate the future, of which he draws attention to at least three. First and foremost is an aspect against which Freud vigorously defends himself – namely, the fictional narrative structure of the clinical account – which today is seen, conversely, as extraordinarily in tune with the *Zeitgeist*, given that the most appropriate epistemological framework for present-day psychoanalysis is the non-positivistic, postmodern approach, within which the Freudian logic of *Nachträglichkeit* operates. Second, I stress the significance of the person of the analyst in analysis; and lastly, I discusses the importance in the text of the image of Raphael's *Madonna* in developing the concept of emotional unison, 'recognition' or *at-one-ment* as a key therapeutic factor in the treatment.

Chapter 7 again interweaves the theme of writing in analysis and that of the inscribing of sociality in the lived-in body, beginning with a re-reading of *Formulations on the two Principles of Mental Functioning*, one of Freud's best known essays and certainly the one that most inspired Bion. Wondering when the reality principle is established in the subject is the same as investigating the process by which the psyche becomes settled in the body. My interpretation focuses on the rhetorical organization of the text, and addresses in particular the famous footnote in which Freud states explicitly that he has adopted the model of an isolated psychic system, and shows himself to be aware of the limitations of this theoretical move. Indeed, he speaks about it as an inevitable fiction, but as a fiction nonetheless, that of a child developing 'autistically', as it were, like a bird enclosed in the shell of its 'egg'. The note can be read as the return of theoretical elements that had been repressed in Freudian theory. This repression will be the starting point for Winnicott and Bion in re-founding psychoanalysis on the ground of the relationship, and in – so to speak – maintaining that the reality principle is born in the intermediate space of intersubjectivity. Nevertheless, it must be said that Freud himself in some ways forecasts these future developments.

The concluding Chapter (8) addresses the theme of truth's role in psychoanalysis. The text develops as a comment on some contributions by other authors representing the main currents in contemporary psychoanalysis which, at Jay Greenberg's prompting, appeared with mine in *Psychoanalytic Quarterly* in 2016. So ideally these papers, that are very easily accessible, should be read first. On the other hand, the inclusion of this chapter here is justified by the fact that it has its own autonomy, as it tries to develop a particular view on the topic of truth in psychoanalysis from the point of view of the concept of phenomenological method of observation – the so called *epochè*. What I seek to argue is that truth, as inflected on a variety of levels, is always at the centre of psychoanalytic discourse. I try, furthermore, to provide a unifying frame within which to depict these various levels; a frame that would also offer the possibility of identifying a new common ground for psychoanalysis: indeed, I consider the method adopted by the principal psychoanalytic models along the same lines as the phenomenological or transcendental turn introduced into philosophy by Husserl, based on his motto which invites us to go back to things. What do I mean by this? That all psychoanalytic models exercise a centripetal attraction on the elements of analytic discourse, even the most concrete ones, those apparently extraneous to the analytic setting; or to put it another way, by using the conceptual device of the unconscious they bring everything back to the here and now of the present relationship. The guarantors of truth in psychoanalysis would be the principles of immediacy and unison.

In this connection, the differences between models, beginning with the various nuances of the way in which psychic functioning is theorized, concern the radical nature of this '*epoché*', to use the term current in speculative thought. The extreme point of this way of keeping truth at the centre of the scene is the Bionian definition of 'truth drive' and of truth as 'food for the mind'. But now the circle closes: what 'lifts' us into becoming subjects is truth based on the 'understanding' of which Freud speaks in the *Project*; in other words, on unison/*at-one-ment* or on the human capacity for cooperative interaction (Tomasello). We are 'sublime' subjects because we are capable of attaining shared truths; obviously not only the conceptual kind of truth, even though the haven of the concept represents the greatest and necessary extension of this process, but also truths that are affective, pre-categorical and semiotic.

If there are also truths like these, then this is how aesthetic experience lived through the enjoyment of art, and especially art inspired by the principles of the sublime, enables us to comprehend these concepts experientially, and not only via an abstract route, as in aesthetic or psychoanalytic theorizing. In the end we manage to glimpse a sort of unitary state in the foundations of the psychic, which in the various contexts of knowledge, exercises its ingenuity, so to speak, in obsessively investigating itself and the conditions of its appearance and evolution. This demonstrates all the profundity of the Keatsian intuition that equates truth with beauty.

One final note is needed as I present this book to the reader. Theoretical discussion predominates in it, and there is little or no space for clinical material, but all its contents are firmly aimed at clarifying the meaning of our practical activity, of treatment and the alleviation of psychic suffering. The implications for practice should be taken for granted. What is outlined in the book is the need for technical elaborations that are more consonant with the theoretical premises presented, since we acknowledge as established the model of the psyche's birth and development which they draw. I am obviously referring to the necessity for achieving a definitive transition, to use the words of Luciana Nissim Momigliano, from listening with a 'suspicious' attitude to the patient to listening with respect, and from an archaeologico–evidential paradigm to an aesthetic–relational paradigm, one that also respects the reasons and discourse of the body.

Chapter 1

Bion and the sublime: the origins of an aesthetic paradigm

A psychoanalysis (of the) sublime

> Auch das Schöne muß sterben![1]
>
> F. Schiller

Bion's work is a resounding example of intertextuality.[2] It makes recourse to a multiplicity of thematic and methodological premises that enable him to open up new fields of experience and to produce surprising constellations of meaning. Hence some of these concepts can give the impression of being heterogeneous and accidental. However, close retrospective examination reveals that they belong to precise symbolic matrices. In this study I shall dwell on one of these matrices: in the slipstream of Carlo Ginzburg (1979), who highlighted the existence of the evidential paradigm in Freud, I shall discuss the possible role of the aesthetic paradigm in Bion.[3]

More particularly I propose to investigate the influence exercised on him by the pre-Romantic and Romantic aesthetics of the sublime, an influence whose most interesting aspects remain unexplored if we generally limit ourselves to examining writers who are contemporary with those whom he most often cites in his books. The hypothesis I shall advance is that some key concepts of Bion's theory may be attributable to the subterranean action of certain principles in this aesthetic. In other words, I maintain that the aesthetic concept of the sublime is a fundamental theoretical operator in Bion's thought. Behind his inspired creativity there would have been at work a tradition that opens out in various directions and stamps an order on the otherwise chaotic variety of his novel ideas. This also means that the frequent quotations from Romantic authors in his work would not be factitious or merely decorative but would reflect an intimate necessity.

Apart from Kant, we do not know how much Bion read and studied the literature to which I refer here. Nevertheless, it would be justifiable to use the sublime as a lens for reading Bion even if we had no interest in demonstrating some direct relationship with the concept; that is, one not mediated by poets and novelists. In any case, there is overwhelming evidence of the weight which the Romantic authors – if not the theorists – bring to bear on his thought. Thinking only of Milton, a Romantic author *après-coup*, so to speak, we may say that the adjective 'Miltonic' is in itself synonymous with 'sublime' (Sertoli, 2002, p. 14).

However, my intention is not so much to work on the sources, as to highlight the greater theoretical coherence of a set of key concepts in Bion's thought by holding their watermark up to the light, and revealing them as an implicit part of a complete aesthetic programme. Therefore, my analysis will not address authors, except indirectly, but the paradigm itself: in other words, style and concepts. It should also be said that, in terms of extent through time and space, and because of the complexity of the literature on the sublime and of Bion's own writing, my contribution may be considered only as preliminary to a more systematic study.

There is nothing on this subject in the psychoanalytic literature, if we except the 1982 paper by the American critic Harold Bloom entitled *Freud and the sublime: a catastrophe theory of creativity*. We do however have works by Harris Williams (2010a, 2010b)[4] and Torres and Hinshelwood (2013). The first of these sets out the exhaustive synoptic framework of the authors by whom Bion is miscellaneously inspired, and also tries to trace the precise derivation of various concepts. The second investigates the influence of Romantic poetry, above all on his autobiographical works. The anthology edited by Torres and Hinshelwood principally assesses the impact on him of other analysts and philosophers. There is also a chapter on aesthetics but it contains no hint of the sublime as a theme.

The critical work that I propose here is more necessary for Bion than for other writers, and in fact more rewarding. The reason lies in the revolutionary nature of some of his formulations, which nevertheless frequently arouse feelings of perplexity and even provoke outright rejection. If we do not make the effort to shed some light on them, we run the risk of simply disregarding them, of seeing them as tending to weirdness, or at least of not taking in their full richness and generative power. The advantage of reading his ideas against a background of the aesthetic of the sublime is that this already has a theoretical foundation (it is a psychology), which is not something we can say of the literary authors of the Romantic tradition in general.

A by no means exhaustive list of principal concepts that in my opinion can be traced back to the paradigm of the sublime would include Negative Capability, Language of Achievement, Faith, Madness, Genius, Infinity, Mystic, No-thing, Night, Noughtness, O, Passion, Without Memory and Desire, Suffering, Mathematical Sublime, Nameless Dread, Stupor, Tiger and so on. However, before reviewing a few of these, it is necessary to recall some general notions about the aesthetic of the sublime.

The aesthetic of the sublime from Longinus to Kant

The aesthetic of the sublime established itself in Europe in 1674 with Nicolas Boileau's translation of the treatise *On the Sublime* [*Perì hìpsous*], written between the end of the first century BCE and the first decades of the next. An earlier translation into English in fact went wholly unnoticed. Discovered in 1554 and first printed in Basel by Francesco Robortello, the treatise was erroneously attributed to Longinus, as a result of which it is often called the Pseudo-Longinus. Passionately discussed and universally admired throughout the eighteenth century, this essay on aesthetics, rhetoric and literary criticism is a source for texts by Edmund Burke (1756a, *A Philosophical Enquiry into Our Ideas of the Sublime and the Beautiful*), Immanuel Kant (1763–64, *Observations on the Feeling of the Beautiful and the Sublime*) and the 'Analytic of the sublime' contained in the *Critique of Judgement* (Kant, 1790) and Friedrich Schiller (1793a, *Of the Sublime*), which inaugurate the Romantic period.

The treatise by Longinus gives as examples of the sublime in art the silence of Ajax in Book XI of the *Odyssey*, Sappho's 'Ode to Jealousy', various moments from the *Iliad*, passages from works by Aeschylus and Euripides; in the Romantic period there are the poems of Hölderlin and Leopardi; the paintings of Turner, Friedrich, Blechen and Schinkel; Piranesi's drawings; the Gothic novel as a whole; Coleridge, Shelley – and also Mary Shelley! – Keats, Wordsworth, Blake and so on.

It must be said straightaway that the concept of the sublime evolves over time and therefore we find it expressed by these varied writers in slightly different ways on different occasions, which makes it complex and almost impossible to grasp. What the various interpretations have in common is the idea of an expressive style that differentiates itself sharply from the traditional canons of beauty, such as measure and harmony. According to the most widely accepted etymology, the word 'sublime' evokes an elevation that runs along not a perpendicular axis, but a diagonal one. In the sublime, altitude is reached by an indirect route, *limis* or *limus* meaning 'oblique' (Bodei, 2008, p. 21). In aesthetic experience what is uplifted is obviously the soul. The ascending movement is also expressed as 'looking upwards' (ibid., p. 25).

But what are we looking at?

Theorists of the sublime have drawn up a rich and detailed catalogue of places and situations that arouse the feeling of the sublime in art, identifying it in the 'highest' points that offer us the spectacle of nature. Such points are also places of the greatest danger: snowy peaks, active volcanoes, impenetrable forests, deserts, fearful precipices, grand ruins, abysses, stormy oceans, manifestations of divine power, scenes of war, etc. However, it is not always a matter of grandiose visions. Everyday objects can also be sublime, as when bottles and items of china are arranged on a table to project their shadow onto the background of a painting, or in those examples of still life in which the fruit is painted at its highest point of maturity [*toppunt*[5]], just before decomposition (ibid., p. 39). The indeterminate, the extraordinary, silence and emptiness can be felt as equally threatening: as can the idea of the infinite, anything boundless, darkness, fog, night, the unconscious and madness.

In the painting of the sublime, man struggles to adapt to nature and also to control it, as in Carl Friedrich Lessing's 1828 picture *Ritterburg* [*Knight's Castle*], showing a castle on a steep precipice.

At other times nature is humanized, as when a gorge deceptively seems to represent a vagina, for example, in Karl Friedrich Schinkel's *Felsentor* [*Rock Arch*] of 1818.

However, an element of mourning is always present: a true theoretical summa of the sublime is Caspar David Friedrich's *Abtel im Eichwald* [*Abbey among Oak Trees*] of 1809–10, which brings together various recurring elements: ruins,[6] trees with their branches stripped bare, a funeral scene, the difference in scale between little human figures and nature.

The aesthetic of the sublime received a strong impulse from the success of the scientific culture of the time. By moderating mankind's claims to transcendence, science confronts us with the terrible grandeur of nature. The sublime reveals in visual forms the fracture that has been created between man and nature, between infinite and finite, between the immeasurably large and the incredibly small.

However, the feeling of deprivation gives rise to an emancipatory impulse. It is a twin movement of the sublime, and simultaneously with it, a deficit in the Ego reveals itself, but at the same time the soul feels relieved (Gaetano, 2002, p. 12). The upward leap is possible precisely because of this deficit. The bowstring is pulled in order to fire the arrow. Revealing itself to be a small thing, a 'straw in the wind', the subject is reabsorbed into the greatness of nature. At one moment one feels dragged down and then (in reality, almost instantly) is seized by something that pushes one up to the heights. This is why we say the pleasure given by the spectacle of the sublime in nature is of a *negative* order, because it arises from the violent contrast with a sense of danger that is an integral part of it.

The verticality that so markedly distinguishes the sublime would not be found in the classical idea of the beautiful. In order to justify the dichotomy of beautiful/sublime on the theoretical level, Burke distinguishes between passions ('organs of the mind', 1756a, p. 52) related to self-preservation and those relative to reproduction/sociality. The first provoke delight, the others pleasure. When they are obstructed, the first give rise to physical pain, the second to (moral) affliction. For Burke, only the passions linked to self-preservation (in the final analysis, to the idea of death) are sublime. 'In the end, the true sublime is death itself' (Sertoli, 2012, p. 24), unless those linked to the beautiful reach such a stage that they carry an equally great risk: the figure of Werther, for example, is certainly sublime. The dimension of the sublime, therefore, refers to the danger of dying, while the dynamic of the beautiful refers to the danger of losing the object. But pain is stronger than pleasure, and so the sensations aroused by the sublime are stronger than those aroused by the beautiful.

For Longinus sublimity is above all a matter of style and rhetoric. The emphasis is on language and on the production of sublime discourse. Burke is more concerned with the effects created in the recipient. From the rhetorical sublime we pass to the psychological sublime:

> It is no longer even a style, but a function of language (poetic and oratorical) that puts two psychic universes into communication: that of the poet/orator

> and that of the listener . . . The sublime is displaced from linguistic experience to extra-linguistic experience: it is no longer located in language but in 'things themselves' (certain 'things') and language (i.e. poetry) is only subordinately sublime inasmuch as it represents (describes) these 'things'.
>
> (Sertoli, 2002, pp. 10–16)

In his examination of the sublime Kant further emphasizes the receptive pole in the psychology of the subject. Sertoli writes (ibid., p. 31):

> Kant does not deny the Ego's moment of vertigo, but subsumes it into a movement that in the end reaffirms and elevates the Ego. Hence the 'negative pleasure' (= delight) inherent in the experience of the sublime: it is not a 'positive joy' (= pleasure), but an alternation of attraction and repulsion consequent upon that movement.

From being an attribute of nature the sublime goes back to being determined by humanity. The same psychologizing line is followed by Schiller (1793a), who recalls man's 'double dependency on nature' (which reminds us of Winnicott's (1955) concept of 'double dependency'), and delineates the subject-matter of the sublime as a conflict between the sensible and the super-sensible, between the natural and moral existence of man.

If faced successfully, however, the conflict gives us a way to make ourselves independent of the object to which we are irresistibly attracted. The experience of the sublime in art is therefore a victory over the subjugating power of the object. The emotion of the sublime – the terrible beauty, the horror rendered thinkable by art – consists after all in the subject placing the right distance between himself and the fascinating but frightening object. In the end, what does 'represent' mean if not placing oneself at a safe distance from a real that is experienced as threatening; if not establishing a meaningful space for vision that reflects the relationships with the primary objects and becomes in addition a set of pre-conceptions for successive experiences?

Bion's sublime: authors, style and themes

I repeat, not wishing this to be a study of sources but rather of one symbolic matrix within Bion's thought, that I shall not go deeply here into the influence that Romantic authors clearly exerted on him. For that purpose I refer the reader, on the one hand, to Harris Williams (2010a, 2010b), while, on the other hand, I shall note some Romantic writers in the sections below, each taking a different perspective.

Discussion of Bion's style is a different matter, a subject that does not appear to me to have been much considered. Bion develops a theory about the Language of Achievement (see *infra*) for the analyst and indeed uses it in his writings. On the stylistic plane we can say that Bion inclines towards the sublime because it is concise – which is less evident in translation – to the point of obscurity, sparing with adjectives, simple, energetic in expression, direct and pathetic (in the sense of impassioned). Its silences, in itself and in words, are no less sublime. The lofty tone, as of someone speaking about dramatic things and for whom it is worthwhile to live and to suffer, and the very choice of words lead us directly to several *tópoi* in the aesthetic of the sublime. The movement of his prose has something of the sublime in itself in the fact that impenetrably dark sentences are sometimes lit up by flashes of brilliant intuition.

It is curious that one of the effects that this style provokes in the reader can be a mixture of persecution, reverential fear and amazement. His writing has to be described using oxymorons such as 'boiling ice' or 'terrible joy' and so on. Bion makes us visit places inaccessible to the psyche. These places of madness give us vertigo, but the same can be said of the theoretical formulations with which he probes into them, because they are always on the edge of paradox, ambiguity, a certain obscurity and indefiniteness. In his writing Bion gives the idea of struggling incessantly with himself, alternating extreme intellectual engagement and detachment, passion and distance. He is both fired up and cold like an officer on the field of battle; and this, as we know, is one of his metaphors, and what is more, one derived from real experiences in his own life.

A sign of this struggle, and we may indeed call it sublime, is its bitter and pungent flavour of irony, bordering on sarcasm, inspired by a degree of ex-combatant animosity and directed at himself as well as at others. As the etymology of the word 'sarcasm' suggests, a laceration of the flesh – a wound never healed? – it is reflected in the style of those who mock the world. But in fact irony is always an appraisal of a defeat. Bion's tone is often, in a word, 'Miltonic', and we may indeed presume Milton to be a direct source of inspiration if we think of the sublime description of Lucifer's fall (*Paradise Lost*, I. 589–94) quoted by Burke (1756a, p. 61):

> He above the rest
> In shape and gesture proudly eminent
> Stood like a tower; his form had yet not lost
> All her original brightness, nor appear'd
> Less than archangel ruin'd, and th'excess
> Of glory obscur'd . . .

As far as themes are concerned, how can we not think of the sublime when in reading Bion we come upon such expressions as 'nameless dread', the unconscious reformulated as 'infinity', the exaltation of the dark night of the soul in St John of the Cross, or of the 'Negative Capability' that Keats places at the foundation of all poetics? Or in the state of sleep, almost 'stupor', which the analyst should reach in order to make himself permeable to the immaterial facts of the analysis (Bion, 1970)? Or again, if we think of the ineffable O? And is the bi-temporal dynamic of the sublime not equivalent to losing oneself in the experience of confusion and persecution (to become 'O' or to be in a paranoid–schizoid position) before eventually entering into knowledge (K)?

Having simply indicated some general motifs and being unable here, for reasons of space, to go into a systematic analysis of them through all of Bion's work, I shall confine myself to some of the more significant examples, drawn principally from *Transformations* and *Attention and Interpretation*. But I think it would be equally illuminating to examine the autobiographical works and the trilogy *A Memoir of the Future* in the light of the sublime (see Civitares, 2017a). In each section I shall begin by recalling an aspect of the sublime and shall then illustrate the psychoanalytic concept that in some ways corresponds to it. For this I have to assume the reader has a minimum familiarity with Bion's thought. In any case, every analyst nowadays should know its essential elements since it is revolutionizing the way we think about psychoanalysis.

O, *awe*, \ ȯ \

In the dialectic of the sublime are represented both directions of the double movement that Bion places at the foundation of thought, when he says it is born from absence: the vertigo of the fall given by rediscovering the condition that characterizes us as human beings, of being cast out into the world, is followed by the moral elevation of self-consciousness (Kant), but also by a certain Luciferine pride, because we nevertheless remain in unhappiness and we never regain the lost Eden.

In *Transformations* Bion (1965, p. 151) quotes Milton 'to represent O', the ultimate reality:

> The rising world of waters dark and deep,
> Won from the void and formless infinite.
>
> (*Paradise Lost*, III. 11–12)

As he explains: 'The process of binding', coincident with K – that is, with abstract knowledge – 'is a part of the procedure by which something is won from the void and formless infinite'. This is a different procedure from what we mean when we say that: 'O is "become".' K is based on the language of logic: becoming O, on the other hand, means knowing something emotionally. Simultaneously meaning origin, zero, vagina (Bléandonu, 1990), darkness, thing-in-itself, real, infinite void, terror (as is suggested by the sound and spelling of 'awe', \ *ȯ* \), O is one of Bion's most ungraspable, and for this reason most subtly troubling concepts. The same series of synonyms for O includes the noumen, Godhead, the divine, God, Tiger (Harris Williams, 2010b); but also the no-thing and noughtness. The *no-thing* is not only the persistence of the 'shadow' of the object that is no longer there, but also the *thing* as it is in the sense of the Real, and not as it appears. From O the subject can 'win' knowledge, thoughts, existence, but there is always risk of being devoured by it.

Nameless dread

For these reasons, 'O' is also the psychoanalytic concept that can in the most immediate way evoke the terror of the sublime in art. For Bion it is the 'void, formless and infinite' with which the infant is confronted when it comes into the world, and indeed even before.[7] And the only thing that can preserve it is the psychological distance in which its mother envelops it.

The state of infantile impotence [*Hilflosigkeit*] noted by Freud, and the severe anguish described by Klein, become in Bion nameless dread. The marked dramatic colouring of the expression he chooses to use in place of Freud's and Klein's continues to disturb us because it powerfully evokes something extreme and irremediable.

Nameless dread, which arises in the newborn when the breast fails in its task of providing meaning (Bion, 1965), is not only a terror so intense that we have no words to define it, but also a terror that literally kills the name (or the symbol), or rather destroys thought (Micotti, 2013). Not only this, but compared to Freud and Klein, Bion adopts a vaster vision of psychic life in imagining fears that are so violent because undergone in the foetal state and therefore need new names, such as 'thalamic' or 'sub-thalamic' fears.

Darkness

It should be evident from what has been said so far that in preaching the necessity of the moment of terror and the sacrifice of the Ego's centrality in the universe, the aesthetic of the sublime may be defined as an aesthetic or 'poetics of renunciation' (Reitani, 2003). The same holds for the aesthetic paradigm in Bion. He too asks the analyst to make a certain sacrifice of the Ego with a view to a gain in psycho-somatic integration.

Bion confronts the theme of darkness brought up in the famous letter in which Freud (Freud and Andreas-Salomé, 1966, p. 45) writes to Lou Andreas-Salomé that in order to concentrate on a problem he needs to illuminate it with a ray of darkness. Freud's example is analogous to the struggle against the senses (Bion, 1970, p. 62) required in the spiritual elevation of the sublime, and to the many occasions when Bion draws inspiration from St John of the Cross and his *Dark Night of the Soul*.

Everything is transparent for Freud. If it is not, the reason lies in the intrinsic difficulty of the material, not in the investigating eye. Freud's (1895 (1950), p. 284) invitation to 'imaginings, transpositions and guesses' [*Phantasieren, Übersetzen und Erraten*] is indeed always in the service of a *théorein*, a seeing, and subordinate to the strictest principle of rationality. It is different from the invitation to imagine extended to us by Bion. For Bion, imagination has the sense of the Leopardian exceeding of a limit that nevertheless sends us back to an infinity that is itself unknowable. For us to be able to imagine infinity we need it not to be visible.

For Freud, it is a matter of rounding or climbing over the obstacle in order to see, as it were, with the senses. For Bion it is a matter of rendering the invisible

visible, of intuiting or rather of renouncing the senses. The self-imposed limit on the exercise of memory, desire and understanding serves in fact to liberate the imagination. Indeed, it is in the imagination that we deploy the psyche's capacity to make things up, to put them in contact with its 'personal myths' that is, with its mythopoeic (or poetic) capacity.

The senses could never supplant the evocative power of the imagination. They could, however, limit its effectiveness. And for that reason it is well worth renouncing them a priori. On the other hand, it is in darkness that the capacity of the unconscious to dream the real, projecting its films onto it, is deployed to the highest degree. We can move forward safely only in darkness, only by obscuring phenomenal reality and the perceptions that construct it. While the beautiful gives itself to be seen, or at least makes us think so, the sublime lives in the tension, destined to remain unresolved, between 'sensuous/sensible' (that which we can perceive with our senses) and sense-able (that which we can sense in a vague and undefined way), between what we can see and what we can only intuit.

Good distance and unison

Burke theorizes the effect of the sublime as a function of the distance between subject and object (Sertoli, 2002, p. 23). By distance, as the key factor in ensuring that the subject is not overwhelmed by the threat represented by a nature that it cannot master, we should understand the transformation of horror into aesthetic experience. It is then that the sublime strengthens the Ego that is passing through a transitory dissolution. Something of that which exceeds it[8] is in substance assimilated and becomes food for the mind.

The individual transcends his own limits by resonating with the great soul [*megalophrosýnes apéchema*] of one who has been able to dominate nature and generate the effect of the sublime through the wise fiction of art. The poetic of the sublime as an art of passion and distance aims to arouse in the reader or spectator a feeling of being at one with the poet, and sets up between them a strong bond of empathy, makes them vibrate in unison.

As a theory of unison, the aesthetic of the sublime is an extraordinary model for showing precisely how Bion imagines the development of the psyche. The sublime describes as elevation of the soul what for Bion is the unison/*at-one-ment* with the object/analyst that makes the psyche develop. Furthermore, in the aesthetic of the sublime the recurring Bionian theme of the drive for truth and of (emotional) truth as food for the mind finds its equivalent in the demand for authenticity (Civitarese, 2013a). Unison is *ékstasis* in the sublime. *Ékstasis* means to be out of oneself: it is paradoxical that the subject constitutes itself exactly when living through moments during which it is 'out of itself' or maximally alienated in the other, but what counts is the emotional tone of this alienation. If positive, then when the subject comes back to itself it is enriched by its temporary merging with the other.

The motif of refuge or of distance from *O* (nature, object) immediately opens up to current psychoanalysis, for example, in discussion of the father or third as a symbolic function and of regulation of the 'good distance' (Civitarese, 2013b). If *O* is threatening, finding the right distance is a question of the greatest importance. Keeping a sufficient distance means making oneself a subject and also respecting the difference of scale between self and object, and not trying to deny it. Denial would in fact be an act of *húbris*. The space that interposes between the defenceless subject and the nightmare that could engulf him or her is a psychological space of safety given by the introjection of alpha function and the capacity for maternal reverie. As is the case with the sublime in nature, we can contemplate the terrible beauty of the object, but only at a certain distance. In Bion, then, the concept of distance could always also be theorized as the indicator of the achievement of a sufficient equilibrium in the ever-active dialectic between narcissism and socialism, between intense focus on the individual and intense focus on the group.

Imagination, fancy and reverie

The poetics of *Bildhaftigkeit* (vividness of expression), the pre-eminently visual character of the 'catalogue' of sublime situations developed by the aesthetic of the sublime, a Nietzschian 'thinking through images' (Reitani, 2003), reminds us of the importance of reverie in Bion.

The suspension of memory and desire that Bion requires from the analyst is not only associated with Keats, but recalls Coleridge's ideas about 'that willing suspension of disbelief for the moment, which constitutes poetic faith', and the 'negative faith of inspiration that transforms reality into a creation of the spirit' (Panella, 2012, pp. 121–122, quoting Coleridge, 1817). Just as the sublime in art creates the distance of safety thanks to the mechanism of scenic or literary fiction, so does analysis which in its own setting dramatizes the 'terror' of nature in madness. Fiction is the necessary refuge that renders it possible to experience compassion and to resonate sympathetically with the suffering other.

For understanding the concept of reverie, Coleridge's distinction between imagination and fancy is also extremely illustrative. Panella comments about this antinomy:

> if *imagination* and *fancy* are two aspects (one – *imagination* – oriented in an active direction, the other – fancy – weakened and constrained to follow the 'normal' laws of mental association and the relationship between sensations, memories and judgements) of the unity that presides over poetic creation, then the poet too who seeks to live at the service of the creative imagination will neglect the relationship of cause and effect (the basis of associationism) and will try to achieve that 'illusion' or 'negative faith' . . . which will permit him to show the truth by means of the unrealistic, the mythic or pure intellectual creation. Setting fancy aside and privileging the formal force of imagination,

> Coleridge attempts to reunite rhetorical form and rational structure, moral passion and a feeling of inspiration in a single dimension in such a way as to bring back into the field of poetry the all-inclusive charge that should mark any true poetic work.
>
> (ibid., pp. 126–127)

In this passage we can find valuable prompts for distinguishing reverie from free association. One takes over from the imagination, the other from the fancy (for us to grasp the distinction it is not essential to accept the denominations proposed by Coleridge). The English poet is here writing an anti-associationist manifesto with a slant to which Bion could have subscribed. He sets the imagination as a faculty for creating new depictions of the real or as the mind's synthetic activity of *poiesis*/poetry, against fantasy as the 'mechanical' capacity of remembering (merely 'a mode of memory') and tying various psychic elements together. It is as if Coleridge were battling with the blackest fantasies born from the Enlightenment, while Bion combats the equally 'Enlightenment' (in the negative sense given to the term by the philosophers of the Frankfurt School) technologization of the Freudian method.

It is not extraneous to this sensibility, and moreover is in harmony with that of the Romantics, to endorse the idea of myth as a domain of extension for the elements of psychoanalysis; and, in the terms of those authors who address the sublime, to value the connection of myth 'not with an original metaphysical revelation that the myth would translate and of which poetry would be the dwindling reflection, but with chaos (Schlegel) and negativity (Novalis)' (Oppo, 2011, p. 264). As we see, there is common ground between Bion and the theorists of the sublime in the distinction between ordinary memory, which Bion requires to be actively shunned, and dreaming memory, 'the stuff of analysis' (Bion, 1970, p. 70), that which generates myths.

Passion

'The final purpose of art', writes Schiller, 'is the exhibition of metaphysics' (1793a, p. 149), to increase 'the moral independence of the laws of nature'. So that this may happen, 'The sensible essence must suffer intensely and vehemently; pathos is necessary', which on the part of the artist implies candour, delicacy, sincerity, sensitivity and lack of regard for decorum. Schiller adds: 'The person who is prey to any pain, is only a tormented animal, but not anymore a suffering human being, for a moral resistance against suffering becomes simply demanded from the human being, through which the principle of freedom in him alone, the intelligence, can make itself recognizable' (ibid., p. 154) and again, 'Hence, in any pathos, the sense must be aroused through suffering, and the spirit through freedom' (ibid., p. 166).

The idea of the pathic sublime finds an echo in the Bionian conception of 'suffering'. The pathetic/sentimental has the same place in the sublime as the emotional element does in Bion. There is a vivid clue to it in the idiosyncratic use of the verb 'to suffer', used indiscriminately to mean 'suffer pain' or 'suffer pleasure' as distinct from feeling pain or pleasure (without 'suffering' them). In such a context, the verb to suffer takes on the meaning of *authentically living* the experiences of pleasure and of pain; or rather, the experience of *being*. This is possible only when we have no rigid defences against experience, as can happen when our personal history is studded with traumas that have blocked psychic growth (Bion, 1970); only if there is a lasting and sufficient openness to the world and the other. It is as if one quality of the anguish that impels us to interrogate ourselves about the meaning of existence and to appreciate the transience of all things cannot fail to be present in the light of any experience of authentic life.

As Heidegger (1927) maintains in the famous sections 50–53 of *Being and Time*, being is being-towards-death [*Sein-zum-Tode*]. What makes us human is to be spoken of by language; or rather, by the practice of discourse, institutions and habits that give us access to the possibility of thinking about our finitude. We are a socio-historical interweaving of past and future. In this future which thus forms a *constituent* part of the Ego, at least once we live in a state of authenticity, there cannot fail to be the knowledge of the ever-imminent possibility of one's own death.

Language of achievement

The art of the sublime exists in the passion of language [*lógon tà páthe*], which is coincident with the art of passion [*páthous tékne*]. Giving space to these concepts, the aesthetic of the sublime anticipates some of the more current tendencies of critical theory which relativize the autonomy of the text. Generally, in this trend, attention moves from the artist and the work considered in isolation to the relationship between artist and audience and to the effects produced on the public. In more contemporary language we could say that the reader becomes the author and that the work is only an instrument for producing certain emotions. In fact, a state of identification is postulated between author and reader, but also a competitive relationship (Bloom, 1982).

In psychoanalysis the same aspiration expresses itself in attention to the analyst's unconscious responses and to the idea that the text of the analysis comes not from one or the other, but is written by them together. One does not give authentic interpretations without an impassioned nature. The aesthetic ends up being re-included in psychology. If the truth of the interpretation is no longer communicated unilaterally but discovered in the sharing of emotion, it is essential to interrogate oneself about the quality of the medium in which the encounter is taking place.

Freud had already wondered what criteria to use for assessing the efficacy of an interpretation, but – as far as I know – nobody before Bion had ever posed himself the problem of forging a Language of Achievement. This is the expression with which he translates into the language of psychoanalysis the 'passion of language' or 'the art of passion' from the aesthetic of the sublime. In the same way, the vitriolic critique that Longinus makes of language that is affected or lacks simplicity finds an echo in Bion's polemic against analysts' jargon, a jargon that is so often turgid, inflated, pedantic and so full of vacuous subtleties as to be entirely equivalent to the ridiculousness of the false sublime.

The concluding chapter of *Attention and Interpretation* (Chapter 13), which is also significantly the last in the series of Bion's great books, bears the title, 'Prelude to or Substitute for Achievement', and is devoted to this very subject of language. There is an obvious allusion to Wordsworth's *The Prelude, or Growth of a Poet's Mind*. It is very hard not to think of this as a truthful transposition, and that the homage is not confined to lexical choices, but extends also to the contents. Moreover, the epigraph to the chapter is the famous passage in the letter of 21 December 1817 from Keats to his brother George, from which Bion took the psychoanalytic concepts of Negative Capability and Language of Achievement:

> I had not a dispute but a disquisition with Dilke on various subjects; several things dove-tailed in my mind, and at once it struck me what quality went to form a Man of Achievement, especially in literature, and which Shakespeare possessed so enormously – I mean Negative Capability, that is, when a man is capable of being in uncertainties, mysteries, doubts, without any irritable reaching after fact and reason.
>
> (quoted in Bion, 1970, p. 125)

Drawing on this phrase of Keats, Bion is here quite explicitly setting up a cardinal principle drawn from the aesthetic of the sublime as a measure of effectiveness in the application of psychoanalysis. Above all, he is on the watch for the multiple risks of deviation from meaning that an analytic encounter must entail. The analyst can speak two kinds of language: one that is equivalent to doing so as not to think, and which is entirely a substitute for action (Language of Substitution); and by contrast a language that is only a prelude to action, and which therefore informs, inspires and directs it. In the second case, and only in this, he embodies the Man of Achievement. In other words, a crucial element of analysis is the passive and active receptivity of the analyst. The principle enunciated by Keats thus becomes the acid test of every session. Bion could not be clearer. '*Any session should be judged*', he writes, '*by comparison with the Keats formulation*' (Bion, 1970, p. 125, my italics: we may note, *en passant*, the typically prescriptive, almost military tone that Bion adopts in so many of his recommendations; that pervasive quality which some have defined as *tankishness* (Souter, 2009). I do not think this contradicts his radically anti-dogmatic stance, but is rather the expression of a profound, and therefore intransigent, ethical passion. For Bion, understanding psychoanalysis as a systematic exercise of doubt requires a severe discipline).

But why is this principle so important?

In the first place, as Bion spells out, because Negative Capability and Language of Achievement always depend on a vertex. They never present absolute perspectives on things, and for this very reason they are the foundation of an ability to observe the events of the analysis. So Bion dwells at length on an enumeration of the various ways in which one can have the impression that there are numerous ideas and dreams, but that they are only and always reiterations of the same idea, in effect a kind of cancerous proliferation of (pseudo) elements of psychoanalysis because greed and envy split off to infinity the idea that might otherwise have been born. Negative Capability would therefore be a dyke against the uncontrolled proliferation of thoughts. However, that implies a more or less lengthy period of suffering. Acceptance of not knowing and not understanding brings with it a temporary increase in a mixed feeling of anxiety and guilt.

But isn't this feeling the same as the moment of dismay when we contemplate a sublime spectacle? Does it make a difference that in our case the landscape is the equally infinite one of the unconscious? In fact, the conclusion of the chapter – we could say of Bion's whole oeuvre, if we leave aside the last brief writings and the various transcripts of seminars and conferences – is extraordinary:

> What is required is not the decrease of inhibition but a decrease of the impulse to inhibit: the impulse to inhibit is fundamentally envy of the growth-stimulating objects. What is to be sought is an activity that is both the restoration of god (the Mother) and the evolution of god (the formless, infinite, ineffable, non-existent), which can only be found in the state in which there is NO memory, desire, understanding.
>
> (Bion, 1970, pp. 128–129)

Firstly, a final note on style. As we see from the quotation, this kind of writing itself arouses a feeling of the sublime. Next, it is especially well suited to the lofty, almost solemn tone of the discussion. We also see in this example how Bion implies a series of equivalences (god = primary object = divinity-as-projection-of-the-parental-imago = ultimate reality, etc.) but without making them explicit as such.

As for the content, what hinders a good relationship with nature (with the object) is quickly stated: a state of greed and envy has been created. The subject has the firm conviction that he is being denied a vital benefit that he lacks while others possess it in abundance. This generates aggressiveness and, as a consequence, guilt (the impulse to inhibit that dries up vitality). The growth of the mind is arrested. Before this impasse, the only thing to be done is to re-establish 'god (the Mother)' and make 'god' evolve. It is not so much a matter of mellowing the Super-Ego as of inclining towards unison with the object. 'God' is the real as 'the formless, infinite, ineffable, non-existent'. 'Restoring god' can have the sense of ceasing to destroy him and hence being unable to use and introject him. Making god evolve could then mean, when the 'restoration' has been successful, being able to give a personal meaning to experience. In psychoanalytic terms we would say regaining contact with the object as a source of significance and therefore of vitality.

Finally, the passage can also be read as inviting us to pay attention in the first place to the Ego's needs and only as a next step to those of the Id (on this distinction, see Girard, 2010).

The genius and the mystic

Exaltation of the genius is typical of the sublime. 'The loftiness of conception, the vividness of the images, the terrible quality of the effects are the prerogative of the genius': so says Leopardi (quoted in Gaetano, 2002, p. 191). But in order to produce *ékstasis* it is necessary for the author to have a 'great soul' and to write with genuine passion. These are the prerogatives of the genius. The genius has vigour, boldness, strength and a great imagination. Something mad and extravagant lives in him. He is astute, penetrating, impetuous, radical and capable of surprising syntheses. It is not uncommon for him to be melancholic, just as his relationship with the society of his time is one of unhappiness and conflict. Leopardi again (quoted in ibid., p. 441):

> The world laughs, persecutes him if need be, and excommunicates him. Nor does it shift from its position, by which I mean it does not accelerate its march. Meanwhile, the average minds, in part aided by discoveries of the great man, but above all by the natural course of things, and by virtue of their own reflections, take half a step. Others repeat the truths taught by them, since they are only slightly at odds with ones that are already received and readily admissible. The world, whether for this reason or by dint of the example set by many, follows them. Their successors take another half step with equal success. Thus little by little, until someone comes to complete the tenth step and reach the point which that great spirit had attained so long before. But he is either already forgotten, or the prevailing opinion regarding him still endures, or finally the world does him no justice, because it finds that it already knows all that he knew, that it has learned it by other means, and does not believe that it owes him anything.
>
> (Leopardi, 2013 (1898–1900); Kindle positions: 1730–1731)

Does this not seem like a portrait of Bion and his fluctuating fortunes?

Bion uses the concept of Language of Achievement to address in the analytic situation the same problem as that faced by the theorists of the sublime: how to produce transport (*ékstasis*) in the public. He identifies the genius and the mystic with the analyst who is also a Man of Achievement capable of speaking the Language of Achievement – that is, of being with the patient in a way that is authentic, passionate, creative, sincere and without regard for decorum. Not only that, but the key point is how to arrive at a conceptualization that allows us to communicate in an efficacious manner not only with the most differentiated aspects of the mind but also with the most primitive ones; how to influence the vestiges of foetal life and the inaccessible unconscious. At the moment in which he re-anchors it to the sensible, Bion interprets the Language of Achievement that – let us remember – expresses a mode of being ('Man of Achievement'), as the language which has the characteristic of being open also to the pre-verbal sensory levels of discourse (Lombardi, 2012).

It is clear that, in having the chance to ask analysts to be passionate but not all to be actually geniuses, Bion introduces the surprising figures of the Genius and the Mystic as allegories of a creative capacity that every one of them should nevertheless actively cultivate. At the same time the Genius and the Mystic are those characters who have Faith in the truth of which they are the bearers and who are capable of entering into contact with O as 'that which is not yet evolved, nor differentiated, but pregnant with potential' (Fornaro, 1990, p. 187). These truths are felt by institutions as potentially destructive, but also as nutritive elements that can make them grow. The same is true on the individual plane for the 'inspired or messianic idea'. Let us note *en passant* how these figures also bring with them the conflict-dynamic of the sublime.

Aesthetic conflict

I think the fortunes of the aesthetic of the sublime from Longinus (2008) to Žižek (2000), and to a large extent – as we are seeing – those of Bionian theory, even more than may yet have been suspected, derive from the fact that they make the essence of any aesthetic experience come to the surface; and this essence lies in authentically accepting the ephemeral nature of all things. If we wanted to express the same thing in the language of Heidegger's[9] philosophy, the horror or truth to which the spectacle of the sublime exposes us, provokes anguish [*Angst*] which, when it is tolerable – and it is beauty that renders it tolerable – reinstates us in the social order of discourse [*Rede*]. Therefore only the idea of death – as 'the structure of nothingness that always underlies my time' (Aho, 2009, p. 93) – gives meaning to life at every moment. In this way the sublime reveals the abyss which existence looks out onto. But here death is not so much physical, biological death as the loss of meaning, the partial loss of meaning, to which – let us remember – any symptom testifies.

The aesthetic of the sublime anticipates the concept of aesthetic conflict inspired in Meltzer (1973; Civitarese, 2011a; Meltzer and Harris Williams, 1988), and which is presented by the former with a splendour lacking in the latter, even though the novelty of the notion is that it also serves to connote certain clinical situations.

Viewed from this angle, the distinction between sublime and beautiful works only up to a certain point because the beautiful also always confronts us with the spectacle of its own transience and loss, and of the inexorability of destiny. The ultra-sensitive probe of psychoanalysis allows us to cross the caesura that in the aesthetic of the sublime binds the two concepts in an antinomian relationship. We discover that we are not in the presence of phenomena belonging to different categories, but of two different expressions of the same phenomenon.

Stupor

'Astonishment', writes Burke (1756a, p. 56) 'as I have said, is the effect of the sublime in its highest degree; the inferior effects are admiration, reverence and respect.' The semantic space around the term is broad: it can also mean surprise, hesitation, suspicion. By definition, astonishment is a feeling of wonder and surprise so intense that it almost wipes out the ability to speak and act, and so for this reason it is paradoxically akin to stupor, the slowing or stopping of ideation in a waking state.[10]

Now Bion says: 'The nearer the analyst comes to suppressing desire, memory and understanding, the more likely he is to slip into a sleep akin to stupor' (1970, p. 47). It is this same condition that enables him 'to "see" what the patient sees' (ibid., p. 40), to intuit his 'hallucinations' (p. 45):

> to appreciate hallucination the analyst must participate in the state of hallucinosis . . . By eschewing memories, desires and the operations of memory he can approach the domain of hallucinosis and of the "acts of faith" by which alone he can become at one with his patients' hallucinations and so effect transformations $O \rightarrow K$.
>
> (p. 36)

Bion uses the word 'stupor' to indicate a mental state of voluntary weakening of focused attention, that is, a suspension of the normal reactivity to stimuli: the aim is to heighten a marginally conscious awareness – which we could also consider equivalent to the capacity for using intuition – directed instead towards the emotions and to all that is not directly perceptible by the senses. A condition of this kind favours the emergence of images, sensations, thoughts that have the quality of 'hallucinosis', by which is meant psychic productions apparently in contrast with the examination of the patient's factual reality, but which are nevertheless equally indicative of important aspects of his psychic reality, or of the unconscious emotional reality of the therapeutic relationship. Only by rendering itself less powerful can the Ego elevate itself to the level of the unconscious and its mythopoeic and 'diagnostic' capacity (Freud, 1917). So Bion postulates an initial moment of identification with the patient that also represents a falling-off of the capacity to symbolize, as happens to the thunderstruck observer dazzled by the sublime. The surrender to 'stupor' should be followed by a re-emergence as a kind of reawakening that makes us leave the 'hallucination' and consequently transforms it into a dream (and this is where the second part of the 'stupendous' experience occurs, the feeling of wonder at the power of the unconscious). There is also the idea that the mind may be unequal to its task. The events of the analysis cannot be touched, seen, smelled, heard, or tasted. The Ego is overpowered by something which transcends it. This is therefore a matter of accepting the limit and overturning it. The price we pay is the indistinctness and indefiniteness of intuition, because the psychological infinite is grasped aesthetically. But if the operation is successful, out of a feeling of inadequacy can arise a feeling of stupor in the positive sense of wonder.

Given that the unconscious as infinity exceeds the possibility of being grasped by logical thought, Bion proposes a systematic restriction of the Ego's faculties. To find itself, the Ego must first lose itself. Only the voluntary limiting of vision can arouse and reinvigorate the power of the imagination. Out of powerlessness before the unknowable comes a psychological revival; from ecstatic ravishment creative resources are revealed; from the abyss of the senseless come the ravishments of daydream and the epiphanies first of hallucinosis and then of dream.

The unbalancing of the Ego before the overwhelming vastness of the natural sublime is an image of the Ego's own limits during the moment in which it wishes to grasp the vastness of the unconscious. A psychological sublime can be modelled on an aesthetic sublime. The natural sublime's very savagery becomes in Bion a granting of access to 'wild thoughts' (Bion, 1997).

Historical reality

Paintings inspired by the sublime often portray an observer in the moment in which he opens himself to the spectacle that instils a feeling of dismay, one which can descend into 'consternation [*ekplexis*], surprise [*thaumaston*], even terror [*phobos*]' (Guidorizzi, 1991, p. 14).

The aesthetic of the sublime is in itself an aesthetic of immanence, of the here and now, of the experience that is neither separate nor independent from the event, but which on the contrary is consubstantial with it. What is thus represented is the infinitesimal moment of emotional fall. In substance we are present at the unheard of threat of the suspension of temporality and, with it, of meaning. In that moment we are all hurtling down like Milton's Lucifer.

This is also a classic theme of the sublime; for example, in Schiller:

> how little the poetical force of some impressions that moral characters or actions can make upon us depends on their historical reality . . . for it is the poetical, not the historical truth, on which any aesthetic effect grounds itself . . . The poetry should not take its way through the cold region of memory, it should never make of learning its interpreter; it should never make egoism one of its advocates.
>
> (1793a, p. 175)

Hence, in the aesthetic of the sublime, the theoretical, technical and ethical necessity to dramatize and intensify the emotional situation with passion *páthos*.

Likewise, in Bionian and post-Bionian psychoanalysis the value given to the intensity of the experience undergone by the analyst and the patient in their encounter, the emphasis on passion as an indispensable dimension of the elements of psychoanalysis, but also on the senses and on the fictional dimension of the analytic setting (myth) all serve to concentrate on what is alive in the here and now of treatment. By 'passion' in particular (see below), Bion means that the analyst must pass through a transformation of his own self, must let himself be impregnated by the patient's suffering – in his terminology become the O of the patient, or as he says elsewhere 'of the session'. In essence, that means renouncing abstract comprehension, the use of theories as 'hallucinoses' for screening himself from the other. Grotstein (2008, p. 202) makes the same point by likening analysis to a 'passion play':

> psychoanalysis constitutes *a drama, an improvisational passion play*, one in which the analysand is the leading actor who unconsciously invites and recruits, maybe hypnotically ensorcels the analyst, all be it through the unconscious agency of the unconscious nouminous 'third subject of the analysis' or the dramaturge, to participate in a play in which the dyad is involved in 'playing' roles that have been unconsciously assigned to them.

There are obvious resonances with the aesthetic of the sublime when by 'passion' we can in some ways mean, in full agreement with Grotstein, a precise 'technical tool' of psychoanalysis.

Transformations

For sublimate, read . . . transform. We need not dwell at length on all the occasions when Bion likens psychoanalytic transformations to aesthetic ones, and compares the figure of the analyst to that of the artist. Moreover, there is an obvious connection between the alchemical meaning of sublimation and that of psychic transformation.

What could be considered more deeply in the light of the sublime would be the differences between the Freudian theory of sublimation and that deriving from the concept of aesthetic conflict as explanations of the aesthetic experience. This is not the place, but I shall just say that I think they retrace – bearing various *caveats* in mind – the dichotomy between the sublime and the beautiful. The idea of an artwork as the concretization of a reverie of the artist and the presenting of an object that contains and transforms (but also, in his own turn, as a request made to the other to see his own anguish accepted and contained), corresponds to the sublime; on the other hand, the idea of a satisfaction of the sexual drive 'promoted' in such a way as to be diverted from its original goal corresponds to the beautiful. But both the beautiful and the sublime express the intimate vicissitudes of the relationship with the object that contains because it is able to give a form to the chaotic experience of the real. The sublime is the beautiful in the moment in which the subject is *obliged* to become fully aware that there is a risk of losing the object – and not only to know it unconsciously and in an ante-predicative way – and therefore is forced to re-appropriate its dignity as a human being.

Catastrophic change

In the light of the aesthetic of the sublime, the Bionian concept of catastrophic change is all the more immediately comprehensible in its positive valency. There is much more to it than reference to catastrophe theory, which applies to physical rather than psychological models. Throughout the eighteenth century and after there was endless discussion about how the dynamic sublime – that is, a literally catastrophic threat (an 'impending disaster'; Bion, 1970, p. 92) – proceeding from a natural context, may give rise to a sense of moral growth. As we have seen, in the interpretations of the sublime by Kant and Schiller this second aspect becomes the dominant theme. We could say that it highlights the functioning of the psychic container and not the isolated fact of the contained.

Bion addresses this argument in Chapter X of *Attention and interpretation*, preceded – and not accidentally – by yet another reference to Milton. Moreover, the catastrophic change adopts and renews the biblical sense of apocalypse, of revelation coming at the end of life (Vitale, 2005). The apocalyptic paradigm, inspired by biblical exegesis, corresponds to the pervasive idea that (secret, hidden) truth is given retrospectively as an unveiling; to be precise, an *apokálupsis*, a Greek term translating the Hebrew GALEH. Hence the idea of the end that, from being imminent, becomes *immanent*; in short, the faith that we will witness a moment of 'absolutely profane illumination' (ibid., p. 105). But here it is a simulated end, as in a theatre, and so to speak in-sight-of-the-end.

Becoming infinite

> Another of the sublime is infinity . . . Infinity has a tendency to fill the mind with that sort of delightful horror, which is the most genuine effect, and truest test of the sublime.
>
> (Gaetano, 2002, p. 331; quoting Burke, 1756a, p. 71)

The centrality of the motif of the infinite in Bion can be seen in the closing pages of *Transformations* which bear the stamp of Pascal. Bion refers to a passage from the *Pensées* – which is also one of the most cited in the literature of the sublime! – 'Pascal's phrase "*Le silence de ces espaces infinis m'effraie*" can serve as an expression of intolerance and fear of the "unknowable" and hence of the unconscious in the sense of the undiscovered or the unevolved' (1965, p. 171). But for Bion the infinite is inflected in the form of several clinical concepts.

First of all, it is the infinity of the unconscious. Second, the void and formless infinite is also 'the beginning of a session' when it 'has the configuration already formulated in the concept of the Godhead' (ibid., p. 171) After an initial setback, as at the sight of the sublime, something evolves; one glimpses a schema with which the analyst tries to enter into contact, and something is pulled from the void. It is the exact dynamic of the experience of the aesthetic of the sublime in two time frames. Bion also reformulates it in terms of the relationship between no-thing and thing (or infinite and finite): 'The personality that is capable of tolerating a no-thing can make use of the no-thing and so is able to make use of what we can now call thoughts' (1965, p. 106).

It is worth noting the role played by all this 'no-' in Bion's theory, but how could it not be associated with the 'negative pleasure' of the sublime? The conflict between the sublime and the beautiful is a conflict between the reality principle and the pleasure principle, though I would say – shifting the discourse to the sublime – between pain and 'delight'. Bion writes: 'The objection to a meaningless universe . . . derives from fear that the lack of meaning is a sign that meaning has been destroyed and the threat this holds for essential narcissism' (ibid., p. 73). We could make a like-for-like transposition of the concept to describe the feeling of terror of the dynamic sublime, but Bion's statement helps us in the specifically psychoanalytic task of translating the insensateness of nature into the Sphinx as a character in the Oedipal myth and then into the absence of the object. But if the absence of the object is circumscribed and tolerable, then at its reappearance we have delight (etymologically, something that is loved because it charms). A deep comfort grows out of the awareness of having been able to bear a hard test, thanks to thought. Lastly, the infinite returns in Bion when he speaks of the object becoming infinite by transformation in hallucinosis. When he illustrates this concept, Bion very evocatively describes the explosion of the object/container, which is then dispersed over an infinite space to the point of producing a concomitant dispersal of time:

> [T]his explosion is so violent and is accompanied by such immense fear . . . that the patient may express it by a sudden and complete silence (as if to go to an extreme as far from a devastating explosion as possible) . . . The patient's capacity for emotion is felt to be lost because emotion itself is felt to drain away and be lost in the immensity . . . The events of an analysis, spread out over what are to the analyst many years, are to [patient] A but the fragments of a moment dispersed in space.
>
> (1970, pp. 12–13)

Perhaps there is no more penetrating image than this for interpreting the drama that is played out in any expression of the aesthetic sublime.

In the presence of the patient's experience of the object becoming infinite, the analyst must also 'become infinite' (ibid., p. 46), suspending memory, desire and understanding:

> The emotional state of transformations in O^{11} is akin to dread as it is represented by the formulation:
>
> *Like one that on a lonesome road*
> *Doth walk in fear and dread,*
> *And having once turned round walks on,*
> *And turns no more his head;*
> *Because he knows, a frightful fiend*
> *Doth close behind him tread.*
>
> The 'frightful fiend' represents indifferently the quest for truth or the active defences against it, depending on the vertex.
>
> (ibid., p. 46)

This is *The Rime of the Ancient Mariner* by Coleridge. Here, too, we can see how Bion's quotation does not by any means have an ornamental purpose, but that it is justified by the existence of an aesthetic that has been debated for at least a century and produced some of the peaks of Western philosophical reflection. It is always here, a few steps behind, as Bion shows the analyst and as we have just noted, in the falling 'into a sleep akin to stupor' (ibid., p. 47).

Tiger

In *The Dream*, the first volume of *A Memoir of the Future*, Bion (1975, p. 112) writes that: 'Psychoanalysis itself is just a stripe on the coat of the tiger. Ultimately it may meet the Tiger – the Thing Itself – O.' The symbol of the tiger recurs in various writings. Harris Williams (2010b, p. 80) underlines how it may be the instrument of his 'most intimate identification' with Blake. But first it is still the tiger which had frightened him and his brother when he was a child in India, the tiger as a figure in fantasies of being devoured.

Psychoanalysis as ZwitterArt

Now, to tie up the threads of our discussion, I think I may assert with confidence that just as the aesthetic of the sublime represents the arrival in the eighteenth century of a new poetic sensibility in reaction to a certain aridity of the Enlightenment vision of human affairs, so Bion bears witness to both the exhausting of a positivistic urge and to the movement, especially in his last works, towards a new paradigm which can itself be defined as 'aesthetic'. The aesthetic of the sublime and the aesthetic paradigm in Bion have in common 'the primacy of emotion over persuasion' (Reitani, 2003, p. 128). In both – along with a de-emphasis on the privilege traditionally accorded to reason – there is the recovery of the significance of the 'inferior' actions of sensibility and emotionality for understanding human affairs.

Giuliano Baioni has spoken of an 'aesthetic of combat' (ibid., p. 129) and this can also be applied to Bion, who expresses an intensely combative vision of analysis. Similarly, Schiller underlines the great beauty of the sublime deriving from the representation of the struggle which, thanks to our capacity, we can deploy to challenge the senses and transcend them: 'Sensibility will, in truth, always fight its enemy, however, never once itself . . . The fight against the affect, to the contrary, is a fight against sensibility; and supposes, hence, something that is differentiated from sensibility' (1793a, p. 156): what, we might wonder as we pass on our way to the field of psychoanalysis, if not Negative Capability? Or rather, the capacity to oppose our senses in order to rid ourselves of memory, desire and understanding?

For Bion the elements of psychoanalysis must extend into the domain of passion: but pathos is another synonym for sublime. Passion means intensity of suffering, intensity of conflict with the senses. The greater the suffering, the grander and more all-encompassing the struggle, and the more intense the aesthetic/transformative effect. And here again is the Language of Achievement.

In summing up, I would like to show once more how the aesthetic of the sublime is an assemblage of concepts which continually refer to each other and which acquire meaning only in this interlinking, and that the same can be said about the secret harmony of their 'derivatives' in Bion's thought. One concept turns back into another like the delicate cogs of a clock to the point where it is impossible or factitious to separate them. Each is necessary to the other, and all belong to an articulate and coherent symbolic matrix. The important thing is to take account of how in Bion too the corresponding transpositions of the various elements in this series connect with each other not only on the plane of the explicitly symbolic matrix represented by Bionian theory, but also on the implicit plane of the aesthetic of the sublime.

So what I have tried to do is to delineate the terms for a dialectical cross reference from the aesthetic of the sublime to the thought of Bion, and vice versa, in the conviction that they can be mutually illuminating. The task seems particularly important if it is true, as it is true, that both the subject of the sublime (Lyotard, 1984, 1991) and the thought of Bion are alive and current today.

Indeed our era sees the concept of truth in a rhetorical and aesthetic tone. As a result, aesthetic experience asserts itself ever more strongly in psychoanalysis too as an important paradigm. I mean that ideally the purpose of this paper goes beyond the aim of highlighting, as I said at the start, one of the symbolic matrices of Bion's full maturity. If truth is rhetorical and aesthetic, psychoanalysis can never become an entirely exact science, but will always be a hybrid – that is, 'whole'– and should perhaps be proud of it.

In his letter to Goethe of 31 August 1794, Schiller describes himself as floating between 'ideas and perceptions, rules and feelings, the technical head and genius' (Schiller, 1794, p. 11). Thus he outlines an aesthetic theory in which there is a hybrid or 'androgynous' state inherent in art, that is if it wishes to be whole (*ZwitterArt*; Reitani, 2003, p. 124).

Bion's idea of the psychoanalytic method is not dissimilar, and seems uncertainly poised between intuition and concept, forever working at reconciling them. To use the traditional categories of aesthetic criticism, Bion's psychoanalysis is a Romantic psychoanalysis, even if it is obvious that each pole contains elements of its opposite. For example, Descartes' hyperbolical exercise of doubt leads us to face the abyss of our ignorance; as a man of the Enlightenment, Freud investigates the magma of the drives and the opacity of the unconscious, etc. Similarly in Bion, where the struggle to make psychoanalysis mathematical, to make it climb a few steps towards the rank of the most formal sciences, comes close to disciplined mysticism. He reclaims for rationality themes and procedures of mysticism in order to bend them to his own purposes, or rather to increase the receptivity of the analyst to the events of the analysis that are not within the range of the sensible. This is the reason why Bion paraphrases Kant when he writes:

> When I tried to employ meaningless terms – alpha and beta were typical – I found that 'concepts without intuition which are empty and intuitions without conceptions which are blind' rapidly became 'black holes into which turbulence had seeped and empty concepts flooded with riotous meaning'.
>
> (Bion, 1977a, p. 229)

Notes

1 'Even the Beautiful must die!'
2 See Kristeva, 1980; Genette, 1982.
3 Clearly the two paradigms are not mutually exclusive, and in fact they can be found together in the detective stories of Edgar Allan Poe.
4 Harris Williams (2010a) devotes only a few lines to the theme of the sublime.
5 Cf. Berger (2000, p. 255): 'Still lives . . . were caught (in the Dutch) at their toppunt: the zenith before the fall; the moment of perfect ripeness before the decay.'
6 In Freud too we find the theme of archaeological ruins, but within a logic quite different from Bion's which is based on an aesthetic rather than an evidential paradigm. Naturally, Freud was also influenced to some degree by Romanticism and he certainly had no difficulty with the subject of 'transience', which is linked among other things to poetry and art.
7 According to Harold Bloom, upstream of any creativity, Freud would presuppose the narcissistic wound of the 'infant's tragic and inevitable first failure in sexual love' (Bloom, 1982, p. 97). The Freudian theory of the genealogy of drives and consciousness would indeed be 'catastrophic' and for this reason is tinted with the negative colours of the sublime. In *On narcissism* Freud wonders 'what makes it necessary at all for our mental life to pass beyond the limits of narcissism and to attach the libido to objects?' and quotes Heine: 'Illness was no doubt the final cause of the whole urge to create. By creating, I could recover; by creating, I became healthy' (Freud, 1914, p. 85). Thus Freud 'transposes from the catastrophe of creativity to the catastrophe of falling in love' (Bloom, ibid., p. 105).
8 For thinking about this excess, see also Laplanche's (2004) concept of traumatic seduction.
9 The reason for my harking back to this controversial German philosopher is that in his existential analysis there can be found a radical and definitive critique of the limitations of thinking about the subject as isolated.
10 Translator's note: the Italian word stupore means both 'astonishment' and 'stupor'.
11 It goes without saying that among the many possible ways of interpreting O, there is also the vocal expression of surprise, as in the onomatopoeia of 'awe'.

Chapter 2

On sublimation

The sublime and sublimation are the key concepts of two theories of aesthetic experience exploring the spiritual emancipation of man. One theory, born in classical antiquity as a principle of rhetoric, acquired a philosophical or psychological–philosophical status in the pre-Romantic period during the second half of the eighteenth century; the other is instead part of the Freudian view of psychic development, therefore presenting itself from the start as a psychological theory. Both theories propose themselves as heuristic tools to investigate the mysteries of artistic creativity at its highest levels[1] and, according to both, the experience of art fruition would afford an 'elevation' of the subject. The contiguity of these two theoretical threads is not only seen in the fact that the terms which define them, namely sublime and sublimation, share the same etymological root[2] – the first referring to the subject's ethically enriching ascent, the second to the set of psychical transformations that the Ego undergoes but it may be argued that their similarity extends to the fields of investigation and, even if through different explanatory routes, to the different theoretical conclusions. There is, however, an asymmetry in the reception of the concepts of sublimity and of sublimation.

In fact, whereas the sublime seems never to go out of fashion, sublimation is somewhat the 'Cinderella' of psychoanalysis. Despite being one of the most debated and widely disseminated concepts in popular culture to the point of becoming a feature of common speech the concept of sublimation still lacks a convincing systematic theorization. It is not therefore surprising that sublimation may suffer from being dated or discredited.

For this reason, and in light of the relative similarity between the two concepts, but also in view of their different 'specific weights' in their respective disciplinary domains, I propose that it is worthwhile revisiting sublimation through the theory of the sublime to assess if, once reinterpreted or 'rediscovered', the concept may still be considered a valid theoretical and clinical tool. To my knowledge, an attempt to compare sublimation and the sublime has not yet been carried out.[3]

A nebulous (sublime?) concept: Freud and sublimation

The concept of sublimation has been marked by a degree of ambiguity since its very origin. We find it for the first time – after a hint in a letter to Fliess dated 2 May 1897 (Freud, 1985) – in the case of Dora, where sublimation possibly arises from the repression of infantile perverse sexual dispositions, and is a feature of transference 'more ingeniously constructed'; transference, that is, which does not take the form of mere 'reprints' but of 'revised editions' of earlier psychic experiences (Freud, 1901a, p. 116). Freud did not manage to write the chapter he had planned in his *Metapsychology* which might have cast greater clarity on this topic (or perhaps it was lost).

But what do we mean by 'to sublimate'? Essentially, we mean the capacity to be able to convert a sexual drive – in Freud's writings a recurring synonym of sublimation is 'sexual abstinence' – into a non-sexual one, and to change its object and aim. The new aim is psychically 'closely related' to the old one, but is 'higher' and therefore 'unobjectionable' (Freud, 1910a, p. 28) and 'more socially valuable' (ibid., p. 54), as it relates to specifically human and socially approved functions and activities.

Not that for the individual a direct sexual satisfaction would not have value, but one attained through sublimation would have value for more people (this doesn't imply that for some sublimation may have no value at all or even be despised). Sublimation therefore refers to a 'displacement of libido' (Freud, 1930, p. 79), where the libido's impetus has been mitigated, 'tamed', and its aim deviated to a 'finer and higher' joy; a joy, even though of 'much lesser intensity than the direct satisfaction of coarser drives [would bring]', that does 'not convulse our physical framework'.

This operation seems intuitively plausible, however there remains a certain degree of ambiguity between true and pathological (compulsive and prevalent) sublimation. Freud's position appears to rest on a precarious balance between considering sublimation as a defence mechanism, whereby the sexual drives (or, better still, their partial and non-differentiated infantile components) are masked and embellished, or treating sublimation as a 'legitimate' collector to control the strength of the sexual drives. Sometimes Freud sees 'suppression by reaction-formation' (Freud, 1905, p. 238), as a sub-species of sublimation; other times he seems to argue that through sublimation the libido is able to take a fast track to effectively mollify the effects of the conflict between psychic demands and prohibition. There are nonetheless limits to the possibility of sublimating sexual libido. Sublimation, Freud writes, is 'accessible only to a few people. It requires special talents and gifts, which, on a practical scale, are not exactly common' (1930, p. 80).

There are three especially contentious points: it is unclear *whether* and *how* the desexualization of the drive is attained; it is also unclear if sublimation has to be intended as a defence mechanism or simply as an 'alternative' release pathway for the flow of the libido, one of gratification rather than repression, so to speak;

finally it is unclear whether, with respect to sublimation, the presence of a special creative talent in the fields of arts or science is necessary. We can immediately see the problems that stem from a spurious, chimerical definition like the classical definition of sublimation, the basis of which is an obscure appeal partly to metapsychology, and partly to sociology of arts and to micro-sociology of patient's biographies. The classical definition of sublimation, in fact, hypostasizes a psychic function by inferring it from the significance created by something unknown in advance (in the sense that it may or may not find effective realization) – namely the capacity to create an aesthetic object. If this is the only possible route for metapsychological thinking, then in the case of sublimation, not only is the psychic mechanism invisible, but doubt is cast upon the very existence of the observable phenomenon from which that mechanism may be inferred. We therefore have the impression that in the case of sublimation we are dealing with a tautological or circular definition of the concept.

The aim of the present analysis will be to explore where these incongruities may lead and whether it may be possible to solve them.

With regard to the first question at issue – how libidinal drives may be desexualized – the view expressed in the first Freudian theory of the drives suggests that this can happen through regression. Libidinal drives, and in particular the perverse ones which fail to integrate with mature genitality, lean on functions which are not directly correlated to sexuality. Later on, with the introduction of the theory of narcissism, Freud provided a second explanation, grounding the pact of sublimation in an exchange between the object-seeking libido (sexual) and the narcissistic libido (desexualized). By identifying with the object, the object-seeking libido turns into the narcissistic libido and henceforth becomes 'transferable' and 'indifferent'. Consequently, sexualized gratification may be substituted by narcissistic gratification. A certain caution is however necessary: if the Ego subtracts too much libido and in doing so is allied with the death instinct, a dangerous drive imbalance may ensue.

To describe this process in *The Ego and the Id* (1923), Freud uses as an allegory of sublimation, or rather of its failure, the pre-Romantic painting by Wihelm von Kaulbach *The Battle of the Huns* (*Hunnenschlacht*), now at the Staatsgalerie in Stuttgart – a picture effectively 'sublime' for the epoch it belongs to (1837) and for its subject and its resonances, for instance in Liszt's homonymous symphonic poem which was inspired by it.

Freud writes: 'The struggle which once raged in the deepest strata of the mind, and was not brought to an end by rapid sublimation and identification, is now continued in a higher region, like *The Battle of the Huns* in Kaulbach's painting' (Freud, 1923, p. 32). And then further on:

> Towards the two classes of instincts the ego's attitude is not impartial. Through its work of identification and sublimation it [the ego] gives the death instincts in the id assistance in gaining control over the libido, but in so doing it runs the risk of becoming the object of the death instincts and of itself

> perishing. In order to be able to help in this way it has had itself to become filled with libido; it thus itself becomes the representative of Eros and henceforward desires to live and to be loved . . . But since the ego's work of sublimation results in a defusion of the instincts and a liberation of the aggressive instincts in the super-ego, its struggle against the libido exposes it to the danger of maltreatment and death. In suffering under the attacks of the super-ego or perhaps even succumbing to them, the ego is meeting with a fate like that of the protista which are destroyed by the products of decomposition that they themselves have created. From the economic point of view the morality that functions in the super-ego seems to be a similar product of decomposition.
>
> (Freud, 1923, p. 44)

Let us note in this passage the dramatic emphasis and the extraordinary Nietzschean metaphor of morality as a product of decomposition. The fragile Ego is forced to invoke 'by way of sublimation' a cumbersome ally, 'the death instincts in the id', which may assist 'in gaining control over the libido, but in so doing, it [the Ego] runs the risk of becoming the object of the death instincts and of itself perishing' (Freud, 1923, p. 44). Eros and Thanatos, the forces that join and disjoin, the vital drives rooted in the body and the devitalizing experience of abstract logics, separate and take arms against each other. We therefore gather that the tactic of resorting to sublimation is never entirely free of risks. As in the painting the battle between the Huns and the Romans is so terrible that the souls of the deceased continue to fight in the skies as they ascend to paradise, so the fight against the libidinal drives, which the Ego cannot overcome on its own, transfers itself by way of sublimation onto 'more elevated grounds' where the Super-Ego may come to the Ego's aid.

In our view, this passage is very interesting as it is the only one where Freud juxtaposes sublimation, the sublime and moral elevation. The passage is even more interesting because, reading between the lines, it contains a theory of negative sublimation, the consequence of which would be an inauspicious dissociation between the drives, in which the rise of the moral impulse is no longer balanced by the anchorage of the libidinal impulse in the body and its needs; or in which there would be no arrival at a level of communicative creativity capable of restoring the interplay of mutual recognition. We should not be surprised then if sublimation often stands as a symptom of a certain 'fragility' and 'instability' of the Ego (Le Guen, 2008, p. 1259), and if it assumes a foreboding, deadening, even destructive aspect that betrays its relatedness to repression and perversion. It is what happens, for instance, even at a collective level, when the Ego ideal sours into a poisonous ideal Ego.

With regard to the second question at issue, in the Freudian understanding of sublimation an important element is the reference to the 'great' sublimations in the arts. A confirmation of this, and of the general weakness of the theory, can be found in the fact that the great majority of authors who address sublimation always refer to patients who are, to some level, engaged with the practical activity of artistic creation, even if only as amateurs. In this way, however, the 'little', ordinary sublimations carried out by people who do not possess an artistic talent (nor consider this in any way a problem), or who are not even capable of extraordinary intellectual attainments, remain excluded from any theoretical framework. Once again, we encounter the difficulty of reconciling a restricted theory of sublimation with a broader one.

Even assessing the social value attached to a specific sublimatory achievement is an uncertain terrain. It has been noted that in Freud's opinion the Surrealists, who we today revere as real artists, were only 'fools'. Furthermore, with regard to the clinical parameter of psychic well-being, the same person may be proficient at sublimating, but altogether suffer from some serious perversion. It is however a fact that even if we allow for the art objects produced to have a wide range of accomplishments, if the reference to some form of artistic creativity falls the concept of sublimation is lost too.

Let us now come to the third question at issue, which relates to the use of the concept of sublimation in clinical practice. Intuitively – I repeat – if we stay within the orbit of drive theory we may adhere without much ado to the Freudian idea that a certain individual, unlike others, may exploit the capacity to divert and channel instinctual resources towards goals that are not sexual in nature; he may thus manage to exhaust the libidinal resources, thereby reducing their subversive capacity to threaten the Ego's integrity, while also earning a narcissistic gain. If however we go back to interrogating what we now seem to be taking for granted, and set aside the problem of the need for extraordinary capacities by considering 'common' sublimation too, we become aware that the distinction between the sublimatory activity that promotes an authentic existence in general and the one that appears as a route to alienation is subtle and almost intangible.

To distinguish between positive and symptomatic sublimation (false, corrupted, artificial sublimation; Loewald, 1988) we in fact find ourselves introducing a subjective judgement value: a judgement which takes one direction or the other on the basis of one's personal conscious and unconscious ideologies. Not that this risk were not inherent to any other clinical assessment that we are continuously required to make, but I would argue that here the vagueness of the theoretical points of reference carries a lot more weight.

First of all, it is worth noticing how a 'metaphysical' prejudice fatally nests itself within the position according to which sublimation is inauthentic; this view, behind the screen of the finest intellectual creations, assumes the existence of a 'true' reality – that of the body and of genitality. On the other hand, a denial of the body and an ascetic idea of 'progress' rests hidden behind an uncritically positive evaluation of sublimation.

Therefore, the sociological 'objective' evidence of the existence of a sublimatory activity is not reliable if it is not considered within the wider scope of the structure of the personality and of the peculiar meaning that it may have for any specific individual. Nonetheless, the issue of sublimation remains elusive. What it might be – whether there is a negative sublimation too or if it is always a positive mechanism, the negative one resulting only from its failure – we continue to not know, as we are left to refer to extrinsic evaluation criteria.

From these brief considerations we may see even at a glance how the concept of sublimation is still deeply incoherent (according to Laplanche and Pontalis (1980a, p. 433): 'one of the lacunae in psycho-analytic thought') and how, even in the best of scenarios, it remains an open question.

Let us now consider some of the classical and recent contributions on this theme. I would however like to state that what will follow will not be a critical review. I intend only to outline some benchmarks which may help us develop our understanding of the concept of sublimation in light of the theory of the sublime.

Sublimation after Freud and according to some contemporary authors

According to Klein (1930, p. 26): 'symbolism is the foundation of all sublimation and of every talent, since it is by way of symbolic equation that things, activities and interests become the subject of libidinal phantasies'. At the root of symbolism, she reminds us, there is identification. And Klein in fact mentions Ferenczi's hypothesis (1915) according to which psychoanalytical symbols differ from others in that they arise from a 'sexualization of the universe'. Ferenczi argues that such a process starts by setting up a series of equivalences between the various erogenous zones of the body which become 'identified' with each other (equalized) by the pleasurable sensations the baby derives from them; subsequently, by the extension through 'irradiation' of such 'symbolic assimilations' to the objects of the world and, lastly, by the repression of the symbolized sexual term. With brilliant insight, Ferenczi highlights that this symbolization cannot be explained as created by analogy only, as if it relied on a rational process, *rather it is produced on an affective and emotional basis*.

On the same track opened up by Klein and Ferenczi we find some contemporary authors. According to Roussillon (2005) sublimation is not a defence, but a transformation akin to the hallucinatory fulfilment of desire that is produced in the absence of the object. Hallucination and sublimation both make a representation concrete: in the case of hallucination, this occurs in perception; in the case of sublimation, this occurs in an object representation. There is a transformation into something external and concrete, tangible, tactile, visual, audible and olfactory. Between sublimation and hallucination there is however a substantial difference. In sublimation the subject undergoes a mourning process and preserves an awareness of the loss of the object; from the process of primary hallucination, which seeks out an identity of perception, through to sublimation, the subject accesses the domain of illusion. As material, the 'object-representations' bear some similarity to Winnicott's transitional objects – the child's first sublimatory activity is play. So described, sublimation approaches what we mean by the term symbolization, without totally coinciding with it.

Rousillon de facto draws a continuum between the various thought processes. The hallucinatory, he argues, is the first step towards representation and not an activity neatly opposed to it. Sublimation places itself at a halfway point in the process of symbolization, where things accede to words and in which the symbol acts as the transitional object.

The 'object-representation' could be defined as a pre-concept or in an oxymoronic way as a 'concrete concept': not yet fully achieved, and not yet completely abstract (*abs-tractus*) and universal as a proper concept would be, but rather it maintains both a specific singularity and a degree of (relative) universality. All thinking beings who are not delusional cannot but share the same concept of a 'tree', the universal notion of 'treehood' [*das Baumhafte*] (Heidegger, 2009); however, many, *but not all*, would be touched reading Leopardi's poems, which we may think of as a 'concept-thing'.[4]

Reviewing sublimation in light of Winnicott's theory of the transitionality, Roussillon points out with great coherency that the development of the capacity to sublimate depends upon the environment and on the primary object-relations. He furthermore specifies that if there were desexualization it would happen at the level of secondary processes, not primary processes. In his view, primary sexualization, namely the libidinal investment in the unconscious fantasy, would instead linger on.

This position is shared by André (2005), according to whom we should talk about sexualization rather than desexualization. He argues that the metaphor-creating transformation implied in sublimation relates itself to and at the same time differentiates itself from the transformation of the dream-work (which he however names 'autistic'), since it is bound to 'the Apollonian constraints represented by form' (2005, p. 1478). With regard to the 'deviation' from the normative direction which drives flow towards, André (2005, p. 1480) also reminds us that according to Freud 'something in the very nature of drives hinders the attainment of a *full* satisfaction . . . not of *a* satisfaction, but of full satisfaction'. Perhaps the notion of sublimation, André concludes, contains in itself a radical criticism of the very idea of aim, as drives would always be somewhat diverted from it. This consideration opens the way to a redefinition of drives, since it is as though a quota of them were always 'forced' to deviate from the aim, creating a gap which then only words may bridge.

Julia Kristeva's contribution (2005) appears consistent with this approach. According to her, a sublimatory process is in fact already inherent in the constitution of language as a '*perverse object*' (Kristeva, 2005, p. 1658), one removed from the domain of 'normal' instinctual gratification. The concreteness Roussillon attributes to sublimated objects is extended by Kristeva to embrace words' material side as symbols used in language. It is by submitting to dependency on the rules of language, and therefore melding the drive into vocabulary and syntax – that is, by sexualizing language – that the subject is liberated from dependence on the real object (Kristeva, 2005, p. 1660). Subjectivity is founded on the constitutive cultural perversion which is the outcome of sublimation. Sublimation moreover accounts for the 'normal' creativity of language. The 'great' creativity displayed in works of art represents only a rare and more conspicuous example of the same process.

This also appears to be the position sustained by Conrotto (2004, p. 1940) who links sublimation, symbolization and mentalization: 'I would argue that the transference onto the word is already the effect of a process of sublimation . . . there is obviously a close relationship between sublimation and mentalisation.' Conrotto (2004, p. 1031) furthermore usefully differentiates between a *primary* sublimation, where it is not sexual contents which are excluded by sublimation, but 'it is the sexual enjoyment of the object that is substituted with an investment in the object in order to come to know her', and a *secondary* sublimation which arises with the resolution of the Oedipus complex.

The theories of Rousillon, André, Kristeva and Conrotto are among the most evocative perspectives in the literature; however they are also the theories which most divest sublimation of its specificity. What difference would there be between using symbols, words and sublimating then? How do we account for the rarity of great artistic and scientific creations? At any rate, Ferenczi's proposed equivalence between identification and symbolization (even if this is limited to psychoanalytic symbols), Klein's proposed equivalence between symbolization and sublimation, the 'hallucinatory' in Roussillon, the unattainability of a 'full' libidinal satisfaction in André, Kristeva's 'perversion', and Conrotto's *primary* sublimation (2004), all bring us back to the idea that psychic birth *in itself* may require a certain sublimatory activity to work through the loss of the object. A 'physiological' loss for humans, since the object cannot be met by the subject in its wholeness, whereas animals, who lack a subjective self, do not perceive themselves as opposed to objects.

This is equivalent to saying that loss is inherent to the constitution of the very process of *subjectivation*. Baldacci and Sechaud's presentations at the Congress of French-speaking Psychonalysts in 2005 centred on exactly these two aspects of sublimation – its *precocity* and its relationship to the process of *mourning*.

These studies – the majority of the most recent ones coming from the French school which is the most committed to furthering conceptual research in the domain of metapsychology – are interesting but not conclusive. They are, moreover, rooted in drive theory, and consequently, although they do refer to the radically intersubjective nature of the processes of psychic birth, they are unable to account for it with the sophistication which, in my opinion, is made possible by the conceptual tools of the latest post-Bionian theories. It is nonetheless true that these authors are among those who prepare the way for us to interpret the concept of sublimation within the framework of a two-person or, broadly speaking, relational psychoanalysis.

But how can we integrate their contributions? Here is where my proposition – to reinterpret sublimation in the light of the theory of the sublime – may prove fruitful. Interpreted psychoanalytically, the aesthetic of the sublime bears a close resemblance to the theory of how psychic transformations of sublimation occur, as we are redefining it – namely as a process of symbolization/subjectivation. The aesthetic of the sublime affords us an X-ray analysis, revealing the dramatic vicissitudes through which this process of (affective) identification takes place – *its genesis*. And it does so both in a rich body of logical-deductive theorizing and in the furtherance of the theory using other expressive tools, those of the concrete artistic achievements which the theory has inspired.

The aesthetic of the sublime and the numerous works of art which paradigmatically illustrate it, may play the same heuristic role for sublimation as was played for Freud by his giving the name 'Oedipus complex' (that is, by borrowing the profound artistic intuitions of Sophocles' tragedy) to a series of infantile fantasies linked to specific relational configurations within the bosom of the family: making available a theory in which we look inside ourselves, one to be lived, and not only to learn. We would have a theory not only made up of the abstract terms of metapsychology, or of the just-as-abstract terms of the aesthetic of the sublime, but one constituted by images of volcanic lava, immense glaciers, impervious tops, stormy seas: the negative side of the object aesthetically revealed.

Sublimity

Due to the vastness of the subject-matter, it won't here be possible to map the whole historical and theoretical field of the aesthetic of the sublime, not even in synthesis. It suffices to say that it is a current of thought that was established during the eighteenth century, based on the translation and reprint of the ancient treatise by Longinus (also known as Pseudo-Longinus or the Anonymous of the Sublime) dated first or second century BC (Grube, 1957).

At the core of the aesthetic of the sublime we find the description of how this feeling originates from a representation of the chasm between the finite domain of mankind and the infinite of nature. Anyone experiencing this chasm becomes aware of a feeling of profound communion with the other, and with the whole of creation and humanity. Simultaneously they will feel the field of their experience expanding and *an ascent* in their sense of subjective self. The spatial metaphor accounts for the perception of seeing things (to 'dominate' from above) from the highest point of a primary emotional experience transformed into thought. The object, which acts as an intermediary for this effect to take place, is perceived as beautiful, and through an awe-inspiring accentuation of beauty as 'sublime', a term that turns the experience of spiritual ascent into a metaphor.

But how does this experience arise?

Longinus's answer consists of a set of rhetorical precepts based on how to achieve the zenith of artistic creation, and therefore evoke the noble feeling of the sublime in the viewer. Centuries later with Burke (1756b) the sublime is no longer presented in terms of rhetoric, style, or linguistics, but rather as a psychological, natural and extra-linguistic phenomenon. What evokes the feeling of the sublime is any natural object that elicits terror because it threatens the survival of the subject: 'Whatever is fitted in any sort to excite the ideas of pain and danger, that is to say, whatever is in any sort terrible, or is conversant about terrible objects, or operates in a manner analogous to terror, is a source of the sublime' (Burke, 1756b, p. 24 II). As long as the threat is real no space is left for the feeling of the sublime, but such a space is created if the subject is far enough from the phenomenon he is observing to be safe from harm.

Nonetheless the process by which the sense of the sublime is attained is not clear. Burke introduces an idiosyncratic distinction between 'pleasure', which according to him would always be 'positive' in the sense of not attached to any other feeling, and 'delight'. In Burke's conception, delight is evoked by the awareness of being safe and by the 'sympathy' one feels towards others who may be in misery. Delight would therefore arise from the combination of a narcissistic and an anti-narcissistic impulse. More precisely, delight arises as soon as we are out of peril but still trembling. It is substantially an apprehension of the 'quiver of death' (Sertoli, 2002); it is akin to taking a glance at the negative: at absence, death, the nothingness that is constitutive of being.

For the purposes of our enquiry, let us agree that for Burke the sublime is the description of a movement towards sociability, followed by a distinguishing of oneself from it. Unlike Kant, who applies a rationalistic emphasis to the same problem, Burke never wearies of underlining how the sublime does not derive from reasoning, but is a strictly emotional phenomenon. Terror is etymologically linked to trembling: the body teeters, is gripped by vertigo. This emphasis on the pathic element is extremely modern, and anticipates the current theoretical emphasis on the role of the body and the emotions in the process of becoming subjects.

In the 'Analytic of the sublime', situated at the heart of the *Third Critique*, more than any other author Kant (1790) explicitly treats the sublime as a theory of the subject. Departing from Longinus, first of all Kant too neatly distinguishes between beauty and the sublime. In his view, the sublime is the feeling evoked in ourselves by the spectacle of elements so grandiose and terrible that they cannot be grasped in their totality by the senses. This initial impasse can be overcome, however, thanks to the intervention of extra-sensory faculties which we then pleasurably discover in ourselves: namely reason. But, on account of this very process, this discovery poses itself as a *negative pleasure*.[5] To put it differently, it is as though the sublime were the experience of 'hitting on the brakes' which makes us discover with relief that we have antilock brakes (ABS) in our standard motor equipment, which allows us to stay on route. However, the sublime is something more than the controlled braking, as it not only reveals the existence of a self-preservation drive, it produces a mysterious elevation of the subject from the domain of sensory apprehension to apprehension governed by reason.

How this shift may happen remains somewhat mysterious in Kant as well, even though we may be able to recall situations from life experiences when we have been rescued by reason and are able to transcend our physical limits. What I would argue is lacking in this theory is the level of intersubjectivity, unless we resort to finding it in the *sensus communis* of the transcendental order, which according to Kant makes aesthetic judgements universal.

We are still within the dynamics of forces that closely approach drive theory, as Kant intellectualizes the process that takes us to the sublime. Using Hertz's (1985, p. 39) expression, according to Kant the sense of the sublime is born out of 'sheer cognitive exhaustion'. It is not anymore a question of horror, or of a sustainable horror (as Rilke (1995) says), of human sympathy and reverence, but a surrendering of the imagination, and therefore of sensibility, to reason. The infinite in nature, which cannot be apprehended by reason, can however be 'thought'. If for instance we wanted to 'imagine', in the sense of apprehending through the senses, all the details of a waterfall, every single drop, it would be impossible; we could, however, by way of thought, imagine being capable of such a thing, since there is an imagination that pertains to the senses and an imagination that pertains to reason. According to Kant, the 'moral' elevation afforded by the sublime is born out of this very tension. The sublime is the agent of a self-revelation and self-elevation, which we experience in the attempt to *represent the non-representable*. For our purposes, it is highly significant that Kant posited a form of 'negative pleasure' at the origin of this spiritual elevation of the self.

Schiller's (1793b) theory of the sublime proceeds along lines not too far from Kant's. It however differs from Kant inasmuch as Schiller develops the theme of caducity, in a way that on the one hand leads us back to Burke's terror, and on the other hand affords us a link to Freud's idea of the *uncanny* (Freud, 1919a). According to Reitani (2003, p. 132), '*The anguish of caducity* is the true starting point for Schiller. Nothing is more terrifying than the representation of death . . . : "*Auch das Schöne muß sterben*", "Even beauty has to die!" is the solemn exclamation of one of his most accomplished lyrical compositions of the *Nänie* [Nenia].' Schiller (1793b, p. 15) writes that 'an object, whose existence conflicts with the requirements for ours, is, if we do not feel that our power measures up to it, an object of fear, fearsome'.

Not every artistic subject is therefore able to evoke the feeling of the sublime, nor any way of representing it. The represented object that is capable of eliciting the feeling of the sublime must be one which more often than not could virtually crush the feeble human's individuality. Romantic art offers us an exhausting catalogue of these kinds of objects: grandiose natural phenomena, catastrophic events, waterfalls, volcanos, deep gorges, snowy mountain-tops, stormy seas and so forth.

Caspar David Friedrich's painting *Wanderer above the Sea of Fog* (1817–18) and Turner's *Snow Storm: Steam-Boat off a Harbour's Mouth* (1842) are good examples. Following Kant's distinction (1790), these paintings are respectively inspired by the 'mathematical sublime' which is linked to the immeasurability of the represented object, and to the 'dynamic sublime', which instead expresses the object's power and destructivity.

As we have seen, in the long history of the aesthetic of the sublime each author emphasizes a part feature of it. But from Longinus to Kant two factors are highlighted as determinants of the transformation which gives rise to the feeling of the sublime: an 'infinite' landscape which evokes awe, terror, anguish and a *rhetoric* that is able to represent it. But isn't rhetoric in literature what the capacity to represent is in everyday life?

Of this capacity to represent Longinus highlights the more aesthetic aspect, Burke the more bodily aspect, and Kant the more intellectual. Longinus insists on the efficacy of the representation, Burke insists on the way a good 'representation' allows us a safe physical distance from what is represented, and Kant stresses the empowerment of the mind's rational faculties.

Now in my view what we need to do with the theme of sublimation is *rediscover the aesthetic sublime as an essential component of the psychological sublime*, reintroducing the importance of form, of the element that – even if already present in Longinus – loses sharpness in all those authors who tend towards a psychological sublime and, unsurprisingly, contrast it to beauty.

The agent of the transformation from pain to pleasure – in other words to pleasurable pain or to negative pleasure – cannot but be *form*, as in a certain type of order impressed in matter. In the intermediate, mediating area of art, in the felicitous[6] meeting of material/perceivable/physical (*aisthetikòs*) impulse and a rational/suprasensible/logical/moral impulse, the effect of personal integration is created: a reconciliation of the intellectual and the intuitive which corresponds to the 'mixed', amphibious nature of humanity. The loss of the body/perceivable/material which abstraction implies is slowed down, and on the contrary, as Amoroso (2014, p. 67) writes in an essay on Schiller's aesthetics,

> Aesthetic truth allows us to retrieve what was discarded, since it takes care of those individual determinations overlooked by logical truth . . . Aesthetic truth therefore constitutes a sort of rescuer of that 'metaphysical truth' or truth of being which precedes the truth of knowing itself.

It is this sublimating property of form that establishes an ideal or 'good' or 'right' distance from what simultaneously attracts and scares us. The right distance, which in the paintings is portrayed through the wanderer's physical position (or through the viewer's presumed one), arises from the transformation into an aesthetic form, from the adoption of an adequate mode of representation. In any case, it is the fruit of a practice which has its rules. In this wholly human capacity to achieve distance through representation – to put the feared object, not the concrete one anymore but a representation of it, 'in front' (Rilke, 1995) – man demonstrates its superior morality as a subject who is free to decide between various options, thereby transcending the limits set by the sheer power relationship between forces which stand at the basis of instinctual reactions.

The sublime in psychoanalysis

Let us now interpret the principal elements of the aesthetic and the psychology of the sublime within a psychoanalytic framework. It will be inevitable to see in the element of nature that frightens the viewer – irrespective of his inclusion in the painting – an object (in the psychoanalytic sense) that evokes the helplessness of the infant (Freud's *Hilflosigkeit*); in the 'good' form we will see instead the capacity of the object, through the generation of order and meaning from chaos, to contain and transform such a fear and thereby facilitate the development of the capacity to think.

We can therefore see the character of infinity which according to the aesthetic of the sublime must be held in the contemplated element of nature, not as one of the many possible attributes, but as the feature of the object which the subject must confront in himself. It will then be up to the 'forms of meeting' with the object – and if felicitous *sublimating* – to transform this infinite into something finite, controllable, conceivable – 'anxiety-provoking' but 'not frightening' anymore, to use the terms of Freud to describe the dream work operating in nightmares in *Beyond the Pleasure Principle*: 'There is something about anxiety that protects its subject against fright and so against fright-neurosis' (Freud, 1920, p. 13). *By way of theorizing on the arts, the aesthetic of the sublime expounds the nuclear experience at the basis of cognitive representation.*

Anyone can intuitively sense that the sublime has to do on the one hand with that 'terrific beauty' described by Rilke in his *Duino Elegies* (2005) – the beauty that terrifies us at the beginning of life – and on the other hand with the possibility of being able to master that terror. One can intuitively sense why the sublime is distinct from pleasurable beauty, and how it came to define the sense of beauty derived from a painful ('pathetic') experience; that is to say, from another perspective which I shall make my own, the sublime unveils the terrific element that is already inherent in pleasurable beauty inasmuch as beauty is, no matter what, a messenger of otherness (Lyotard, 1991).[7]

As with the infantile playing with the bobbin reel described by Freud (1920), in the theatre of the sublime the play we stage is always a 'sadomasochistic' one: the representation of a trauma where the protagonist is exposed/exposes himself to the 'blows' of nature (of the object). 'Thrown into the world', to become a subject he has to position himself at an adequately safe distance.

What affords the subject this distance?

I believe the answer could be the process of subject–object identification described above, which creates the foundation for the capacity to make representations of things – conscious and unconscious, but in any case rooted in the symbolic. The fascination of the natural object (for example in a painted landscape) stands for the attraction exerted by the object. The object's capacity to 'regret' deserting the subject or taking unfair advantage of it, and therefore to showing him its love in reverie, is what triggers a 'sublimating' identification.

This capacity, which in everyday life resides in being able to dream the trauma, is in the aesthetic of the sublime identified with the poetic ability to aesthetically convey such a transformation. The reverie provides the same function as the artist who is identified with a maternal internal object. The feeling of the sublime in the arts is equivalent to the feeling of shifting from dread to anxiety thanks to the object's proof of love.

The discarded matter which is inexorably lost in the process of constructing the Ego (and which in every way equates with access to language) is first of all the materiality of the mother's body. Before any 'subjective' determination, our primitive being lies in the undifferentiated relationship with the mother's body; this is the experience of a state-of-being entirely made up of an indistinct flow of sensations, which can only be theorized *a posteriori* but perhaps has some remnants in embodied memory. Physical separation from this corporeality, which Julia Kristeva describes in the concept of *abjection* (1982; and see also: Civitarese (2012a), precedes psychic separation, which can only take place when the first separation can be *thought*. Physical detachment stands as a prototype for the relative detachment from things which takes place thanks to language in the process of symbolization. The ascent (which is an ascent of thought) is to remove oneself from the mother's body. The manifold relational experiences with the primary object are sedimented in presymbolic and symbolic experiences. This corresponds to the idea, again put forward by Kristeva (1982), that at the origin of the symbol is an imaginary matricide (Sechaud, 2005).

For the sake of clarity, at this point I think it might be worth rephrasing the hypothesis I proposed in this chapter: the aesthetic of the sublime makes us grasp the most valid aspect of sublimation, once this is identified as a process of symbolization/mentalization/subjectivation, not (only) in exceptional artistic creations, but in the importance of the sensorial form (of emotions) in normal psychic development: so to speak in our everyday molecular sublimations. In turn, the concept of sublimation, seen in the light of the aesthetic of the sublime, helps us to grasp more clearly the intimate essence of symbolic processes.

In fact, the art of the author who manages to express the sublime 'lies in a sort of supreme excellence of language' (Anonymous, cit. in Panella, 2012, p. 35). But if we accept the principle of identity between humanity and language, wouldn't excelling in the use of language mean being profoundly (more profoundly than others) in accord with the community of those who speak it? As highlighted by Panella (2012, p. 36), the originality of Longinus's treatise on the sublime (and here we may add on the theory of sublimation) resides in the fact that 'for the first time there, the aesthetic (ethical-subjective) dimension prevails on the normativity of the level of rigorously prescriptive rules and injunctions of institutional character'. Doesn't regard for form express the awareness of the risk of 'sublimating' only on the level of logical abstraction, of being removed from the vital sources of existence, of losing body, or of rising too high above its needs?

As we know from psychopathology, the outcome of the struggle to exist (*ék-sistere*) is not given *a priori*. Thanks to the aesthetic of the sublime we discover that representation is not to be taken for granted but has something 'heroic' about it. After all, don't we look with spontaneous enthusiasm to young children's first verbal acquisitions and don't we intuitively treat them as 'heroic'? From this perspective we may understand the reason why the sublime is defined as 'negative pleasure': sublimity can adequately be described as the process of sublimating in the sense of *transforming dread into pleasure* (or rather into the pleasurable anguish intrinsic to self-awareness) – but isn't becoming *human* based on this very capacity? The fact remains that the first stage – though the experience presents itself to consciousness as simultaneous – is absolutely necessary. For the sake of logical coherence, we cannot help but to make this first stage coincide on the psychological level with the fright stirred up by the object's vanishing or by its overbearing presence. If such fright causes a trauma then representation is suspended.

Sublimation seen in light of the aesthetic of the sublime

From what has been said so far we may see how sublimity – but *not* the Freudian concept of sublimation – has two intrinsic features: *loss* and *precocity*, the latter understood as the coincidence between sublimation and the dawning capacity to use symbols, Laplanche's *dès l'origine* (1980) or Baldacci's *dès le debut* (2005). This is the missing link, without which we could not re-engage with the topic of sublimation, but which is restored to us by passing through sublimity: the role of a *traumatic factor*, a factor not even imagined in the classical theory of sublimation. It is a logical precocity that we are talking about since, from a psychoanalytic perspective, we recognize in the protagonists on the stage of the sublime – namely Nature and its spectator – respectively the immense and threatening primary object and the infant experiencing a condition of absolute impotence and dependency.

On the basis of what we have said so far sublimation can be understood less in terms of a deviated, partial and obscure drive satisfaction, and more in relation to the notion that *any* satisfaction is partial in its own right. Gratification is partial because the advent of language marks the loss of the Edenic condition of full and unperturbed satisfaction: a loss that recapitulates the mythical transformation of our primordial nature into humanity. If we could ever regain an Edenic state of plenitude it would mean the erasing of meaning and the death of the self. At the bottom of *being* there is a void that can never be filled again.

Man's spiritual elevation caused by sublimation is an ascent towards the concept and to abstract thought. A battle is necessary to conquer the condition of humanity, what we also call subjectivation. In this process of subjectivation we lose the 'body'. Like an aerostatic balloon from 'above' the subject can gain a perspective on his own animality, on things, on himself and on the object, but only at the cost of giving up his proto-emotionality. To sublimate is equivalent to *abstrahere* – to abstract, that is to categorize (to simplify through identification). The higher we fly the more we become 'moral' and universal. But here is what the renunciation of drives intrinsic to sublimation might mean: a certain renunciation of animality, of the object and of the body. Here is how we may interpret the vertical axis around which the figures of the Virgin and Child are arranged in many *Sacra Conversazione* in classical paintings.

If however the distance becomes excessive, we get lost in the infinite space as do the protagonists of the film *Gravity* (2013). Instead of 'losing body' to form emotional and intellectual categories, we 'lose the body' that is our sensory knowledge of emotions. In the traditional concept of sublimation, what we gain from renunciation is benevolence from the Super-Ego; however, it is not clear why the process may have an obvious limit in that it is true that we are not *only* animals but we are still *also* animals. Dividing the two aspects and being split by a potent blow into a good and an evil part, as in Calvino's *Cloven Viscount* (1998), would be disastrous.

As we see from these brief annotations, the aesthetic theory of the sublime lends itself to a creative revisiting of the theory of sublimation, conceived at the outset as a possible destiny for the drives. At the very least the aesthetic sublime affords this theory depth and colour. It is true, in my opinion, that, in a productive circularity, only a psychoanalytic reading is able to bring this conceptual richness to the surface and properly appreciate it.

Not even Klein's descriptions, focused as they are on unconscious fantasies and therefore on the 'ideational' aspect even though somewhat 'aesthetic' in their own right in configuring with great expressivity the horrific visions of a primitive world never explored before succeed in effectively theorizing the properly aesthetic element of form as the central factor in the sublimative transformation.

This is not to say that the psychoanalytic literature on sublimation fails to evoke the themes of mourning, precocity, trauma, the coincidence of subjectivation and symbolization, etc., but it has happened at random, like a simple set of options, and sometimes with no congruence between one and another. The aesthetic of the sublime in my view offers instead the opportunity to articulate some of these themes in an effective and coherent narrative (or a modern myth). Furthermore, through the artistic creations that the sublime has inspired, it affords us an understanding of its object which is not only theoretical, but also empathic. To sublimate is what we mostly do without being aware of it, and what we instead become aware of when art and life move us.

For a new theory of sublimation

Beyond the already obvious and meaningful convergences, let us now wonder then what is left of psychoanalytic sublimation if we review it from the vantage point of a metapsychology that we may define (post-)Bionian, and 'rediscover' it starting from the principles of the aesthetic of the sublime? From a clinical perspective, the concept loses a true theoretical workability, if not as a generic reference to the importance of unspecific and aesthetic factors of the treatment. What we obtain instead is a richer vision of the very process of symbolization which stands at the foundation of becoming a subject. The theory of sublimation and the theory of the sublime become two myths which, enlightening each other, on the one hand recount the birth of the subject in a compelling way, and on the other hand help us bring into focus three key factors with a sharpness we would not afford otherwise. The first factor we may define as the 'socialist' factor, the second as the 'aesthetic' and the latter as the 'traumatic'.

The 'socialism' of sublimation

From the perspective outlined here, sublimation is regarded as the felicitous unfolding of the process of subjectification, which after all is always, from the beginning of life, a social process. The idea of sociality implied by the traditional concept of sublimation in the 'downstream' reference to the creation of an object of art (*socially* valued) needs, in my view, to be brought back 'upstream' to the origin of creativity in the nascent mind; here we would look at the origin of the capacity to generate 'ideas' (or object-ideas) and thereby grow, thanks to another mind. Neither the Freudian idea of sublimation nor those of the authors we have outlined so far are anchored to a 'post-drive' theory of how the mind develops; a theory, that is, centred on the 'creativity' of the mother's mind as an index of her capacity to contain the infant's anxieties and therefore of her capacity to sublimate. To anchor our concept of sublimation to such a framework would instead mean to free it from the theory of drives (or it would imply a redefinition of the concept of drive at least).

I propose that symbol-formation, one way or the other, relies first of all on the creation of this primary symbol where the mother comes to *stand for/become* the child and vice versa, without erasing the differences; the creation of this first symbol would then stand as a basis for every successive symbolization involving other objects of the world. The auto-erotic pleasure described by Ferenczi (1915) as the invariant allowing the symbolization of an erogenous zone with another, and of these with other objects of the world, has to be seen as always mediated by the intense emotion of reuniting (to be at unison with/*at-one-ment*) with the mother.

In the process of interaction with the object taking place from birth onwards, the 'sublimating' factor would then reside in the transmission of the object's creativity, namely her capacity for reverie, to the infant's nascent subjectivity. In other words, the 'sublimating' factor would lie in the maternal capacity to provide the infant developmentally tailored opportunities to absorb these functions so that the child may develop psychically, which means being able to think and individuate. Sublimation thereby becomes nothing else but the theoretic exaltation of this process of recognizing and being recognized by the other: a 'socialist' drive, in the sense Bion (1965) gives to this term, referring to the overcoming of individual narcissism and identification with the group. From this standpoint, rather than a deviated satisfaction of the libidinal request, the concept of sublimation comes to express a specifically human capacity for cooperation and bonding.

An 'aesthetic' theory of subjectification

Apart from the 'social' birth of the mind, what sublimation most draws attention to with its obsessive reference to the concrete and public creation of artworks – perhaps the theoretical aspect which most deserves to be rediscovered in order to be saved from oblivion – is that even when it is not properly reflexive, but pre-(self-)reflexive, in the sense of bodily – that is, composed of sensomotor-procedural schemes and emotional categories, self-consciousness should be thought of as also constituted by a pre-reflexive dimension that is not situated outside language, the communicative medium which, as an essentially social fact, differentiates us from things and animals. There are modalities and human significations which give meaning to experience without passing through words, and which, when they do pass through words, 'signify' thanks to their 'body'. In essence, the aesthetic experience in art has its antecedent in the aesthetic experience which the mother capable of reverie is able to bring to life in her child.

Perhaps, without realizing it, what Freud was aiming at in the concept of sublimation does indeed revolve around the enigma of artistic creation, but only as a way of solving the enigma of the aesthetic pole of the subject: in other words, one's way of experiencing and constructing meaning that is not based on concepts, and is if anything a higher function than that, but not on this account external to the community, to the *sensus communis*, and indeed may even be more bound to it than the concept. It is as if Freud intuited that he had to remedy a shortcoming in his theory: that he had turned the Cartesian subject upside down, but without passing beyond the conceptual horizon of which it is the expression.

Sublimity, viewed as inscribed in it in the same way as a figure that only appears in a watermark, helps us see that Freud's theory of sublimation has to do with the 'production' of this 'aesthetic sense' of things and is the embodiment *tout court* of a theory of the aesthetic. So here is another reason to go back to investigating the concept of sublimation; because it happily contains the idea of a process which, to the extent that it develops successfully, elevates the Ego towards the concept, but a concept understood not only as the container of a thematizable content, but also, so to speak of a content whose meaning is semiotic, rhythmic and bodily, and intrinsically un-sayable.

We could say that sublimity forces us to reintroduce the object on the stage of sublimation – and by way of the object, reintroduce culture – not only as the aim but as the very origin of the subject. Sublimity forces us to reinscribe sublimation into a 'social' psychology. The specificity of sublimation is found in the way it shows how becoming a subject means to attune to the Other and gradually form more and more distilled concepts of things by discarding all the inert and inessential matter. But above all, sublimation shows that this process of simplification which stands at the basis of the most sophisticated forms of thoughts does not have to dissociate the emotional from the intellectual; on the contrary, sublimation ideally proceeds in parallel on the logical and sensory, rational and intuitive, intellectual and physical axis. The more we are capable of sharpening our logical concepts and our affective-emotional categories (we may call them following Carbone (2008) 'sensory ideas'), the more we become human. Ideally, an individual should her/himself be capable both of the most abstract rationality and of the greatest sensitivity towards the minimal details of the human and natural world.

Instead, we encounter dissociation whenever we meet someone extremely brilliant in logical reasoning but illiterate on the emotional level. It is this reference to the concrete/material/bodily/emotional that we find in the theory of sublimation (and not in other descriptions of subjectification) in its reference to the concreteness of the artistic object that compels us not to discard it as a psychoanalytical concept. *As a key element in the classical definition of sublimation, the concrete work of art becomes an allegory not only of the 'elevating' and concrete/aesthetic quality of the emotional unity which is the foundation of the subject, but also of the 'sensory' nature which our ideas need to maintain in a healthy process of subjectivation.*

So if we maintain the reference to art, it will not be in order to observe that sublimation has to take concrete form in a particular artwork, but because we see art as a metaphor for a process of psychic working-through aimed at the subject's construction of itself as an entity capable of abstract thought that does not cut it off from its bodily roots, but rather draws vital sap from them to nourish its growth into maturity. When this happens, sublimation coincides with an authentic process of personalization or somato-psychic (re-)integration. Through a new theory of sublimation, the object of art then recalls first of all the originally and exclusively sensory-affective root, and then the sensory-affective aspect – which coexists with the semantic one – of the idea.

Along a continuum these 'sensory ideas' interconnect with one another in a chain reaching up to, in the most fortunate of cases, the greatest heights of artistic creativity. In one case and in the other the meta-psychological meaning of the transformation that elevates would be identical.

Catastrophe and fright ↔ anxiety oscillation

Furthermore, and this is our third factor, what sublimity evocatively adds to the concept of sublimation/symbolization is the idea of a subjectivity whose establishment is conditioned on the presence of a catastrophe (in Bion's sense), which has always both *already happened* and is going *to happen* (is *imminent*), or of a *traumatic factor* which, as we have seen, *frightens* and therefore imposes a mourning process. But why define the effect of reality on the subject as traumatic, if by definition trauma means an overstimulation producing psychic wounds in the form of gaps of meaning? Because the infant is necessarily unprepared to cope with the stimuli which assail him. Paradoxically, such an exceeding (micro-) traumatic quota is necessary to establish the Ego, is a necessary element for symbolization and therefore self-awareness. Along the same lines of dream work in traumatic neurosis, we may imagine this work of mourning as 'endeavouring to master the stimulus retrospectively, by developing the anxiety whose omission was the cause of the traumatic neurosis' (Freud, 1920, p. 32), and to whom Freud assigned a 'function of the mental apparatus which, though it does not contradict the pleasure principle, is nevertheless independent from it and seems to be more primitive than the purpose of gaining pleasure and avoiding unpleasure' (Freud, ibid., p. 32).

The normal or exceptional character of this traumatic factor (which, with a more abstract term, we may call 'the negative') may perhaps explain the difference between 'ordinary' and 'exceptional' sublimations. If we therefore have the concept of sublimation interact with the theory of sublimity, it becomes apparent how it contains the idea of loss too, and specifically the one of precocity. One example of this could be the transposition of the infantile helplessness towards the object into the disproportion between human finitude and the natural infinite which we find in Romantic art inspired by the sublime. The unpleasurable, painful or pathetic element inherent to the sentiment of the sublime, which we should conceive as simultaneous rather than antecedent, can be figuratively identified with the *catastrophe* in the sense of a re-opening and overcoming of a standstill, and in the sense of a ruinous downfall, which we can see so often represented in Romantic paintings. Moreover, at an emotional level, the same unpleasurable, painful or pathetic element can be identified with the anxiety which as we have seen Freud presents to us as the guardian of the Ego.

In conclusion, living an 'aesthetically' rich life would then be proof of a normal sublimatory capacity. On the other hand, having the capacity to actually create an object of art would paradoxically denote the presence of some sort of 'upstream' psychic wound, giving rise to an obsessive drive to 'excess'. It could then be true, as Baldacci (2005) hypothesizes, that sublimations of exceptional level (and I would add, following Freud, in conjunction with a special talent) may derive from a disturbance in the earliest sublimatory processes: '*En d'autre termes, "le don de la nature" essaierait de compenser les exces ou les carences du don provenant de l'objet primaire*'[8] (2005, p. 1466). In such unordinary cases, to 'rise' would then take more decisively the meaning of a rising from dust, of an attempt to overcome a 'collapse' which took place but could not be experienced (Ogden, 2014). In which direction? A rise towards the peaks of the Ego ideal – but running the risk of chasing a dark ideal Ego – that is the overrated expectations of the object. In these cases of productive restlessness,[9] to distinguish between successful and unsuccessful exceptional sublimations would however be problematic. They might even share an identical profile at a metapsychological level, leaving talent only to account for the differences in actual artistic quality. The question remains open.

Notes

1 Furthermore, from Freud onwards, the capacity to sublimate, intended in its broader sense, has also been seen as one of the goals the patient should attain through analysis.

2 'Sublime' comes from the Latin word *sublimis*, composed by *sub* 'below' and *limen* 'threshold', meaning 'which reaches just below the highest threshold'. As a noun it translates the Greek expression *perì ipsous* (περὶ ὕψους), the title of a treatise written

in Neoplatonist circles by Longinus in the first or second century BC. 'Sublimation' translates the neologism *Sublimierung* first introduced by Freud and thereby different from the German term *Sublimation*, even though related to it. To synthetically refer to the aesthetic of the sublime in this chapter I will adopt the term 'sublimity'.

3 In their dictionaries of psychoanalysis, Moore and Fine (1990), Laplanche and Pontalis (1988) and De Mijolla (2005) make only the briefest of references to a possible derivation of the term 'sublimation' to, beyond chemistry, the aesthetic of the sublime. Le Guen (2008, p. 1256) raises the affinity between sublimation (*Sublimierung*) and sublime (*Erhaben*) and solicits that 'such a semantic proximity may be further explored'. The proximity between the two terms is self-evident in Latin languages with regard to the common etymological root. It is not in German, however on the one hand Freud knew the word 'sublime', which he used on at least a couple of occasions in French and German; on the second, the term Erhaben, chosen by the German translators to render the title (*Perì hìpsous*) of the Hellenistic period treatise *On the Sublime* by Longinus (Grube, 1957), still refers to a process of elevation/heightening of the subject towards an out-and-out rationality. Bloom (Arensberg, 1986, p. 7) considers Freud 'the last great theorist of that (sublime) mode', and argues that his essay on *The Uncanny* (Freud, 1919a) might be 'the only major contribution that the twentieth century has made to the aesthetics of the sublime'.

4 If truth be told, we should however add that even a person who is delusional continues, to a large extent, to dwell in language; and furthermore, that the thingly nature of what, within any word, expresses the concept prevents a complete disanchoring of the element of 'pure' meaning from the materiality of the body and therefore from the singularity of the entity it refers to.

5 Kant uses the adjective 'negative' as equivalent to Burke's 'horror', thereby immediately imparting a more abstract reading of the phenomenon.

6 That is created through a form perceived as beautiful.

7 See Szondi (2007) on the crisis of this distinction in Hegel.

8 'In other terms, the "gifts of nature" strive to compensate the primary object's excesses or deficiencies of provision.'

9 In Italian, 'smania' – *s-mania*.

[illegible]

[illegible]

5 [illegible]

6 [illegible]

7 See [illegible]

8 [illegible]

Chapter 3

Masochism and its rhythm

Freud (1924) addresses the scandal inherent in his investigation of 'the pleasure in pain' (p. 161) that is found in masochism, in three key texts written over a period of five years from 1919 to 1924 ('A child is being beaten', *Beyond the Pleasure Principle*, and 'The economic problem of masochism'). He categorizes the varied manifestations of masochism's broad spectrum in the realm of Oedipal conflict. Today, however, most hypotheses are no longer (or not only) centred on Oedipal conflict but on the role of pre-Oedipal factors. Masochism is seen more as the derivative of traumas in the earliest object relations.[1] My aim here is to propose a re-reading of Freud's three texts that emphasizes elements illuminating aspects of the new theories.

My account necessarily addresses interlocking themes, each of which would deserve to be dealt with in its own right, but what I hope gives it unity is the particular perspective I adopt: I dwell on the significance of two sets of remarks by Freud on the *rhythm* of pleasure (and hence on the rhythm of pleasure and pain) contained in the 1920 and 1924 texts, and I re-read these in the light of Gaddini's concept of 'fantasy in the body' (1982). If, as numerous writers have noted, masochism derives from many levels of psychic organization (see, e.g., Markman, 2012), Freud's remark's on rhythm may help us clarify which of these are the most primitive, belonging to the threshold of psychic birth, and less accessible to interpretation – unless, perhaps, it is an 'interpretation-in-action' (Ogden, 1994).

I take for granted the numerous insights about the meaning of masochistic suffering and the many useful technical suggestions for treatment available in the literature, too many indeed for me to review here.[2] Nevertheless, even though the hypothesis of the role played in masochism by factors in pre-Oedipal life has been put forward by various writers, as far as I know none of them has discussed it from the starting point of Freud's hint on the rhythm of pleasure–unpleasure, still less seen it as the expression of a kind of 'nightmare' experienced in the body.[3]

The genesis of masochism

'The economic problem of masochism' marks the conclusion of Freud's reflections on a symptom that in 1924 he still considered 'incomprehensible' (p. 161). He writes that in masochism it is as if the guardian of the psyche, the pleasure principle, were to find itself under the influence of a drug even more dangerous than its counterpart, sadism. Freud had begun his investigation a few years earlier, in 1919, with 'A child is being beaten', in which he studied the beating fantasies of neurotics. Here he enthusiastically expressed the conviction that he had finally discovered the essence of masochism. Between these two texts stands the great restructuring of metapsychology with the introduction of the two classes of drive, of life and death. I am of course referring to *Beyond the Pleasure Principle*, published in 1920. There is a continuity in these three works. This is how we are to understand the letter to Ferenczi of March 17, 1919 (Falzeder and Brabant, 1996, p. 335), in which Freud notes that he has completed 'A child is being beaten' and has started 'a second [work] with the mysterious heading, *Beyond the Pleasure Principle*', giving the impression that he wished to do no more than draft a new chapter on the same theme.

'A child is being beaten' is based on work with four women patients and two men, though Freud makes clear that he had a broader range of clinical material available. The fantasy has a three-stage development in the women ('*My father is beating the child*' → '*I am being beaten by my father*' → An adult is beating a child) and two-stage in the men ('*I am being beaten by my father*' → '*I am being beaten by my mother*'). Freud derives the scene from an incestuous fixation on the father, nourished by the normal Oedipus complex in the girl and by the inverse Oedipus complex in the boy, and by the consequent sense of guilt. To defend herself from the awareness of the forbidden desire, the girl changes the subject of the action and puts a boy in her place, while the boy instead represses only the sex of the parent. In the girl the conscious fantasy becomes sadistic; in the boy it remains masochistic. He represses his homosexuality but retains a feminine disposition towards his mother. The second stage of the development of the fantasy in the female, Freud notes, is the same as the first stage in the male; unlike the subsequent stages it is unconscious and can be reconstructed only in analysis. The other frequently encountered aspects described by Freud are the excitement that accompanies the fantasy; the seemingly coercive resort to masturbation; the familiar array of moral masochism including feelings of guilt and the experience of shame; the hesitation or reticence of the patient about speaking of these fantasies in analysis; the possibility of the fantasies evolving and being modified over time; the fact that they can give rise to an impasse and to negative therapeutic reactions during treatment; and the absence from the anamnesis of real experiences of beating.

However, in explaining the genesis of the beating fantasies, Freud did not limit himself to considering a genital factor, but hypothesized the interaction between a genital factor and a sadistic pre-genital component. The sense of guilt linked to the Oedipal factor would not be sufficient in itself to justify the overthrowing of the sadistic fantasy ('My father is beating a child') into a masochistic fantasy ('I am being beaten by my father'). Something else is needed: 'a share must also fall to the love-impulse' (1919b, p. 189). Indeed, Freud writes, primed by the repression of the underlying incestuous fantasy, 'there is another result as well:

a regressive debasement of the genital organization itself to a lower level. 'My father loves me' was meant in a genital sense; owing to the regression it is turned into 'My father is beating me (I am being beaten (loved) by my father)' (p. 189).

In this way, the punishment itself is eroticized, having not been, so to speak, a minute before. The beatings no longer represent only the necessary punishment to placate the sense of guilt aroused by the forbidden genital fantasy, but also its regressive substitute: that is, an expression of it according to the direct mode whereby it would operate at a more primitive stage of psychic development, when biting or being devoured, destroying or being destroyed, are the same as loving or being loved. Then we grasp how not even the self-defensive overthrowing of love in the hate expressed by the fantasy 'I am being beaten by my father' (the stage of the beating fantasy's evolution that is invariable in females and males) can ever remain in consciousness: because from one point of view in pre-genital unconscious life, which interacts with Oedipal life, it is entirely equivalent to the fantasy 'I am loved (sexually) by my father.'

In regression, the fantasy is strengthened and coloured by an excitatory quality. The masochist is excited by the beating fantasies because he or she[4] unconsciously 'sees' in them what others are unable to see. For the masochist the beatings are not only a punishment for the incestuous desire, for which there thus remains – as in any symptom – a certain indirect possibility of satisfaction, but also its actual realization. The beatings testify to the object's love. In other words, an old, previously dismissed *way* of loving is unearthed again, but it evidently is still there as a deep layer of the psyche, and in normal situations it remains on the margin of sexual life. Freud adds: 'The abnormal sexual constitution, finally, has shown its strength by forcing the Oedipus complex into a particular direction, and by compelling it to leave an unusual residue behind' (1919b, p. 192).

The pre-history of beating fantasies: rhythm and primary masochism

In attributing the etiopathogenesis of the beating fantasies to an effect of posteriority, Freud (1919b) seems to express the need to go back to a 'prehistory' of the subject: 'So it may quite well be that they have an earlier history, that they go through a process of development, that they represent an end-product and not an initial manifestation . . . The first phase of beating phantasies among girls, then, must belong to a very early period of childhood' (p. 184). That is, he seems to assert the idea that in order to understand masochism – perhaps along with tendencies other than that of regression to an old way of loving – we cannot hold on only to the Oedipal or indeed to the level of genital organization. For this reason he postulates that there may instead be a regression to aspects of (amorous) cruelty that are in fact proper to the archaic phases of psychic development, in particular to those linked to the second phase of the oral stage[5] and the anal-sadistic phase (Abraham, 1924). Such pleasurable cruelty is the element that allows the pleasure of biting to be ranked equally with the beatings. (As we have seen, it is thanks to regression that the beatings would stand for 'a passive (feminine) sexual relation' to the father (Freud, 1924, p. 169)).

Anticipating the whole literature on the role of narcissism and the early object relations in masochism, in order to understand the cause of masochism, the tendency to go ever further back, from the life history of the subject to his 'prehistory', is also evident in *Beyond the Pleasure Principle*, in the passage where Freud (1920) characterizes masochism as primary:

> [sadism] now enters the service of the sexual function. During the oral stage of organization of the libido, the act of obtaining erotic mastery over an object [the original sadism] coincides with that object's destruction; later, the sadistic instinct separates off, and finally, at the stage of genital primacy, it takes on, for the purposes of reproduction, the function of overpowering [and therefore no longer of destroying] the sexual object to the extent necessary for carrying out the sexual act

In a change from what he had previously claimed, Freud adds that 'masochism, the turning round of the instinct upon the subject's own ego, would in that case be a return to an earlier phase of the instinct's history, a regression', and that 'there *might* be such a thing as primary masochism' (1920, pp. 54–55).

Re-reading these texts in sequence today, we have the impression that Freud was being held back from the possibility of advancing his understanding of masochism by remaining anchored to the drive theory and to his essentially monadic theory of psychosexual development as evolving through a series of stages. His treatment of the subject sounds abstract, coloured by its biological foundations and by the weight attributed to constitutional factors. Yet the extraordinary thing here is that we are again witnessing one of those leaps forward in which he opens new paths for psychoanalytic reflection. Indeed, in the present case we can identify this return to the origins of psychic life as a feature that will mark all post-Freudian psychoanalysis, both as a general tendency and in the particular case of the interpretation of masochism.

And there are other indications of this tendency. I am referring to passages in *Beyond the Pleasure Principle* and 'The economic problem of masochism' where, to avoid making the pleasure principle the slave of the Nirvana principle, which is in turn an expression of the death instinct, Freud addresses the *rhythmic* character of pleasure–unpleasure. Indeed, he speculates that the sensations of pleasure and unpleasure depend not on 'any directly proportional ratio', but on 'the amount of increase or diminution in the quantity of excitation *in a given period of time*' (p. 8).

My proposal is that we read the brilliant observation on rhythm, which remains obscure not only in Freud but also in all the vast literature on masochism to follow, in the light of the pages on the significance of dreams in traumatic neuroses and on the wooden reel game, pages that immediately ensue in *Beyond the Pleasure Principle* and that create an interesting effect of *après-coup* in relation to it.

If we do so, we will see that Freud, in the very same moment in which he uses dreaming and the normal behaviour of a child at play as a model of pathological masochism, suggests a continuity between the negative/unpleasurable experience of tolerable frustration, inflicted by the object, that leads to symbolization and, at the other end of the spectrum, excessive and painful experience that produces pathology. Emphasizing this continuity allows us a new perspective on masochism and its tendency to endlessly resurface.[6]

Traumatic dreams and the fright ↔ anxiety oscillation

In these fascinating pages, Freud (1920) tries to untie the knot of evident contradiction existing on the theoretical level between the nature of traumatic dreams and the general principle of the dream as a hallucinatory satisfaction of infantile desire. How? By postulating a function of the dream *prior* to establishment of the 'sway of the pleasure principle' (p. 20), and hence independent of it, going back to a period in which the demands are different and due to '*a compulsion to repeat . . . more elementary, more instinctual than the pleasure principle which it overrides*' (p. 23; emphasis added). Dreaming would obey the need for 'mastering the amounts of stimulus which have broken in and of binding them, in the psychical sense, so that they can then be disposed of' (p. 30). 'These dreams', Freud concludes, 'are endeavouring to master the stimulus retrospectively, by developing the anxiety [*Angst*] whose omission was the cause of the traumatic neurosis' (p. 32). In fact, he goes on, anxiety offers protection from fright (*Schreck*), which instead always risks creating a breach in the psychic apparatus. Isn't this surprising? Dreaming would serve not to satisfy hallucinatory repressed infantile desire but to develop anxiety! Anxiety would be the GPS that guides us safely through the minefields of reality.

It is certainly the case that, if we broaden the meaning of what Freud is asserting, it is as if the dream were the servant of two masters: first the Ego ('it is only consistent to grant that there was also a time before the purpose of dreams was the fulfilment of wishes' (p. 33)), whose wounds it works hard to heal, and only afterwards, or as a second step, the Id. This regime of the dream would therefore apply to those regions not yet subject to the lordship of the Ego, or to those that are alienated from it by trauma, and indeed would have the very aim of extending this dominion.

But couldn't this interpretation of the function of dreaming be extended to the whole of psychic life? In fact it is easy to take the view – as Bion does when he characterizes the dream as a function tasked with the creation of meaning – that this function of strengthening the Ego, being in itself 'masochistic' in that it entails the revisiting of a traumatic scene, could remain active throughout life and continue to be primary ('more originary') in relation to the other. From the viewpoint of ontogenesis, this is surely the case. The id's impulses can be consciously experienced only if an Ego has been constructed in the meantime. If we accept this hypothesis, it is of no consequence if we adhere also to the corollary that the ultimate goal conjectured by Freud for masochism may then be a reduction of the ego's tension in the service of the death instinct, of the return of the 'living vesicle' to the peace of the inorganic.

And so when, immediately afterwards, we read the description of Freud's eighteen-month-old grandson Ernst playing at making a cotton-reel – symbolically, his mother – disappear and reappear, and as Freud adds in a footnote (p. 15), subsequently makes himself disappear in the mirror in which he had been reflected for a moment, it seems obvious to us – and this is what constitutes the *après-coup* effect – that it is as if Freud were claiming that in essence *any* trauma is nothing but the re-experiencing of the first trauma of birth and then that of the object's disappearance, and that the reel game is merely the child's attempt to 'dream' (by playing) the traumatic event: that is, to insert it into a story with meaning. The aim of 'mastering [in Italian: *legare*] the amounts of stimulus which have broken in and of binding them, in the psychical sense, so that they can then be disposed of' (p. 30), would become the general model of psychic life; in the language of Bion, *picturing emotions*, transforming beta elements into alpha elements and dream thoughts; in Freud's terms, transforming unpleasant elements 'into a subject to be recollected and worked over in the mind' (p. 17).

Now let us see why an ordinary children's game, the cotton-reel game, should help us in understanding masochism and what they have in common; and moreover, if we develop Freud's intuitions on the rhythm of unpleasure–pleasure with a certain quantity of that 'extreme line of thought' to which he lays claim (Freud, 1920, p. 37 n), what they unexpectedly have in common with art and aesthetic experience in relation to the task of psychic representation.

The cotton-reel game

I will introduce this section with a clinical example.

S tells me that as a little girl she used to beat the doll that was dearest to her, and then fell into despair – 'Real, not pretend!'[7] she explains. Then, filled with shame, she would hug the doll repeatedly. When she was a little older, she felt the urge to do much the same to the family cat. Now she does it to her boyfriend. This scene holds within it the sense of the more mentalized aspect of masochism, which is that of reawakening the love of the object by making it pay the price of guilt, if we think – and this is the other instructive aspect of the vignette – that in the game S puts a double identification into action: with herself as a child and with the parent who used to beat her and of whose love she compulsively needed reassurance.

'Real, not pretend!' makes us stop and think because, in relation to the primary traumatic event, any repetition really does have the character of make-believe. Even in clinical perversion the primary love object is never present. There are only its stand-ins, actors ready to perform, but in search of an author; exactly as in the cotton-reel game of Freud's grandson. If we now re-read S's childhood recollection in the light of this game, we will gather from it also the less mentalized essence, so to speak, consisting in the *rhythm* set up by the game. What we see is that Ernst creates a dramatic, theatrical performance in two acts. He is the playwright and, along with the reel and the string to which it is tied, a character too. The child violently throws away the reel, exclaiming 'a loud, long-drawn-out "o-o-o-o,"' which (not by chance) his mother, who is present at the scene, interprets as a '"*fort*" [gone]' (act I); then, little by little, he pulls it back, exclaiming *da* ('there!') (act II). Freud's interpretation is that the child stands for himself while the reel represents his mother. The role of the string, however, is more mysterious. Interpreted, the story would be: a child and a mother are separated in a violent manner (or rather, a child is abandoned by his mother) and then find each other again. The finale is joyous.

However, in these justly famous pages[8] Freud makes it clear that during the game of 'disappearance and return . . . *as a rule one only witnessed its first act, which was repeated untiringly as a game in itself*, though there is no doubt that the greater pleasure was attached to the second act' (p. 15; emphasis added). What is repeated 'untiringly' is above all the 'distressing experience' of the first gesture, which is configured as a true form of 'pleasure of pain', or rather masochism. We are here confronted by another scandal following those just mentioned, concerning people who derive pleasure from beating fantasies or from masochistic behaviour, and who continue always to have the same traumatic dreams. Nested within the discussion of masochism in *Beyond the Pleasure Principle*, and introduced by the hypothesis on the significance of traumatic dreams, the wooden reel game represents its most illuminating model, even if the former is a pathological event and the latter a normative one. Freud could not have intended this in any other way.

So the child seems to feel pleasure in something that in itself is painful: that is, the disappearance of the object. How might this be explained? According to Freud, an initial explanation is that the disappearance is *a prelude to rejoicing* at the reappearance. A second is that *active repetition of a suffered event* is preferable to suffering the event passively. A third is that throwing away the reel offers the possibility of *avenging* oneself on a substitute for the frustrating object. In relation to this last, Freud gives us a further indication by hinting at a significant 'instinct for mastery [*Bemächtigungstrieb*[9]] that was acting independently of whether the memory was in itself pleasurable or not' (1920, p. 16), a concept that resonates with that of 'obtaining erotic mastery over an object [which] coincides with that object's destruction' (p. 54) in the oral phase of libidinal organization. Apart from anything else, this association confirms our proposition that the reading of the cotton-reel game should be superimposed on the interpretation of primary pre-genital sadism, to which, as we have seen, Freud assigns a key role in the understanding of beating fantasies and the origin of the perversions. Nevertheless, all of this is still insufficient to account for why the child repeats the first part of the game above all, as if it were a full game in itself. But what is Freud saying here? Or rather, what can be intuited from what he is saying? And what affinities are there with the theory of the function of the dream in the traumatic neuroses?

Let's go back to the game. It is of course customary to emphasize that by throwing away the reel the child controls the disappearance of his mother, who from Freud onward has been identified with the toy. What is not seen for the most part[10] is that the child does not only throw away 'the mother', but throws *himself* away. Freud has already suggested this idea when a few lines later he describes the boy making himself disappear from the mirror. As in the case of S, a double identification would be in play: first with himself as he makes his mother disappear, and second with the reel-as-child that is thrown away.

This is evident in the light of another brief vignette of a patient of mine. R tells me that in his early infancy he used to sleep alone with his mother when his father had the night shift at work. On such occasions he felt an intense mixture of pleasure and fear. His brother, a few years older, had to sleep in his own bed as usual. R almost cries while commenting, 'Who knows how much he must have suffered!' But it is easy to intuit that the compassion for the brother is a displacement on him of his own sense of agony when he had to separate from his mother. 'After some time', he recounts, 'she realized that it was wrong to let me sleep alone with her in the marital bed, and she threw me away!'

Whether the reel is identified with the child or with the mother, the first act is (or rather, *appears* to be) always masochistic, because the child procures a form of pleasure by means of pain. This should already make us think that we are dealing with a pleasure different from that of concrete reunion, which he feels when he pulls the reel back with the string and makes it reappear, joyfully exclaiming '*da!*' Indeed, Freud adds, 'the child may, after all, only have been able to repeat his unpleasant experience in play because the repetition carried along with it a yield of *pleasure of another sort* [*ein andersartiger . . . Lustgewinn*] *but none the less a direct one*' (p. 16; emphasis added).[11] But what pleasure?

A new 'aesthetic'

At this point, Freud surprisingly hints at the 'highly enjoyable' experience (*hoher Genuß*) (p. 17) that can be derived from being present at a tragedy (not from suffering it!), and stops there. We know where this will end up: in the death instinct. But could there be an alternative explanation? And what if we could formulate this explanation in such a way as to endorse the first passage on rhythm and the invaluable link back to aesthetic[12] experience that he makes by referring to tragedy (and to art in general)? May we not postulate pleasure of a different kind in the pure repetition of a rhythm? A pleasure linked to the genesis and stabilizing of the Ego rather than to the satisfaction of the impulses of the Id? A pleasure that is the fruit of the urge-to-be and that derives from confirmation of the feeling that one exists? But then this repetition would only *appear* to be 'blind'. While being opposed to the pleasure principle according to the traditional notion, it would have nothing to do with the death drive, or else would necessarily entail its redefinition. Significantly, Freud himself hints that a new aesthetic, 'some system of aesthetics with an economic approach to its subject-matter' (p. 17), could lighten these processes. In my opinion, such an aesthetic could focus on the significance of rhythm in the trans-individual constitution of the subject.

Contemporary psychoanalysis, centred on the model of psychic birth from the first object relations, gives us the tools for probing deeply into this new aesthetic, but it was Freud himself who tried to do it first. We have the impression that this is exactly what is expressed by the title of our third text, from 1924, 'The economic problem of masochism'. Interestingly, the very title of this text carries a reference to an economy (we could say an 'aesthetic') of the sensations of unpleasure–pleasure at play in masochism. What would this aesthetic consist in? What is the 'tragedy' at which we are present in masochism? To know more, we must look more closely at the other actor in the *pièce* entitled 'The Wooden Reel Game': the string. *What does the string stand for?*

Curiously, the Italian word *filarino*, which derives from *filo* (string) and *filare* (to form a sequence, to make sense), means 'the perfect love', and denotes a pair of lovers who have a perfect understanding. *Filare*, however, also stands for *amoreggiare* (to flirt).[13] The string, both in the case of its identification with the mother and in that of self-identification, is the operator that enables recovery of the reel (reel-object in the first case, reel-child in the second). Can we not see this string as the string of memory, as a device that permits us to evoke images of the beloved object, an act that is often prelude to the possibility of finding it again concretely? And would not the first memories we can imagine take the form of ordered rhythms of sensations inscribed in the body?

But then perhaps we would have revealed the secret of the wooden-reel game and the justification for the 'different' pleasure (but now we could say, with greater precision, 'enjoyment') that the child experiences in throwing away his toys. The object *seems* to disappear (and concretely it does: here the cotton-reel *stands for* the word – that is, for the psychic representation of the object) but never does so entirely, because *contact is maintained with the string!* The pleasure of the representation (sublimated, or rather transformed into something that allows sight of the 'other') takes the place of the pain of the direct/non-mediated contact with the object that has previously behaved as a frustrating object, and functions as a 'preliminary pleasure' in relation to that experienced at the moment of actual reunion. We see here at work the basic function of emotions of *linking* (in Italian, *legare*) objects together that according to Bion (1959) is at the very foundation of thinking.

It is important here to be careful about what we mean when we refer to the 'presence' or 'absence' of the object. An object (and ourselves) can be present to our eyes only if we are able to represent it to ourselves in a human sense. However, we can say that, even when concretely present, it is absent to the extent that we cannot help but refer to it in symbolic terms. This is the paradox of language: we can name things only by making them in some way 'disappear' into signs. Heidegger (2009) hints significantly at the effect of 'losing' reality that the concept seems to imply. Hallucination and perception are not absolute opposites; rather, each is the premise of the other. This fact has been well expressed by Žižek (1989): 'as soon as the reality is symbolized, caught in a symbolic network, the thing itself is more present in a word, in its concept, than its immediate physical reality. More precisely, we cannot return to the immediate reality: even if we turn from the word to the thing – from the word 'table' to the table in its physical reality, for example – the appearance of the table itself is already marked with a certain lack – to know what a table really is, what it means, we must have recourse to the word which implies an absence of the thing' (p. 131).

So what does the child gain from the play? Some control over the object, a degree of distance, a certain security, a deferral of trauma. The annihilating terror of dread is transformed into a tolerable and protective anxiety. Throwing a toy and getting it back is of course not the same thing as suffering abandonment by one's mother. Beyond Freud's vignette there is a further factor relating to pure play, because, by impoverishing itself of some qualities, ludic action – Freud (1924) calls the perverse action 'a carrying out of the [corresponding] fantasies in play' (p. 162) – it is abstracted/transformed into language (*fort/da*). The word now *stands* first of all for the ludic gesture, which it still accompanies, and then for the Other *tout court*. As Moravia (1998) writes, evil is dreadful but the representation of evil is redemptive (see Civitarese, 2012b). Where it seemed that the child was throwing away the mother (and/or himself), he was in fact only restraining it (restraining himself) in the symbolic representation. In the game – and by now we are no longer on the concrete plane but a symbolic one – there *is* separation, because it has been enacted, and there is *not* separation: or rather its effects are largely mitigated precisely because the child and his mother remain linked by the string.

As Chemama and Vandermersch (1998) astutely write, at a very basic level it is the 'bond of opposition between two syllables of the language with the repetition of the loss and reappearance of the desired object, pleasure and pain, [that] which can define enjoyment' (p. 143). But then can we not see in this game of syllables a pure rhythm expressed in a kind of song? And rhythm itself as the first vehicle of a musical or semiotic meaning, so to speak, which precedes the semantic meaning of the word? In the interpretation that little Ernst's mother, Sophie, gives of what begins as a simple game of syllables, we see this transformation which is always on the point of completion, but also of being undone, and the inevitably transindividual or intersubjective dimension (the *string*, the *bond*, the *linking*) that is the only one in which it can happen. If we did not take account of the role of the other's presence and of language even in its purely rhythmic component, we would not understand how representational concepts are formed, or how the ability to think is developed.

Despite Lacan's insistence on the unconscious as a discourse of the Other, in his discussion of the episode of the *fort/da* game, the role of Sophie (of the maternal presence) as the agent that actually helps turn a signifier into a linguistic sign is not explicitly emphasized. In fact, the *fort/da* game is one composed of two distinct parts: the *fort* and the *da*. In each of these, the first stage consists in throwing the cotton-reel and the second (in reality simultaneous) in holding on to it by its name *thanks to the* mother's *interpretation*. The child can make his mother, identified with the cotton-reel, 'disappear' and 'reappear' only because she is discreetly present in the room. What is more, her gaze is seconded by that of Freud, who is present at the scene and so can act as the guarantor of a wider consensuality, a thirdness in relation to the accuracy of the mother's interpretation. The scene recounted by Freud is therefore a masterly example of a mother – and of a father, represented in this case by Freud – who knows how to keep a good distance between herself and her child.

In reflecting on masochism, Freud comes close to rounding off this area of study, though in my opinion the Lacanian reading and the intersubjectivist, post-Bionian psychoanalytic perspective are still necessary for its full theorization. But then, even when Freud sees dreaming as a 'binding' of the stimuli that erupt into the psyche in order to master them, he cannot help but consider dreaming 'social' and, in spite of appearances, never purely individual. Moreover, it is obvious how the first 'masochistic' stage of loss intervenes: only something from which one has been temporarily separated can be bound in the mnemic traces. We can clearly see that the sublimating transformation that gives birth to the subject requires some psychic work, a suffering that we could actually call a *suffering of pleasure*. If we exploit the lexical assonance with the word 'bond' [*legame* in Italian], we can also intuit the possible nature of the process Freud described as 'binding' [*legare*] the mass of stimuli that erupt into the psyche in trauma.

In normal development, in play, and in symbolic representation in general, the child evokes the sense-making/flirting of which this very capability is the fruit, and does so before there is any specific representation of reunion with the object. It is like saying that *any* happy representation stands by its very nature for a perfect sense-making with the object. Since at birth the infant enters a state of impotence, at its origin primary symbolization cannot help coinciding with symbolization provided by the mother's love, a love that expresses itself in her concrete presence and in her capacity for mental presence, or rather for reverie (the first string). Gradually assimilated by the child, this function becomes his own capacity for symbolizing/representing[14] (the second string). With the development of more highly evolved psychic functions, this level of representation will enable self-consciousness and hence responsibility and guilt.

As we see in the clinical vignette of S, it is only at this point of development, if the subject identifies with the object that maltreats him, that he can hope to arouse guilt in it and then a reparative impulse of love. If in turn he attacks the object, he will fall prey to guilt in the same way and will strengthen himself in his positive feeling of reparation towards it. When in relation to the cotton-reel game we emphasize the aspect of control exercised by the subject over the object, we sometimes neglect the fact that there would not be much point to this control outside a link of dependency and love. At the same time, Freud emphasizes that the masochist – considering now 'non-normal' development – only accepts being ill-treated by the love object.

Seeing masochism as reflected in the first act of the cotton-reel game –and even more in the first autonomous game, of the twos observed by Freud in Ernst, of simply throwing small objects under the bed while saying 'o-o-o' – in the terms stated above also means foregrounding the *relationship*, the bond [*legame*], in relation to the instinctual discharge, as it is nevertheless more or less implicitly in Freud's interpretation of the beating fantasy as sexual love of the father (in a regressive form) and a symptomatic realization of the incest fantasy. So if, as we observe in clinical work, masochism is placed in the service of sexuality, a different explanation of this fact would be that the subject makes use of the masochistic scene, which is set up in a variety of manners, not because through regression the pain would recall an old way of making oneself (sexually) loved by the parent, but because, in this way he reassures himself of the object's love through the string of the bodily rhythm of pleasure–unpleasure that connects him to the object, an equivalent of Ernst's saying 'o-o-o' and Sophie's interpreting it as *fort* (of course, in adult life the current partner is identified unconsciously with the parent).

When this has been done, it becomes possible for the subject to live in a state of intimacy that does not feel persecutory and thus also to accept sexual pleasure. This is how the masochistic fantasy eventually concurs in the increase of sexual excitement, by clearing the way for it. We can say in other words that the 'other sort' of pleasure of masochism consists in the acquisition of the object's tenderness, and thereby opens the way to sexual pleasure. In Winnicott's terms (1965), we would say that the Ego's 'orgasm' anticipates the 'id's orgasm' or, alternatively, that the stimulation of the erogenous zones that procures the preliminary pleasure noted by Freud, and that increases the excitation aimed at by the sexual discharge, has a linking function. Masochism would be a way of caring for a deficient Ego, of procuring the pleasure of the relationship with the object, with a view to instinctual satisfaction. *Although sexual pleasure may be more intense, the pleasure of tenderness would seem to be of pre-eminent importance.*

It goes without saying that the more fragile the bonds of love are felt to be, the more the subject needs incessantly to repair them. This is how he is granted permission to pass into a life of more intimate affective relationships. If he is reassured about the love-bond, or rather about the component of tenderness that connotes the relationship, and that paradoxically he can confirm for himself only though a kind of passage from the hell of masochism, the dread that he feels in the presence of the object, that can sometimes be so great as to extinguish any form of affective life, is reduced to a bearable level of anxiety. The subject is prepared. He will no longer be taken by surprise. But why then is understanding not enough to free the patient from the repetition of the masochistic scene? Why does he need to pass through pain? Why, as Bion (1970) would say, must he 'suffer' pleasure?

To clarify this point I turn now to Freud's remarks on the rhythm of pleasure–unpleasure, which are reprised in the 1924 paper. But I am anticipating what seems to me the only possible explanation. On the one hand, as we have seen, the pleasure of representation emerges *simultaneously* with the pain of separation (there would be no need to see the two moments as separate, because the pain receives immediate compensation from the pleasure of the sublimatory urge to differentiation); on the other hand, if it is to be effective, representation can only start from the pain really inflicted by the trauma, and hence must involve the body and be 'aesthetically' as happy as possible. In other words, in order to be transformed into a representation that is richer in significance, it must find its own language of achievement, it must become 'e-motional'. This can happen only within a new affective experience that is both lasting and profound. The concept of rhythm brings back into view the essential role of the object in the process of 'binding' the traumatic stimuli. As we said, it should not be forgotten that in the scene of Ernst's game the key factor is that there is a mother who is present and interprets the 'o-o-o' as '*fort*'. Only after this event can the child interiorize it and become capable of playing the same game even when he stands alone.

The qualitative element of the rhythm of masochism

At the start of 'The economic problem of masochism', Freud declares that he wants to return to some questions left unresolved in *Beyond the Pleasure Principle*. So he introduces the reader to the dramatic change of perspective that follows formulation of the concept of the death instinct – the theoretical move that makes masochism, rather than sadism, primary – with this rhetorical turn: from 'if mental processes are governed by the pleasure principle' to 'we have taken the view that the principle which governs all mental processes is a special case of Fechner's "tendency towards stability"' (p. 159). Between pleasure principle and Nirvana principle, Freud opts for the latter.

The term, synonymous with the constancy principle, is a singular echo of the powerful 'drug' he had a few lines earlier hypothesized in order to explain why in masochism the guardian of the psyche appears to be stunned. In any case, to demarcate the pleasure principle from the Nirvana principle, Freud reaffirms that unpleasure is not given by *any* increase in psychic tension (from its absolute value), just as pleasure is not given *only* by its diminution. And it is here that Freud returns to the observation already present in the 1920 text, and which on his way through the three key texts on masochism he thus works out as an *après-coup* game. The circle had opened with rhythm and it closes with rhythm:

> It seems that in the series of feelings of tension we have a direct sense of the *increase and decrease of amounts of stimulus, and it cannot be doubted that* there are pleasurable tensions and unpleasurable relaxations of tension. The state of sexual excitation is the most striking example of a pleasurable increase of stimulus of this sort, but it is certainly not the only one.
>
> Pleasure and unpleasure, therefore, cannot be referred to an increase or decrease of a quantity (which we describe as 'tension due to stimulus'), although they obviously have a great deal to do with that factor. It appears that they depend, not on this quantitative factor, but on some characteristic of it which we can only describe as a qualitative one. If we were able to say

> what this qualitative characteristic is, we should be much further advanced in psychology. Perhaps it is the rhythm, the temporal sequence of changes, rises and falls in the quantity of stimulus. We do not know.
>
> (Freud, 1924, p. 160)

One of Freud's aims in this passage is to differentiate the pleasure principle from the Nirvana principle, but to our eyes his insistence on rhythm is surprising and intriguing because it forcefully introduces the theme of temporality. My interest in beating fantasies and masochism has been aroused precisely by the reference to this *qualitative* aspect that he has identified in rhythm, a point common to both the 1920 and the 1924 texts. Re-read in the light of the inter- or transubjective paradigm of contemporary psychoanalysis, these remarks of Freud's open the way to new interpretive perspectives on the genesis and nature of masochism or, at the very least, make clearer the hypotheses that take it back to the action of the earliest narcissistic injuries.

Then why is Freud's hint at rhythm so challenging? Because it highlights the purely sensory and pre-representational dimension of the primary relation to the object that is encrypted in the infant's body. In the particular rhythm of pleasure–unpleasure in masochism we can see imprinted like a watermark the vicissitudes of this mainly inter-corporeal link. When in the 1924 text Freud expatiates in a highly ingenious manner on the fusion and defusion of instincts, we intuit that this has a background in the thoroughly concrete vicissitudes of relationships: that he is addressing the less mentalized, or altogether *un*mentalized, components of the nascent subject, physical tensions and their relief due to the *quality* of the primordial bond with the object, but before there is really a subject. That is to say, they exist as a *fantasy in the body*[15] (Gaddini, 1982); as the 'somatic', or rather 'semiotic' (Kristeva, 1974), pre- or sub-categorical *aesthetic* equivalent of what will later become a beating fantasy or a real masochistic perversion. In fact, on the axis of ontogenesis the rhythmic/sensory/implicit/semiotic precedes the semantic/representational. But it is a priority that we can also read on the axis of the multiple ways through which we always give meaning to experience, and which extend from the more primitive (i.e., affective-corporeal) to the more differentiated (i.e., logical or rational).

In other words, such a mode of production of experience, typical of the phase in which the infant is not yet differentiated from the object, will continue to exist and have a powerful influence on more evolved psychic life (see Bion (1977b), who speaks of foetal life and of 'thalamic' or 'subthalamic' fears). That is, we are addressing a sensoriality that is unrepresentable but nonetheless a carrier and producer of meaning. This sensoriality can either make an active contribution to development or, since it is a traumatic memory in the body of arrhythmic care provided to the infant by the object (arousing tactile, acoustic, visual, gustatory, kinaesthetic and proprioceptive sensations), it can block development and give rise to expressions of pathology.

Recording these rhythmic sensations in the body, these fantasies without representations, can give rise to psychic syndromes of a defensive nature. Their significance might therefore be simply that of reasserting and stabilizing the primitive process of differentiating the self, a process occurring at birth. Gaddini (1982), for example, notes in a case of dermatitis that the condition served to reinforce the line of the patient's bodily boundaries that due to early pathologies of detachment from the object, were ill-defined and were not been well defined.

So, agreeing with the many authors who acknowledge the role of pre-Oedipal factors in the etiopathogenesis of masochism, I hypothesize, along lines suggested by Gaddini, that the pre-Oedipal does not simply intervene by regressively sexualizing the punishment for incestuous fantasies of the Oedipal phase, but rather that it contains within itself, already stamped on the body's memory, the single or cumulative traumatic event that *directly* caused the perversion, or at least an inclination to seek perverse solutions to psychic conflicts. It is at minimum another determining factor. Then the incest fantasy will present itself as the photograph now developed from a negative that has always been present, or as the psychic representative of a fantasy in the body.

On the one hand, one might think that a masochistic perversity produced by the laying down of 'fantasies in the body', corporeal fantasies bearing the imprint of relationships experienced with the object, cannot in itself explain the conscious eroticization present in the beating fantasies of adults and their being placed at the service of sexual excitation even before the establishment of an Ego. On the other hand, we may also think that this is not the case because, inverting the order hypothesized by Freud, there could be Oedipal fantasies to be eroticized *a posteriori* in primordial sadomasochistic ways of relating to the object – of 'loving it'. Additionally, even before the infant has been endowed with an Ego, the behaviour of the object is instilling such fantasies in it and eroticizing them.

We might conjecture that such infusion occurs in the same way in which Laplanche (2004) says that the unconscious is constituted in the child by means of the transmission of *enigmatic* sexual messages from the mother. If we think of an infant, it is hard for us to presuppose its awareness of the erotic significance of devouring/being devoured: that is, a real awareness of the link that binds it to the object. This distinction may not yet have been set up. But if we consider the psychic dyad formed with the mother, we can identify in this the source of the eroticization, which, as soon as the situation is favourable to it, then like a subterranean river rushing to the surface, it arises into the light of consciousness. Naturally, the child is not yet capable of self-consciousness, nor can he experience guilt (even unconsciously), which for Freud is at the heart of masochism.

A new interpretative hypothesis on masochism

To repeat, the idea is that Freud is coming close to theorizing the unrepressed unconscious (if we see it from the child's side), insofar as it is not representational, but that it is nevertheless 'repressed' if we see it from the side of the mother as a component of the couple, with her giving rise to it in the child as a dynamic constellation of fantasies in the body. Although Freud hints at the possible role of a marked and congenital tendency to sadism, he does not theorize the co-incidence of pleasure and pain in the pre-Oedipal as the site where a precociously masochistic relationship may be set up, but only as a primitive mode of relating. However, he then notes the rhythm of pleasure–unpleasure as a mysterious 'qualitative' factor. But again, if we want to extricate ourselves from the darkness into which we are plunged by concepts like those used by Freud – physiology, biology, constitution – this rhythm can be understood only if it is reconnected to the organizing action of the object in relation to the chaotic life of the infant at birth, of the sole entity capable of creating conditions favourable to the identifications that are the basis of the creation of subjectivity.

In fact, any true rhythm can be considered only within the 'semiotic *chora*' (Kristeva, 1974) or 'matricial space' (Chetrit-Vatine, 2012) within which the relationship to the object develops; it cannot be interpreted other than as the true, primordial psychic skin that surrounds the first glimmer of subjectivity and gives it form. In our reading of Freud's texts we have identified the mysterious qualitative factor of pleasure and unpleasure with the rhythm given by the sequence 'o-o-o'→ *fort*, an action that acquires its meaning thanks to the intervention of the other, and then by the sequence *fort* → *da*, seen as the interiorization and transformation, in action-language, of the play of absence/presence that is the essence of the cotton-reel game.

If that is the case, then we should be able to find traces of this originary, metric foundation of being across the whole range of expressions of masochism and sadism. Viewed according to a far more 'relational' model of mental development than Freud's, the buildup of pleasure–unpleasure will be nothing more than the measure of time the object takes to reappear after having been emotionally or physically distant when the infant once again finds himself in a condition of 'double dependency' (Winnicott, 1955), that is, of complete impotence. Or, to be more precise, it is the alternation of pleasant or unpleasant sensation that the object, in its function as a provider of stimuli, makes him feel by her presence/absence, thus creating the 'typography spacings' that help him to start attributing a personal meaning to experience (Ferro and Civitarese, 2015).

Coming straight after the pages on traumatic dreams, the cotton-reel game tells us that any trauma is experienced unconsciously as a detachment from the maternal body and that, for the subject, any traumatic dream (we could say any dream or its equivalent) is a dream of reconnection to the maternal body, a patient weaving of symbolic/sublimatory representations of the trauma as if they were the string that could reunite him with it. Then both the pages on traumatic dreams and those on the cotton-reel game can be read as an implicit interpretation of the remarks on rhythm that precede them and anticipate their meaning. The concept of rhythm would not emphasize a purely economic factor in the variation of the body's tension – a mere mechanics or hydraulics of the drives, so to speak – but a variation that is closely linked to the *qualities* of the object and to the earliest phases of the relationship with the object, to its capacity for love by means of physical action and reverie (Bion, 1962).

At this point the rhythm of unpleasure–pleasure, the *fort/da* game, and the traumatic dream present themselves to us as equivalent models not only of the beating fantasy and masochistic perversion but also of symbolization at its most basic level. This chain of equivalences might seem disturbingly provocative to some, but I must say that I am only trying to follow up on and expand Freud's hints, though in the light of my own theoretical framework. Although at a very abstract level of discourse, this is what our close reading of passages from the most important Freudian texts on masochism tells us: maybe even more of a 'scandal' than that of pleasure in pain: so long as disturbing factors do not intervene, the coinciding of pain and pleasure now appears to us to be essential and foundational for the process of becoming a subject. From another point of view, this coinciding could also be called a constitutive *non*-coinciding of the subject with itself:[16] a differing from itself, which constitutes the rhythm. The human being is indeed characterized by this capacity for transforming pain into pleasure by virtue of the fact that, thanks to the other (also written with a capital 'o': Other), we have access to the symbolic. Pain can be 'sublimated' in the process of becoming a subject.

It is in this pleasure of representation intimately and *simultaneously* connected to the negative of the object's absence that it may be possible to revise our conception of the primary character of masochism – that is, as a functional element in the constitution of the subject – and also find an acceptable meaning for the concept of the death instinct. Language is an apparatus for deferring trauma, but the trauma is always in the background. The threatening object, death, is at a distance but still visible. Could we not interpret the death instinct in this way, as this tending towards the end while at the same time deferring it as long as possible? Couldn't the death instinct be the 'masochistic' drive towards the pleasure of symbolization – that is, to a higher degree of self-organization that moves us towards the anxiety of self-consciousness, as the empty sign that reveals us to ourselves and opens the possibility of existence to us? Ultimately, couldn't the death instinct correspond more or less to what is expressed by Heidegger's concept of being-toward-death? Is there much difference between this philosophical concept and Freud's assertion (1920) that 'instinctual life as a whole serves to bring about death' and that 'the organism wishes to die only in its own fashion' (p. 39)?

From this viewpoint, representation and concrete object are not antithetical but *dialectical* terms: one negates the other by affirming it and vice versa. The logic of the subject's functioning is a logic of correlatives, of unsynthesizable opposites, of co-belonging, of conflict without synthesis (Bottiroli, 2015). The Ego (the enjoyment of tenderness) is at the service of the Id (sexual pleasure), while the Id (sexual pleasure) is in the service of the Ego (the enjoyment of tenderness).

As S's vignette shows, if the moment of the *fort* appears masochistic, in reality it is also 'sadistic' in that it makes the object disappear,[17] 'destroying' and negating it (or, rather, it is an attack on the concrete link with the object, an act of revenge). The same can be said of the *da*, because it too is only a *symbolic* rejoining, thereby containing both the 'sadistic' destruction/negation of the real object, which continues not to be concretely present, and the masochistic consequence of paying the price for symbolization in the coin of its absence.

This is why we could maintain that representation is in itself a 'sadomasochistic' movement. We intuit that what appears masochistic always contains a sadistic impulse and vice versa: sadistic because, by replacing it with the symbol, the subject 'destroys' the object; masochistic because in so doing it transforms it into a *no-thing* (Steiner, 1978), while making it remain as a simulacrum, thereby avoiding its turning into a *noughtness*. Thought is what is gained here, the distance that the subject succeeds in placing between himself and the horror of the void. What the subject reaps from this is the fruit of the work of psychic elaboration that allows him to keep himself safe from a feared event/object while enduring in a state of ecstatic admiration, a feeling that testifies to the bond of dependency that still links him to the object, as well as indicating the value the object retains for him.

The child that will become an adult who suffers from a masochistic perversion or who coactively dallies with beating fantasies could have experienced a traumatic relationship with the object in early phases of life. Because of his immaturity and the lack of distinction between subject and object, there would be only bodily traces of such traumatic experiences, necessarily organized into *rhythms or, rather, specific arrhythmias* of pleasure–unpleasure. The need to master [*legare*] traumatic experiences would be expressed in the specific 'aesthetic' repetition in masochistic forms of relationship (in direct sensations or sensations provoked by specific representations). The Oedipal fantasy would intervene *a posteriori* to translate the masochistic fantasies in the body and/or to combine with them.

In this perspective the repetition of the trauma is never 'pure' repetition, because it is instead a representation, though by no means abstract or intellectual. On the contrary, only the success of this representation – in the theatres of life or analysis – can bring about transformation of the trauma and achieve the disappearance of the symptom. I hypothesize, therefore, that in general we can assign repetition to the field of condensation (of metaphor). A 'metaphorizing' function is active in repetition,[18] a way of mastering the experience *that is in itself pleasurable*, even if it passes through pain.

In other words, in the tendency to repetition we can see the reaching towards realization of a transition from multiple experiences to a 'concept' (a being-common) of these experiences (obviously in treatment these would possibly become gradually 'happier' revisions, thanks to the availability of the analyst to transform them). Repeating is letting ourselves be interpreted by what we are repeating, ultimately by the object at the origin of the vital rhythm – in masochism, a return to a stage of *Hilflosigkeit* in order to make ourselves like wax, ready to receive new inscriptions of the other.

So we rediscover that the pleasure of pain is the mark not only of masochism but, at its most basic level, of representation. Like the cotton-reel of Freud's grandson, pain itself, even if only 'in fantasy', stands metonymically for the object that originally caused it, or rather for the string of the ability to bear absence, that which is in itself life-giving and pleasurable. I repeat, the secret of the first act, the *fort*, lies in its non-specific repetition, which becomes somatic (and semiotic) categorization of experience and then specific imaginative representation.

In the clinical setting, if the subject finds a mind that helps him contain the emotions in play, through repetition of masochistic schemes of bodily signification, he is given the opportunity to 'conceptualize' the experience and gradually master it. This transformational capacity of the object would be the equivalent of the formal qualities that makes a tragedy pleasurable: in neither case is success guaranteed. Thus, the subject passes from the negative of representation to the representation of the negative. We could call this a sublimatory transformation, a transformation that is pleasurable in itself. At the start of life, but then always alongside more evolved forms, this is a subor pre-categorical – that is, somatic – representation. On this terrain, by transduction and grafting, the incestuous Oedipal fantasy will secondarily be implanted.

But the important thing to grasp is that significant repetition has the structure of a rhythm; that whatever has meaning for us *is* rhythm (organized difference) because it is in temporality that meaning is constructed; and, last, that rhythm per se, even the most banal musical rhythm, is always composed of a first 'unpleasurable' moment of increased (or decreased) tension, and then of a second 'pleasurable' moment of relaxed (or increased) tension. Set in the context of rhythm, it is not problematic to admit that masochistic fantasies, acted out or not, have all the meanings that have been underlined by various authors: controlling the object in the sadomasochistic *mise-en-scène*; expiating Oedipal guilt; avenging oneself on the object by turning sadism on oneself. But these also show themselves to be a way of weaving the string of representation, imitating – as in the cotton-reel game – the disappearance and magical reappearance of the self and the object. In other words, the masochistic magic 'binds' the object not only externally in the concrete setting up of a sexual masochistic scene or virtually in a masochistic fantasy, but in *any* representation.

By the way, discovering masochism as the common denominator of various dimensions of human experience also affords us the possibility, which is essential in clinical work, of freeing ourselves from the negative connotations of the term, as likewise of the term *perversion*, and from the tendency to adopt more or less subtly moralistic and antitherapeutic attitudes. Besides, from what has been said, what should become clear – at least as regards treatment – are the limitations of a static and taxonomical tabulation of the masochistic symptoms in their numerous variants.

The perverse analytic field and its cure

Every perverse *mise-en-scène* represents a 'carrying out . . . in play' (Freud, 1924, p. 162) of the perverse fantasy and tends towards the 'highly enjoyable' nature of tragedy (Freud, 1920, p. 17). This, in my opinion, is the key to masochism. It is therefore neither the immediate, instinctual satisfaction of making oneself loved sexually by the father, as Freud claims, nor an expression of the death instinct, but negative pleasure mediated by representation. We are introduced to this dimension by the indications scattered through Freud's pages on rhythm, on meter as an embryonic poetry. We should not confuse the pain that wounds with pain that is mitigated and mastered by representation, and hence pleasurable.

The history of the relationship with the object emerges in the subject first like a script written in the body and its sensations. But the imprint of this relationship is also represented 'aesthetically' in the analytic field by these very fantasies in the body, and not only by the psychic contents. The masochistic scene, both in fantasy and in masochistic perversion, appears as an attempt at 'dreaming in the body', *but also in the body of the setting and of the analytic field*, the traumatic traces left by the primary relationship with the object. The aim is that of reanimating a body – a body that has now become the site of the treatment – by means of a compulsion to repeat understood not as enslavement to the death instinct, but as a work of somatic/semiotic 'categorization' and then as a work of figurability. It goes without saying that the theatre in which the drama is replicated, within and without an analysis, can always burn down and thus produce a new, real traumatization.

In any case, the treatment of masochism passes through the construction of the perverse subject of analysis (Ogden, 1996). If, as we have seen, masochism is the dream in the body (but not only this, naturally) of a trauma relating to the gaps in the primary relationship with the object, we would expect that analysis might wholly or in part become this shared dream/nightmare. It is not that the trauma is reproduced. At least, this should not happen unless the theatre, as it were, goes up in flames. As we know, it is not so easy to avoid the risk of a new traumatization, especially with patients who have suffered severe trauma in their history. In any case, we should not confuse the trauma that destroys the apparatus of symbolization with the representation of the trauma, which instead attempts gradually, and not always successfully, to give it more 'aesthetically' efficacious and transformative versions performing their parts.

From Freud onward almost everyone concerned with masochism has for the most part interpreted it with reference to the external, biographical context and the structure of the patient's psyche. This approach, while helpful, must be integrated with another perspective if the treatment is to be efficacious: masochism seen as a narrative that indirectly illuminates the ongoing formation of oneiric thought in the waking dream-thought in the group-mind of the analyst–patient dyad at work. For this we need the Bionian concept of 'transformation' (Bion, 1965) in order to grasp in the most precise way possible the meaning of the current emotional experience in the session. From this point of view it is as if we were pretending to see the masochistic symptom for the first time. It loses its specificity as a symptom of the individual, but acquires another, more current role, as a hologram of the functioning of the analytic field.

Bringing everything back to the dream of the session makes it easier for the analyst to have a more capacious 'aesthetic' view – that is, as immersive and personal a view as possible – of what takes place, and even more so than if he makes reference only to the instrument of the countertransference. Why? Because if, on the basis of a radical conception of the dream of the session and of the analytic field, he brings all the narratives of the analysis systematically back to centripetal movement (everything, even if it relates to past or external events, is virtually attracted by the centre of the current therapeutic relationship and read in its light), he brings into effect in the most radical manner the type of phenomenological reduction (somehow 'impossible' and paradoxical) that constitutes clinical work in analysis (Civitarese, 2016a). He has more data at his disposal and so more possibilities to get in touch with the patient. I believe it to be the case that this new method of reading the events of the session may, in itself, be clinically more effective in treating disturbances on the spectrum of masochism, even though it is not specific to this type of pathology: in my opinion, it is certainly more effective and more transformative than readings that concentrate on the here and now of the session but only in a partial manner, as in some interpersonal or relational approaches (Ferro and Civitarese, 2013).

It would be much more difficult to 'prove', using clinical material, my interpretive hypothesis about the role of rhythm in the repetition of masochistic episodes (though no harder than it is to prove the existence of the death instinct), whether on the macro level, so to speak, or on the molecular level, and the specificity of a type of treatment deriving from my interpretation of masochism, which stands partly on a clinical basis and partly on a speculative metapsychological basis. But it can be said, nevertheless, that a better theoretical understanding would make us more sensitive to hitherto neglected aspects of treatment: for instance, the various ways in which the semiotic/sensorial dimension of treatment is revealed (to give just one example) with the conceptualization of the 'bodily reverie' (Civitarese, 2014a).

At the bottom of masochism we find a nuclear experience of psychic death as the basis for a form of perversion in the analytic relationship. In the analysis this sense of psychological death is frequently translated into the scant vitality of the analytic process, the chronic sense of falsity in the discourse corresponding, as sometimes it is only discovered later, to a secret eroticized dramatization of the relationship itself. Thus what Ogden calls the perverse subject of analysis is created, which we could theorize as the necessary illness of the analytic field.

It is an illness the analyst cannot fail to contract, but whose presumed origin it is appropriate to place between brackets. We would then concentrate on the transformative processes that make the mind grow: that is, the ability of the pair to give meaning to the shared emotional experience. It goes without saying that this conceptualization requires the analyst to be much more sensitive to the 'music' of what occurs in analysis. This is reflected, I think, in the idea expressed by Bion (1977b) when he says he is fascinated by the 'rhythmical communications' (p. 31) of which musicians are capable.

Notes

1 Loewenstein (1957) sees masochism as a 'seduction of the aggressor' (p. 40); Berliner (1958) as 'a pathologic way of loving' (p. 40); Valenstein (1973) underlines the painful pre-verbal experiences in the early relationship with the object.
2 For a guide to the state of the art in the understanding of masochism, see Holtzman and Kulish (2012).
3 There is no mention of rhythm at all in Holtzman and Kulish (2012), and only one very superficial reference in Glick and Meyers (2013); Chasseguet-Smirgel (1993) quotes Ferenczi in a note, mentioning his observation on the continuity between the primary rhythmicity of the infant and of adult sexual life.
4 For brevity the masculine pronoun is used elsewhere to cover both genders.
5 See Abraham (1924): 'The secondary level of this phase differs from the first in that the child exchanges its sucking activity for a biting one . . . In the biting stage of the oral phase the individual incorporates the object in himself and in so doing destroys it. One has only to look at children to see how intense the impulse to bite is – an impulse in which the eating instinct and the libido still co-operate' (pp. 450–451).
6 A similar line of thought characterizes the way Aulagnier (1975) differentiates the necessary from the unnecessary and traumatic 'violence' of interpretation, or Laplanche the primary seduction from traumatic seduction.
7 It is striking how this expression by S let us think of Lacan's theory of the intrinsically traumatic quality of the Real (Mitchell Wilson, personal communication), and also of the verbal assonance between the words (wooden) 'reel' and the French 'réel' (real).
8 There is an extensive literature on these justly celebrated pages of Freud, which I cannot go into here. I will confine myself to recalling that Freud's pages have received very considerable attention from scholars, especially those of the Lacanian school. Unlike Freud, who privileges the significance of actively mastering the trauma of separation from the object, Lacan (1966) instead underlines the significance of the episode about the game as primordial access to symbolization. Among the other authors who have concerned themselves with this, we cannot fail to mention, in philosophy, Derrida (1980), who focuses on the relationship between Freud and his dead daughter Sophie, mother of Ernst; and in the field of literary criticism, Barthes (2007), who connects the *fort/da* to the relationship between rhythm, meaning, and the origin of aesthetics.
9 On the meaning of this term, see White (2010).
10 But see Fornari (1977) and Derrida (1980).
11 Here I roughly follow the Freudian texts' implicit distinction between (perverse) enjoyment (*Genuß*), pleasure (*Lust*), and (sexual) satisfaction (*Befriedigung*).
12 In this text I use the word *aesthetic* in two ways, which I hope are clear from their contexts: on the one hand, in reference to what we understand by aesthetic experience in art; on the other, to indicate the properly 'aesthetic' dimension, in the emotional-sensory-motor sense of the term (as we know, *αἴσθησις* means 'sensation'), within which the process of primary symbolization takes place. So when I refer to an 'aesthetically' successful process, I mean that through the repetition of a pathological configuration – as Freud observes of a dream's work in enabling the passage from fright to anxiety – the subject (which includes those just coming into being, on the threshold of subjectivity) succeeds in some way in mitigating the inscription of the trauma in the body.
13 Obviously we can take advantage of the additional sense brought by the Italian translation of the term *bindfaden*, which comes to play a full part in the paratext (Genette, 1982, 1987) of Freud's paper. The German word is composed of *bind*, which means, among other things, 'to tie up with bonds', 'to make captive', and 'to stick together', and *faden*, which means 'thread'.

14 By 'representing' I mean an imaginative process that takes place within a symbolic setting.

15 By 'fantasy in the body' I mean a way of organizing sensory experience given by 'forms' corresponding to schemes of impressions in the body at the limit of objectuality and on this side of representation, i.e., of emotive-sensory categories or 'concepts' of 'embodied' scenarios. They are close to Tustin's 'self-generated forms'(1972) and to the forms of Ogden's contiguous-autistic position (1989). Strictly speaking, we should not speak of 'fantasy' if by this term we are implying an unconscious scene in which the subject is present insofar as it relates to an object. There cannot yet be repression at this point unless it is 'heterologous' (coming from the object, as the imprint of its influencing action), but a production of sensations without ideas, or rather without *perceptible* ideas, 'a sort of "tactile hallucination"' (Genovese, 1995, p. 55).

16 See Rimbaud (1871, p. 85): 'I is another.'

17 See Lacan (1966): 'the subject . . . destroys the object that it causes to appear and disappear by *bringing about* its absence and presence in advance . . . the symbol manifests itself as the killing of the thing, and this death results in the endless perpetuation of the subject's desire' (p. 319).

18 See also on this topic Roussillon (2001): 'Mais la contrainte de répétition pourra, à l'inverse, être signifiée comme l'effet irréductible du désir et de la vie, comme . . . le travail de symbolisation et d'appropriation de la part d'inconnue qui le constitue, elle sera alors pulsion de vie, exprimera le primat du principe de plaisir' (p. 68).

Chapter 4

Whirlpools, rhythms, ideas

Aesthetic experience and intersubjective constitution of the individual

In some recent papers I have suggested seeing the psychoanalytic theory of sublimation and the aesthetic theory of the sublime jointly as theories of subjectivation (Civitarese, 2014b, 2016b, 2017b). The challenge of the aesthetic as a discipline is to investigate in form the mystery of art and the feeling of beauty that it arouses in us, and which we experience as something that lifts us towards the human and towards authentic existence. This is not dissimilar to the challenge of psychoanalytic theorizing to develop a discourse that can say indirectly how the early forms of the psychic come into being. In my opinion, the aesthetic experience in art and in psychoanalytic practice are concerned with the intersubjective or social constitution of the individual, understood at its pre-reflective or intercorporeal level. In order to fine-tune some instruments that may help us intuit where the intersection between these two modes of human experience is located, and following some suggestions from my reading, I shall try here to interweave the figure of the whirlpool with the concepts of rhythm and idea (or rather, of sensible idea).

Whirlpools

I take my inspiration for proposing the image of the whirlpool from a note by Walter Benjamin, who makes it an emblem of origin immanent in the present. However, I owe my knowledge of the note to a book by Giorgio Agamben, *The Fire and the Tale* (2014).

A whirlpool is created when a flow of water comes up against an obstacle or by the meeting of two currents of water running in opposite directions. This struggle between forces becomes a new form characterized by its own rhythm. The new form attracts nearby elements into its movement. The status of the whirlpool, observes Agamben, is *singular*. It is a form in itself, enclosed and clearly circumscribed, but at the same time confused with the medium of which it is part. It follows its own laws, but nothing belongs to it specifically.

The key word here is 'rhythmical'. What the author is describing can be entirely superimposed on the idea of rhythm as something that undermines (in Italian: *intacca*) the measured time of the chronometer and this way defines the singularity of the subject. But unlike rhythm, and even though the term can also be used metaphorically in reference to the non-musical, the figure of the whirlpool lends itself better to representing the movement and play of forces.

Let us think of portrayals of whirlpools in literature and painting: of the fascinating story by Edgar Allan Poe, 'A Descent into the Maelstrom', or JMW Turner and his *Snow Storm: Steam-Boat off a Harbour's Mouth*. Obviously what interests us in these finely crafted forms is the thought of them as allegories of emotional (or sensory and emotional, or senso-motoric) whirlpools which are the foundation of psychic birth. The (emotional) 'whirlpools' of the primordial mother–infant relationship or the analytic field (the therapeutic relationship) are potential opportunities for the subject to be (re)born; situations in which lines of tension emerge and are shaped into dynamic, ordered and directed structures. One indication which confirms our intuition can be found in *Signs*, by Merleau-Ponty (1964, p. 40), where the author makes use of the image of the whirlpool to portray 'the whole of the spoken language surrounding the child'; a whole in ordered movement which sucks him back inside himself, bringing him from the chaos of the sensory to sense. Let us now go more deeply into the concept of rhythm.

Rhythms

I have always found this sentence of Winnicott's (1949, p. 184, my italics) illuminating about the meaning of music-as-container of the most primitive anxieties:

> Belonging to this feeling of helplessness [at birth] is the intolerable nature of experiencing something without any knowledge whatever of when it will end. . . . It is for this reason fundamentally that form in music is so important. Through form, the end is in sight from the beginning.

These lines came to my mind when I subsequently came across a chapter in another book by Agamben, *The Man without Content*, which deals with rhythm and is entitled 'The Original Structure of the Work of Art'. The *incipit* is flashy. Agamben quotes Hölderlin: 'Everything is rhythm, the entire destiny of man is one heavenly rhythm, just as every work of art is one rhythm, and everything swings from the poetizing lips of the god' (1994, p. 94). Then the author wonders wherein consists this original character of the work of art which the poet assigns to rhythm. So, making reference to ancient philosophy he assimilates rhythm to the concept of '*structure*, schema, as opposed to elementary and inarticulate matter' (ibid., p. 97). The original being of any work of art would simply be ῥυθμός ('structure') (ibid., p. 98). But what structure is in question here? Not structure as number but as 'ουσία, the principle of presence that opens and maintains the work of art in its original space' (ibid.). The term 'rhythm' comes from the Greek ῥέω, to pass, to flow. Whatever flows, flows in time. But into this unstoppable flow of linear time, impersonal and unclaimed, rhythm bursts like:

> a split and a stop. Thus in a musical piece, although it is somehow in time, we perceive rhythm as something that escapes the incessant flight of instants and appears almost as the presence of an atemporal dimension in time. In the same way, when we are before a work of art or a landscape bathed in the light of its own presence, we perceive a stop in time, as though we were suddenly thrown into a more original time . . . but this being arrested is also a being-outside, an *ék-stasis* in a more original dimension . . . it is the original ecstasy that opens for man the space of his world.
>
> (ibid., pp. 99–100)

If I understand Agamben correctly, I would say that this is a question of identity and difference. Rhythm takes us out of ourselves, immersed as we are in the unnoticed flow of time, and by making us rediscover this crucial dimension it constitutes us as subjects. Rhythm roots us in the consciousness of time as the original domain of our being. In this, the echoes of Heidegger are obvious.

In order to explore further the suggestions coming from Agamben, it is useful to read them in the light of the beautiful book, *Listening*, by Jean–Luc Nancy (2002). In this study he perhaps clarifies better the sense of rhythm as a 'continual differing from oneself'. Nancy writes:

> Perhaps we should thus understand the child who is born with his first cry as himself being – his being or his subjectivity – the sudden expansion of an echo chamber, a vault where what tears him away and what summons him resound at once, setting in vibration a column of air, of flesh, which sounds at its apertures: body and soul of some one new and unique.
>
> (ibid., pp. 17–18)

For the human being, any seeing is seeing oneself seeing (*Vedersi vedersi* is the title of a beautiful book on Valéry by Valerio Magrelli (2007)) and any hearing is hearing oneself hear. And thus openness to the world is established and the space for interiority is created. But if there is a 'rhythm' of seeing, this notion becomes yet more pregnant when we consider listening. Seeing is already compromised by association with the rational pole of being (θεωρέιν means 'to look', 'to see'), with representation – and it is on the centrality of representation that Freud erected his theoretical edifice. Hearing, however, is still further beyond language. It has more to do with sense than with meaning. More to do with the body than with the intellect. Rhythm cuts out strips of time and in doing so subjectivizes it. Furthermore, it introduces a sense of space. Only time makes it possible for the spaces which typesetters place between words to become effective in constructing the meaning of the sentence. Technically this is called 'spacing'. The word is an addition to time and space, or rather, to duration which makes itself into space. 'Rhythm', writes Nancy, 'separates the succession of the linearity of the sequence or length of time: it bends time to give it to time itself, and it is in this way that it folds and unfolds a "self"' (ibid., p. 17). And he wonders, 'isn't the subject itself the starting of time in both values of the genitive: it opens it and it is opened by it? Isn't the subject the attack of time?' (ibid., p. 75).

The notion of rhythm returns insistently when we find ourselves faced with the key theoretical crux of contemporary psychoanalysis, the unrepresentable: that is, the dimension of sense that both precedes and then accompanies linguistic signification, but which withdraws from any kind of translation that is not essentially intermodal (from one medium to another). It happens that I have addressed this on at least three occasions: in relation to aesthetic conflict, in a chapter of *The Violence of Emotions* (Civitarese, 2011a), in the essay on Ferro entitled, appositely, 'Spacings' (Ferro and Civitarese, 2015), and lastly in a recent study of masochism (see Chapter 3). In the last of these the concept of rhythm becomes the keystone of an attempt at an alternative theorization of masochism from the starting point of Freud's annotations in two of his three key essays on this subject, in *Beyond the Pleasure Principle* and 'The economic problem of masochism.' In these wonderful works Freud gets to grips with the enigma of pleasure in pain:

> It seems that in the series of feelings of tension we have a direct sense of the increase and decrease of amounts of stimulus, and it cannot be doubted that there are pleasurable tensions and unpleasurable relaxations of tension. The state of sexual excitation is the most striking example of a pleasurable increase of stimulus of this sort, but it is certainly not the only one.
>
> Pleasure and unpleasure, therefore, cannot be referred to an increase or decrease of a quantity (which we describe as "tension due to stimulus"), although they obviously have a great deal to do with that factor. It appears that they depend, not on this quantitative factor, but on some characteristic of it which we can only describe as a qualitative one. If we were able to say what this qualitative characteristic is, we should be much further advanced in psychology. Perhaps it is the rhythm, the temporal sequence of changes, rises and falls in the quantity of stimulus. We do not know.
>
> (Freud, 1924, p. 160)

If it is a question of rhythm and not of absolute values, this also means that the first moment of unpleasure at the increase of tension is nevertheless a component of the pleasure, and that every pleasure can be called a negative pleasure.

A further extraordinarily fertile suggestion about rhythm can be found in Nietzsche (2001, p. 84). In an aphorism devoted to the origin of poetry he speaks about the power of rhythm 'that reorganizes all the atoms of a sentence', and constrains not only the body to a certain cadence of movements, but the soul itself, and even 'the souls of the gods', enabling us to draw closer to their ear and almost oblige them, so to speak, to keep time with us and receive our prayer. As Nietzsche observes, 'even the wisest of us occasionally becomes a fool for rhythm, if only insofar as he *feels* a thought to be *truer* when it has a metric form and presents itself with a divine hop, skip and jump' (ibid., pp. 85–86).

Ideas

'Contact of the nipple with the baby's mouth' (writes Winnicott (1964, p. 40)), 'gives the baby ideas! "perhaps there may be something there outside the mouth worth going for."' What is intriguing in this sentence is the word, 'ideas'. We cannot think that these are ideas in the true sense: that is, belonging to someone who can think their own thoughts. It must mean a special, rudimentary idea, the body's idea. In the same way, Bion speaks of the 'conception'which arises from the encounter of a pre-conception with a realization. Unlike 'concept', the word 'conception' has more to do with an idea of process, and lends itself better to indicating a dimension of experience which is more of a pre-reflective or non-verbal order, as in a dance in which one is engaged with the other, than a psychic content of a representational type.

I hope it is clear at this point what model I am proposing in order to identify the point at which aesthetic experience in art and in psychoanalytic practice conjoin: when the turbulences of sensations and proto-emotions become rhythms, and ideas arise from the calming rhythms, proto-ideas or sensible ideas at first, and then, after words are added, concepts. I hope it is also clear what I mean when I speak of an aesthetic paradigm in psychoanalysis: nothing aestheticising or vaguely 'artistic', even if there is an undoubted artistic component in our work.

However, the aesthetic experience in psychoanalysis must make reference to the intersubjective constitution of the individual. The term 'intersubjective' (perhaps it would be better to replace it with 'transindividual'; Cimatti, 2015) is often mistaken for interaction between two separate subjects (as would be the case within the frame of an interpersonal model) instead of an intermediate area or space that stands *between, in the middle*. In the more specific use I propose, the term instead refers above all to the social birth of the individual, but understood in Husserl's and Merleau-Ponty's sense of *Ineinandersein* (Szanto and Moran, 2015, p. 108) – that is, one being in the other – of the interconnection/interweaving, initially concrete/sensory and only later involving ideas, which makes us subjects.

Creating concepts of things, abs-tracting, means simplifying, reducing a variety of objects to a common feature, eliminating differences and grasping similarities. This is how – through a sublimating transformation – we attain the status of subjects.

From a psychoanalytic viewpoint, the emotional unison between mother and baby is *a sort of primordial abstraction* – an expression which Cesar and Sara Botella (2001, p. 44) instead reserves for the synthesis which arises from the encounter between the hallucinatory and the perceptual – and occurs first in the dimension of the purely sensory and indistinct, and then in that of the affective/sentimental space (which is, however, always a conceptualized space if we take account of its being provided for the system-couple by the mother). The possibility of synthesising the con-cepts of logic is created only at the end. As Wittgenstein (1969, p. 96) writes, 'Knowledge is in the end based on acknowledgement [*Das Wissen gründet sich am Schluß auf der Anerkennung*]'. The body that is 'lost' in the ascent to the concept is the body as a source of dark and imprecise sensations. In this sense, subjectivating oneself does not mean losing but *taking* body in the sense of endowing oneself with the necessary emotional categories, the ‘sensible concepts’ indispensable for life.

But in this sense the prototype of a ‘concept’ is the area that gives calming sensations corresponding to the surfaces where the baby’s cheek meets the mother’s breast. Is it not the case that the institution of this area of contact consists in identifying a being-common for two different terms?

In conclusion, it is important to realize how unision (being-one) is always really a finding of unity in diversity. It is thus, in generating the unity in which the concept contains being-common, that the object (but also art) fulfils the task of ordering the infant’s multiple representations; and those of the ‘infant’ in the adult, an expression which allegorizes the endurance in the adult of the (emotional-sensory or semiotic) level of functioning that I have tried to illustrate with the figures of the whirlpool and of rhythm, and additionally that aspect of the adult which is still plastic and susceptible to evolution.

Chapter 5

Hypochondria and the politics of narcissism

I would like here to try and situate the concepts of narcissism and hypochondria against the background of some starting points offered by the Heideggerian theory of *Dasein*, because I am convinced that we can derive from it some useful suggestions for deepening our knowledge of these concepts. In so doing, I shall draw with some frequency on the recent volume by Kevin A Aho, *Heidegger's Neglect of the Body* (2009) on the problem of the (presumed) omission of topics relating to the body in the German philosopher's work.

The psychoanalytic concept of narcissism takes into account the way in which the subject places himself in what Heidegger calls Being-there: that is, existence as the product of a sociality made of discursive practices, institutions, habits, which precede the subject and pre-determine its essence on a bodily and pre-reflective level. Overruling the visual, which we usually choose automatically, to illumine philosophy with psychoanalysis in order to rethink narcissism in the light of *Dasein*, helps us to orient ourselves in relation to the disputes about the best theory for treating psychic suffering; that is, whether it is more appropriate to maintain the perspective of the isolated subject (drive theory) or better to view the events of the analysis with a theory about the inevitably intersubjective constitution of the mind (in a broad sense, a relational theory); positions which, at the cost of some over-simplification, we identify with Freud and Bion respectively.

Indeed, in Freud narcissism designates the direction of the investment of the libido (or sexual energy): towards the object or towards the subject. This corresponds to a vision of the mind as an agency which differentiates itself in order to find some responses to the endogenous urge incessantly exercised by the drives. In Bion, by contrast, it is not the drives but the emotions which bring about this differentiation. Unlike the drives, the emotions are postulated as always deriving from relationships – of love, hate or knowledge – with the object. For Bion the mind is intrinsically relational, from the start. Narcissism as a measure of libidinal investments, is therefore always infused with the qualities of the object (or rather, with the relationship with the object). This is the secret outlined, onto which is woven the fabric of what is visible phenomenologically. But what, in substance, does Heidegger say about the subject, if we do not let ourselves be intimidated by the complexity of his thinking?

For Heidegger, 'discourse' (*Rede*) and not 'rationality' translates the Greek term *lógos* ('an unfolding, linguistically structured space of meaning that is always already "there" [Da], occurring in and through the social acts and practices of humans', comments Aho, 2009, p. 74), because reason/rationality refers to the Cartesian subject seen not, as it should be, as the site of a rationality that is diffuse and precedes it, but as a static, objective presence: *a body that encapsulates a mind*. But, for the German philosopher, we are born into a historical and social context where no distinction is given between internal/external and no intentionality that directs itself *towards* or stands *against* a material world independent of objects. On the contrary, objects form part of this network of meanings already given. We always encounter them from the starting point of *Dasein*. What the body obscurely knows anticipates, and then always accompanies, perception. Perception is already situated, oriented by *praktognosia* (ibid., p. 35). The body does not stand in space but institutes it. 'The embodied perception is already determined by the "primacy" of Dasein' (ibid., p. 47). Discourse/*lógos* is the medium in which the subject is born and is the sole possible precondition by which it is capable of thinking about its existence: 'we are human not because we speak but because we are "bespoken by language"' (ibid., p. 89).

As we can see, Heidegger's existential analysis can be an extraordinarily useful tool for justifying the necessity in psychoanalysis to pass from the vision of the isolated subject to the vision of a holistic totality (a background) of social relations of which the subject is only one point, in turn both product and artificer; to reaffirm how what we are concerned with in psychoanalysis is the field of the *lógos*, in the sense that I specified earlier, and of its crises; to abandon definitively any type of mind/body dualism; also to move beyond Merleau-Ponty's conception, although it converges with psychoanalysis on many points, because – for all that it gives priority to the body and to perception – it does not bind them indissolubly to the manner in which culture has already stamped itself on them. What is primary is not perception but *Dasein*. For Heidegger – and he seems to be commenting on the misunderstandings that can arise from discoveries such as that of the mirror neurons – as Aho (ibid., p. 66) again reports:

> empathy does not reveal a "primordial existential structure", because the experience of empathy is always mediated in advance by a temporally structured familiarity with the other; the other, to some extent, already matters and makes sense to me. Thus for Heidegger, individual experiences such as empathy are themselves made possible by Dasein.

The notion of *Rede* thus anticipates the psychoanalysis conceptions of an intermediate area – field, third, middle kingdom, intermediarity: all, of course, concepts thought of as circumscribed by the analytic situation – though no notion of the unconscious is developed within it, and it is only considered a type of 'atmosphere in which we first immerse ourselves in each case and which then attunes us through and through' (ibid., 92).

Now, two pernicious dichotomies afflict our conception of the body. The first is the Cartesian duality of mind and body – further reinvigorated, though largely unnoticed, by the neurosciences in the binary form brain/body (cf. Barile, 2013) – the second between nature and culture. But since human beings have acquired the capacity to think about their own thought – that is, a mind – given the way we commonly understand it as a product of culture, it makes no sense to split it off from the body: for one simple reason, because a reciprocally and recursively generative relationship exists between the two. It is not enough to say that our cognitive structures represent projections of how we are made biologically and how we move – that is, that the body creates sense – but also that, entering evolution as a potent factor of adaptation, however scandalous it may seem, the mind also creates/models the body.

The world in which we give a meaning to experience, whether of a semiotic or procedural kind or strictly linguistic or semantic, is always the fruit of an indissoluble interweaving of biology and sociality. For us, the biological can never again only be the biological, nor can the cultural ever again be absolutely detached from the body. Indeed, as has been said, the body is an incarnate metaphor. If metaphor is the way in which thought is given, even in the most abstract case, then clearly the body is thought. What does the body think about? In its whole being, at every moment, it must think, or rather transform, the primary emotionality which is born out of the encounter with the real. At the start of life, this real is the object: the uterine cavity, then the flux of sensations of the semiotic maternal *chora* (Kristeva, 1974) and, later still, the mother's face.

At birth, then, Nature too always presents itself in the guise of the object: Nature *is* the object. Subsequently, when the individual is faced with it, it will now inevitably be a Nature read through the lens of the first relationships with the object and the residual fantasies associated with it. But this also holds for the schemata of relationships that pass through the body. At every moment, the body interprets the world (Civitarese, 2014a). On the one hand, we find something of the kind already in Freud, because if it is true that the drives arise from the body, as a whole they already record the impact that culture has produced on them, otherwise we would speak not of drives but of instincts; on the other hand, my thesis is that even though Freud asserts that the Ego is the projection of the bodily surface, no such intrinsic bond between body and object and between the body and its mind is evident in his thinking. The body Freud is writing about is still the objective body of science.

The critical theory borne on the wind of postmodernism has called this vision radically into question. After Foucault and all the feminist literature of recent decades, the body, in all its materiality, appears as the elective location for practising the politics of the production and repression of discourse. The body's expressions are by no means entirely natural, but powerfully pervaded by the normative effects of sociality. Where bodies can go, what postures they can assume, how they must show themselves, be touched, seen, hidden, is minutely and obsessively regulated. Bodies are both materially real, concrete and socially constructed. The question 'What is a body?' would be very difficult to answer.

And yet, what is more familiar to us than bodies, than our body? The fact remains that, however counter-intuitive it may be, the body's limits are felt as dangerously fluid and, for this reason, laws must be written about them (or in them) to guarantee that they are respected (Longhurst, 2001); this is obviously helpful, but can also produce forms of rigidity and suffering.

For example, there are simple products or symptomatic manifestations of the body which cause the distinctions between internal and external to waver, and which therefore become (or, rather, we are induced to find) abject. It would be enough to think of the bodies of hysterics, but also the mute body of somatosis, the depersonalized body of psychotics. This does not mean a denial of the body's materiality; the fact is that we never have access to a pure materiality. Our access to the material body is always mediated by language. Foucault (1963) wrote definitive pages about this in *The Birth of the Clinic*. Could it be the case that the simple fact of acknowledging a materiality which does not depend on language, could never be located outside language. Couldn't it ever, like the noting of a fact, nevertheless entail a point of view, a discursive strategy, in the last analysis an ideological option, could we say with Derrida, a textuality? Even if the paradox is that also our linguistic access to what we can postulate as the Real, the substance, the absolute exteriority, it can only pass through the materiality, in itself equally obscure, of the linguistic signifier. That is, we cannot do without the body when thinking about the body. Or we cannot think about the body without the body.

Turning now to hypochondria, we can ask ourselves: what is specific about the hypochondriac symptom/body? That, unlike other forms of psychic pathology, it is an incessantly inspected, investigated, interrogated, scrutinized, diagnosed body. The hypochondriac shows rather than says (it is Foucault who . . . confines himself to 'saying'!), making a spectacle out of the misunderstanding on which our naïve mind/body dualism is based. The hypochondriac is a perspicacious philosopher, without knowing it. He is a narcissist because he folds his own body back on itself – as if regressing to a state of sleep while still awake;[1] he is absolutely anti-narcissistic because he interrogates the other, even with a certain 'violence', and does not at all resign himself to the naturalness of physical illness (although, obviously, the reason for this is that he does not accept the diagnosis he is being offered). We can say, therefore, that the body is also the expression of a political conception. But what is the hypochondriac seeking if not to restore the condition of familiarity with his own body? And doesn't the word I have used, 'familiarity', already present us with the thing in itself?

We do not really know why a presumably similar emotional conflict leads to the development of different symptoms. Many factors are always in play. An interesting hypothesis of Bion's is that the subject develops different symptoms according to how far he has to hurl the untransformed emotions he is trying to get rid of. On hypochondria, he writes,

> Hypochondriacal symptoms may therefore be signs of an attempt to establish contact with psychic quality by substituting physical sensation for the missing sense data of psychical quality.

> It seems possible that it was in response to his awareness of this difficulty that Freud felt disposed to postulate consciousness as the sense-organ of psychic quality. I have no doubt whatever of the need for something in the personality to make contact with psychic quality.
>
> (Bion, 1962, pp. 53–54)

So we could say that the hypochondriac's narcissistic investment in his own body is not very different from that of the adolescent and the psychotic who is suffering depersonalization. It stands half way between physiology and serious pathology. But isn't the adolescent engaged in mediating the spaces in which his or her body can *legitimately* be situated – that is, happen? And isn't delusion by definition the discourse that withdraws from consensual validation (not, however, entirely, something on which we never reflect enough)? The hypochondriac's narcissistic withdrawal is by no means a detachment from the object, but on the contrary an obsessive re-interrogation of it. This will only appear evident to us if we see the body as continually produced by sociality and not as something material that belongs only to whoever possesses it.

However, this request is very often so intolerable that it provokes reactions of rejection, among which I would place the rigidly technical responses of diagnostic procedures. Ever more invasive, these sometimes end up dramatically mimicking what must have been the relationship with the primary object: that is, a cold, mechanized and intrusive relationship. To Bion's sentence I would add that the hypochondriac symptom does not so much seek to re-establish contact with psychic qualities as, going still further back towards the source, with the psychic qualities of the object which were deficient in the nurturing relationship. So we could say – I repeat – that the hypochondriac deconstructs the presumed naturalness of the biological body, just as he deconstructs (or shows in a new light) the classical concept of narcissism. It is as if he were saying, 'What? Don't you realize?! You persist with a body of which you only see the matter, but this body isn't only matter; it's also the Other.' That is, the hypochondriac needs to mend a breach in the symbolic order from which he feels his own Ego bleeding. What the hypochondriac represents to himself as diseased is in fact a part of himself felt as abject because no longer redeemed by communion with the other.

If we move from the body to the social body, narcissism understood in the most negative Freudian sense is epidemic. The cause lies perhaps in the crisis of ideologies and in the technologization prompted by the forms of our existence. The physical and virtual nomadism of the period in which we live denies us any possibility of not being exposed to contagion from the other. The equilibrium between living for oneself and living for the other has become precarious. Hypochondria of the individual and hypochondria of society mirror each other. It is now a stereotype, but no less true for that, that contemporary identity has become liquid. To sex, gender and sexual orientation we must now add the avatar with which we present ourselves in the virtual forum. But with each new articulation, it becomes more difficult to harmonize the various components into a sufficiently unitary identity, however much we may want to move beyond the binary male/female system – as Celenza (2013) writes, half-quoting Faulkner: 'The binary is not dead; it is not even binary!' Isn't the easy availability of cosmetic surgery equivalent to the diagnostic techniques and surgical interventions which the seriously hypochondriac sometimes succeed in obtaining? What is hypochondria if not this melancholy leaning over oneself with one's gaze turned to the past? Hypochondria is an illness of our century, just as hysteria was in Freud's century, but a more 'narcissistic' illness than hysteria?

We really seem to be witnessing a phenomenon of the return of the repressed. The digitalizing of identity merely makes manifest what was latent: in other words, identity has always been 'diffuse and social' even when there was no Twitter and Facebook. We will find hyperbolical rather than suggestive Derrida's thesis that most of the elementary information processes in the living cell are also a type of writing 'and one whose system is never closed' (Kirby, 1997, p. 61), because it is actually now possible to write (manipulate) cellular DNA.

The topic of the specificity of the symptom is always quite slippery. It is a fact that, although we know little about it, no other symptom lends itself as well as does the hypochondriac symptom to parodying and self-parodying the idea of the body as substance, constantly putting its inadequacy on show. The doctor who denies substance to the hypochondriac symptom is not yet putting himself in the different perspective of a crisis of the sense of belonging to a social order made flesh, to actualization in a given context of *Rede*. He confines himself to rejecting the patient's suggestion, but from the same level of the material body, and not from that lived in a given context – that is, of a body 'spoken', albeit 'implicitly' by language. Exclusively using the technological perspective of the body-machine, he perpetuates the alienation which the patient is trying to get rid of.

During an analysis a patient claims to be convinced that he is suffering from hypertension. How should we listen to what he is telling us? It depends what role we have. If I were his cardiologist, I would invite him to have a series of complimentary examinations, I would give him a diet, I would advise some hygiene measures and I would prescribe him a drug. As a psychologist I might think that, on one plane of reality, if my patient has developed a heart condition it might be because of an excess of stimuli which has been unable to transform and which are therefore a source of stress. As an analyst I could relate the symptom to unconscious aspects of his own behaviour, and for example hypothesize that there may be a connection with a chronically repressed rage that is activated in certain Oedipal situations, outside and inside analysis. This would help him to have new points of view about things and perhaps modify his behaviour. There is also another possibility: of considering that, from the perspective of the field, hypertension ('HYPER-tension') is entering the fictional dialogue of the analysis as a character to express something that pertains to the unconscious communication in the here and now. I could try more subtly to develop this character's narrative. The aim would be to ensure that the patient equips himself with better instruments for reading his reality, and hence for giving meaning to certain situations without the need for the hyper-tension-character to intervene (like a kind of Hulk always on the brink of exploding).

Which is the most effective of the procedures described? In my opinion, the one that best sees what is happening on the unconscious plane of communication, and which ultimately most respects the Freudian method of exploring the unconscious. Naturally there is nothing to stop the analyst talking about the relationship between hypertension and conflicts in the patient's working life, knowing that he is talking about something that is happening there. In this way, he uses an integrated, binocular, vision and does not risk splitting off current emotions, encapsulating them in presumed realities external to the analysis, or in one-way transference/misunderstandings.

In another of my patients there was a very evident to and fro between the emergence of hypochondriac anxieties – the idea of having cancer of the liver – in the periods when he was living as a kind of reject from society, one condemned to a life of solitude because of his physical ugliness and the repugnance he aroused in women, and the easing of this pain when he succeeded in making a few shy steps towards the other sex: steps, it goes without saying, made possible by the authentic investment he had felt being made in him by me, by my tenacity and patience. In fact it took many years before we could scratch the surface of a thick narcissistic barrier made of a mixture of irritability, a feeling of abjection and yet also a subtle arrogance, with which he protected himself. The hypochondriac symptom objectified still further his presumed (objective) ugliness, but still left some margin for relational play: after all, don't we say that beauty (or ugliness) is in the eye of the beholder? And so doesn't ugliness go back to having been ugly for one's mother?

In hypochondria it is the prop of existence that is being urgently sought, that which is 'mute, tacit, unexpressed and inexpressible' and which inevitably characterizes experience, 'the opacity of feeling' which stands alongside 'the transparency of representation (Lanfredini, 2011, p. 76). As Merleau-Ponty writes (1945, p. 306–307, my italics):

> The subject of sensation is neither a thinker who takes note of a quality, nor an inert setting which is affected or changed by it, it is a power which is born into, and simultaneously with, a certain existential environment, or is synchronized with it . . . Just as the sacrament not only symbolizes, in sensible species, an operation of Grace, but is also the real presence of God, which it causes to occupy a fragment of space and communicates to those who eat of the consecrated bread, provided that they are inwardly prepared, in the same way the sensible has not only a motor and vital significance, but is nothing other than a certain way of being in the world suggested to us from some point in space, and seized and acted upon by our body, provided that it is capable of doing so, so that *sensation is literally a form of communion.*

It is this knowledge, that we lost since we started to look at the world with a 'Godlike' eye, which the brilliant installations of Richard Serra (for example, 'The matter of time', at the Guggenheim in Bilbao) or of Anish Kapoor seek to reawaken, giving us a sense of how we construct experience in the very act of passing through space.

Wishing to try to go still deeper and going back to pick up some starting points from Heidegger's thought – since, after all, what has been said so far is still elliptical – we can ask ourselves again: what then does the hypochondriac symptom express? I believe it may be the manifestation of an incapacity of the individual to derive safety from society in order to bear the anxiety about death; an anxiety about death which is intrinsic to the human condition, to *Dasein*, and which cannot by any means be repressed. *Dasein* is born with access to language, which makes it possible for us to think thoughts about existence. We can see how the essence of what makes us human resides in a no (cf. Aho, 2009, p. 95); or rather, it may be continually involved in the oscillation between the Bionian 'no-thing' – the absence that we are able to tolerate or, rather, an absence that is a quasi-presence: that is, 'a negativity or circumscribed absence' (Carbone, 2011, p. 29) – and the risk of falling into the abyss of 'noughtness'. As Heidegger maintains, being is being-for-death. What makes us human is being spoken by language, or rather being pervaded by a significativity that precedes us and grants us access to the possibility of thinking about our finiteness, the reason for the essential unhappiness of all narcissism. We are a socio-historical interweaving of past and future. In this future, which therefore becomes part of the Ego *constitutionally*, at least as long as we live in a state of authenticity, there cannot fail to be the knowledge of the always immanent possibility of our own death. Is this not enough to make us intuit the sense of inauthenticity which strikes us so acutely in clinical work with narcissism?

I believe that the success of the aesthetic of the sublime, from the Pseudo-Longinus to Žižek and, even more than one might suspect, in much of Bionian theory (with concepts such as Negative Capability, O, infinity, nameless dread, etc.), derive from the fact that they bring the essence of any aesthetic experience to the surface, an experience which consists in acceptance of the ephemeral nature of all things. The horror or true shock to which the spectacle of the sublime exposes us, arouses anxiety [*Angst*] which, when it is tolerable – and it is beauty which renders it tolerable for us – reinstates us in the social order of *Rede*. Only death, therefore, gives sense to existence at every moment. Thus the sublime unveils the abyss [*Abgrund*] of *Dasein*. But here death is not physical, biological, but the loss of meaning, 'the structure of nothingness that always underlies my time' (Aho, 2009, p. 93): loss of meaning, to which any psychic symptom testifies, and in particular that of hypochondria, anchored as it is to the body.

So, by the expression 'politics of narcissism' I mean that even the direction that the individual imprints consciously or unconsciously on the libido – towards or away from the object – reflects *the political* in its broadest sense as the theory and practice of the social management of power. Yes, even on the unconscious level; the unconscious with which psychoanalysis is concerned, being none other than the field of the symbolic: 'The concept of politics', writes Derrida (1994, p. viii), 'rarely announces itself without some sort of adherence of the State to the family, without what we will call a *schematic* of filiation: stock, genus or species, sex (*Geschlecht*), blood, birth, nature, nation – autochthonal, or not, tellurian or not.'

But I also mean something else: that in the politics of narcissism there are also the politics of psychoanalysis, and that adopting one theory or another is not an indifferent matter. In one case, hypochondria is a problem of the other; in another, of myself *with* the other (and with the Other who constitutes me in that I am a human being). In one case I am sufficiently master of the situation, while in the other I have to admit that I too am played by the unconscious, and that only by looking behind me can I hope to grasp something with which to orient myself in relation to what is happening.

In the end, the narcissism of psychoanalysis is also in play: whether, as with the hypochondriac crisis in the narcissistic organization of the subject, to take shelter in a 'hypochondriacal' and dogmatic defence of what we already know or, on the contrary, to apply to this knowledge the instruments we have acquired from critical theory. The implied question is rhetorical; it should be clear that only the second way seems viable to me if we are once again, as Freud has taught us, to turn a fragility into a position of strength.

Note

1 An extraordinary image of a narcissistic drive expressed in sleep, but in this case in that of the loved object, can be found in Proust, that extraordinary creator of modern myths. In relation to this, see Carbone (2011, p. 14):

> It is well known that the desire for subjugation exercised by the Narrator over Albertine seems to find here a momentary appeasement only in the beloved's sleep, once she is like an object in being without consciousness, but at the same time always a subject, and as such able to offer her lover the acknowledgement he seeks.

This is the passage from Proust in question:

> By shutting her eyes, by losing consciousness, Albertine had stripped off, one after another, the different human personalities with which we had deceived me ever since the day when I had first made her acquaintance. She was animated now only by the unconscious life of plants, of trees, a life more different from my own, more alien, and yet one that belonged more to me . . . In keeping her in front of my eyes, in my hands, I had an impression of possessing her entirely which I never had when she was awake. Her life was submitted to me, exhaled towards me its gentle breath.
>
> (2006, p. 503)

The passage has also been commented on by Sartre (1965, pp. 416–417). On the theme of the unseeing object who in sleep cannot return the gaze of the subject, see also Lemma (2013).

Chapter 6

Dora

The postscripts

The modernity of *Dora* lies, I would argue, in what its author sees as its manifest outdatedness – that is, in the involuntary exhibition of the essentially rhetorical and narrative nature of any truth. In showing itself to be so clearly at work in the text, the historico-naturalistic paradigm – or the archaeologico-evidential paradigm, according to Carlo Ginzburg's famous definition (1979) – is reversed into its opposite, the aesthetic paradigm. However, the same major transformation pervades present-day psychoanalysis and renders it absolutely consistent with the ethos of our so-called postmodern age. It is furthermore obvious from *Dora* that Freud, while willy-nilly espousing the positivistic vision of an ultimate, transparent truth, was one of those who contributed to its corrosion.

Whereas the detective-like approach adopted by Freud in *Dora* induces us to opt for the same method, it will nevertheless not be *precisely* the same: our aim here will instead be to undertake a 'metanarrative' analysis of the textual rhetoric, rather than endeavouring – as some might, abandoning themselves to resentful and unempathic rivalry with the author – to compete with him in interpreting the many details of the case without, moreover, having been present in the concrete situation and without even a modicum of contextualization. Such attempts can readily lead to arbitrary interpretations, forced associations and highly dubious constructions. My intention here, on the other hand, is different: I aspire to re-read the text creatively (Ogden, 2012) in search of original resonances and suggestions, with a view not to arriving at a definitive explanatory formula, but to expanding the field of possible meanings.

This vertex (Bion, 1970) is in line with our current conception that the principal therapeutic factors in analysis are no longer abreaction, the surgical extraction from the psyche of pathogenic memories as foreign bodies, or systematic interpretation of the transference, but instead development of the transformative capacity of the mind and growth of its symbolizing functions by way of the greater emotional attunement that becomes possible between the two members of the analytic couple. Drawing the patient's attention to the emotions aroused in the analytic field; creating with him[1] apt metaphors for transforming and containing these emotions; and playing and bringing oneself into play with the whole of one's being so as to achieve an ideal level of receptivity – these are now seen as more appropriate guides to our daily work. Many principles of classical psychoanalysis are retained – in particular, the central importance of the setting, of dreams and of the unconscious. However, these concepts have now each been reformulated: the first in accordance with Winnicott and Bleger as the repository of the most primitive parts of the personality (Civitarese, 2004); the second as the poetizing activity of the mind (Civitarese, 2013c); and the third, due to Bion, as the psychoanalytic function of the personality (Civitarese, 2011b).

It is extraordinary to see how, in *Dora*, Freud somehow shows himself to be already aware of the problems I have mentioned, at least in four key points, where he apologizes for writing a short story; for having breached professional secrecy; for having frankly discussed improper matters with his young female patient; and, lastly, for having failed, given that Dora broke off the treatment because he had omitted to interpret and 'resolve' her transference on to him. If read in this way as a pre-conception of future psychoanalytic models, the text reminds us of the celebrated note 4 in 'Formulations on the two principles of mental functioning' (1911). In it, Freud – here again in effect asking to be forgiven – openly confesses the limits of his conception of child psychic development, a conception he describes as a necessary 'fiction'.

As with that note 4, I propose that *Dora* can be re-read by considering the points where Freud defends himself against the above charges as implicitly paving the way to the new intersubjective paradigms of psychoanalysis. Let us now address in order the four 'symptoms' set out above.

'If I were a man of letters . . .'

In certain passages of *Dora*, Freud confronts head-on the issue of the literary nature of his essay; to avoid misunderstandings, he writes:

> I am aware that – in this city, at least – there are many physicians who (revolting though it may seem) choose to read a case history of this kind not as a contribution to the psycho-pathology of the neuroses, but as a *roman à clef* designed for their private delectation.
>
> (Freud, 1905 (1901), p. 9)

Note first the insecurity inherent in the adjective 'revolting', which seems to us emphatic and surprising. Elsewhere Freud is concerned to stress the essential correspondence of his account with the actual course of events. In so doing, however, he causes a second crack to appear in his positivistic approach, because he admits that 'absolute' fidelity is neither possible nor necessary: 'Thus the record is not absolutely – phonographically – exact, but it can claim to possess a high degree of trustworthiness. Nothing of any importance has been altered . . .' (ibid., p. 10). A further comment conveys a similar impression: 'I shall present the material produced during the analysis of this dream in the somewhat haphazard order in which it recurs to my mind' (ibid., p. 95).

The evidential paradigm and the underlying paranoid and subtly moralistic emotional background (Terman, 2014) are perhaps nowhere as manifest in any other of Freud's writings. While the case of *Dora* is a thriller, it is a thriller *à clef.* This is because, first and foremost, each character corresponds to someone who actually exists (including, for that matter, Freud himself as a character and intradiegetic narrator as opposed to Freud as the author in reality); and, second, because the entire narration revolves around the deciphering of the riddles represented by two dreams. One of the effects on me of re-reading *Dora* was a kind of *déjà vu*. There came a point when I said to myself: 'Well now, this is Freud *à la* Hitchcock!' – in other words, it is no longer possible to read Freud except on the basis of the paratext (Genette, 1982, 1987) of all the cultural productions, especially those which are most popular and involving, inspired by his work. 'Freud *à la* Hitchcock' – the idea of the analyst derived from Hitchcock's films – seems to us to be more 'real' than the real Freud. Ginzburg's essay has made this obvious to us. Furthermore, the style and rhythm of Freud's investigation directly call to mind some of the best known tales of Edgar Allan Poe and Arthur Conan Doyle, as well as their unforgettable detective protagonists, Auguste Dupin and Sherlock Holmes respectively.

For example, phrases such as the following constantly recur: 'conclusion'; 'signs which tended to show its true character'; 'a cloak'; 'she admitted'; 'I had hit the mark'; 'a malingerer'; 'I was led to imagine'; 'betray her secret'; 'At such points the physician is usually faced by the task of guessing and filling in what the analysis offers him in the shape only of hints and allusions'; 'I was obliged to point out to the patient'; 'it was justifiable to suspect that there was something concealed'; 'the solution to this riddle'; 'led me to see that . . . its opposite lay concealed'; 'she would not hear of going so far as this in recognizing her own thoughts'; 'a disease which still remains as great a puzzle as ever'; 'taking into account certain other of the patient's peculiarities, which were otherwise inexplicable'; 'the mystery'; 'I have formed in my mind the following reconstruction'; 'the problem is not solved by'; 'the men she secretly loved, lest its regularity should betray her secret'; 'solution of this riddle'; 'reproach of malingering'; 'human interests which the patient keeps hidden from us'; 'and the whole disorder, which up till then had shown the greatest obstinacy, vanishes at a single blow'; 'I ought to have guessed'; 'numerous details'; 'But the conclusion was inevitable that'; 'I was on the point of abandoning the track'; 'which fitted in very well with my view'; 'scepticism . . . astonishment and horror'; 'take the dream bit by bit'; 'inquiry'; 'confession'; 'pantomimic announcement'; 'I expressed my suspicion that'; 'He that has eyes to see and ears to hear'; 'showed how entirely correct all of this was': 'if I were a man of letters engaged upon the creation of a mental state like this for a short story, instead of being a medical man engaged on its dissection' . . . This last phrase is significant because Freud's secret concern – that he might be 'a man of letters' – is inherent in it!

Publication

As stated, one aim of Freud's defence of his approach is to remind the reader that what he is about to report is 'real'. However, because it is real, it breaches professional secrecy and the undertaking of confidentiality made to the patient. From this perspective, one might comment that it is a pity it is not merely a work of fiction! With regard to his own time, too, Freud is fully aware of the risk of abuse: 'I naturally cannot prevent the patient herself from being pained if her own case history should accidentally fall into her hands' (Freud, 1905 (1901), p. 8 f.). Even if he made sure that she could not be recognized by others, Ida Bauer – the patient's real name – could recognize herself in Dora. In fact, the first statement – that only Dora could have recognized herself even where her own time was concerned – was also qualified, as Freud honestly admits in the following note added in 1923:

> In Dora's case the secret was kept until this year. I had long been out of touch with her, but a short while ago I heard that she had recently fallen ill again of other causes, and had confided to her physician that she had been analysed by me when she was a girl. This disclosure made it easy for my well-informed colleague to recognize her as the Dora of 1899 [1900].
>
> (ibid., p. 13)

Given our sensitivity as Internet users and hence as dwellers in a world in which information cannot be confined to limited, specialized groups, it seems obvious to us that Freud's act of writing may not only be tantamount to an act of violence, but also that it is, for precisely that reason, the symptom of a traumatic nucleus which the analyst–patient couple has not succeeded in 'dreaming' – that is, in transforming (Ogden, 2003). Even today, it can hardly be seen as anything other than one of the 'symptomatic acts' which he so eloquently describes in the text. However, what else is he asking us to forgive him for? Could it be something to do with Dora which not even he can precisely identify? It is a fact that, here again, the issue of secrecy arises with regard to what is real or fictional in the text, but is not thereby resolved.

Pornography

The third charge that Freud is answering is, in essence, that he is a pornographer and a pervert. A pornographer is someone who takes pleasure in observing explicit sexual scenes, with 'scepticism [but also] astonishment and horror' (Freud, 1905 (1901), p. 48), who dares 'to talk about such delicate and unpleasant subjects to a young girl' (ibid.), who engages in conversations with her that are full of 'pruriency' and concern 'such revolting things' (ibid., p. 50). One is surprised, too, at the almost contemptuous tone of Freud's remarks about the perversions, even if its purpose is to anticipate and rebut his detractors' objections: 'which regards the perverse nature of her phantasies as horrible . . . aberrations of the sexual instincts' (ibid., p. 48 f.); 'precisely the same content as the documentarily recorded *actions* of perverts' (ibid., p. 50).

Here, Freud's defence takes the form of alternate retreats and lightning-swift advances. He asserts that, as a physician, he calls things by their names (*'J'appelle un chat un chat'* – ibid., p. 48), but also that he has used the necessary tact ('From the very beginning I took the greatest pains with this patient not to introduce her to any fresh facts in the region of sexual knowledge' – ibid., p. 31). He then turns the accusation back on his critics: 'it would be a mark of a singular and perverse prurience to suppose that conversations of this kind are a good means of exciting or gratifying sexual desires' (ibid., p. 9). What is more, he adds spitefully, these critics, being excluded from the special intimacy he enjoys with his patient, 'appear to envy either me or my patient the titillation which, according to their notions, such a method must afford' (ibid., p. 49). Continuing the cut and thrust of his attack, he hints at the possibility of holding them up to ridicule: 'I shall avoid the temptation of writing a satire upon them' (ibid.).

However, here too the Freud we thought we knew seems a little unsteady. It is unlike him to fail to demonstrate the contained *pathos* that is otherwise always in evidence, even when he uses the rhetorical device of engaging in a dialogue with an imaginary critical reader, in this case instead threatening ludicrous retaliation against his ignorant or disingenuous adversaries.

But here again, what is it that Freud the pornographer 'sees' and ought not to see on the basis of the then prevailing theories of scientific knowledge?

The 'great defect'

Lastly, we come to the fourth 'symptom', negation of the transference. Freud addresses this point in the Postscript to *Dora*.

He begins with a general defence of psychoanalysis, of its scientific nature and its method, and of the obvious character of its discoveries about the unconscious functioning of the mind, thus continuing in the same vein as before. Indeed, this seems to serve as a means of transition from the previous plea for the defence to the argument to come, which concerns him more closely as a person and as a professional, on the handling of Dora's case. Freud mentions three reasons for his composition of this paper: (a) to supplement *The Interpretation of Dreams*; (b) to illustrate the complexity of the psychic factors at play in hysteria and the subtle mechanism of psychoanalytic therapy – namely, the transformation of representations that are inadmissible to consciousness into normal representations; and (c) to demonstrate the role of sexuality, 'the motive power for every single symptom, and for every single manifestation of a symptom. The symptoms of the disease are nothing else than *the patient's sexual activity*' (Freud, 1905 (1901), p. 115). By expressly setting out his intentions, he is therefore taking the stage all the more in the first person as a character in his narrative – and this is already unusual, because a scientific text ought to be based on neutral reporting of facts and on the originality of its author's discoveries.

During the treatment, Freud explains, the neurosis produces not new symptoms but transferences, impulses and fantasies transferred from the historical person on to that of the physician either directly or by 'sublimation'. These detailed considerations form the basis of Freud's fourth argument in his defence: the 'great defect' (ibid., p. 118) in Dora's analysis lay in his having disregarded the role of the transference. Since he had consequently been unable to resolve it, Dora had actually treated him as if, owing to an 'unknown quantity' (jealousy? money? – ibid.), he *was* Herr K and taken her revenge on him.

More precisely, Freud blames himself for having overlooked an allusion to the transference in the first dream (Dora's decision to leave Herr K's house as a disguised advance warning of her decision to break off the treatment). In the second dream, too, he confesses that he could have apprehended a number of clear allusions to the transference. For instance, on the edge of a thick wood, Dora asks a man how far it is to the station. The reply is *two and a half hours more*. Freud subsequently comments that, at the time when Dora tells him the dream, he had only *two hours* more left for their work, and that he should have noticed the parallel between the refusal to be accompanied and the refusal to continue with the treatment. The element of *two hours* had then recurred in the account of the trip to the lake. Here again, had she walked round the lake, it would have taken two hours. Freud then points out that two hours was also the length of time Dora had spent at the Dresden gallery in contemplation of Raphael's *Sistine Madonna*.

The painting first appears in the text as an association to the first dream, in which the unknown town is connected with Dora's visit, alone, to the picture gallery, after declining to be accompanied by a male cousin. Freud does not fail to emphasize the particular quality of this representational element (as well, however, as others, such as the photograph album and the picture of the nymphs in the wood) as a 'nodal point in the network of her dream-thoughts' (ibid., p. 96). By immediately afterwards laying stress on the formal aspect, he is drawing attention to the subject of the painting, the Madonna, or virgin mother.

Freud's smile

The structure of *Dora* is a pre-eminent example of the role of the paratext. Here the paratext emerges from the background to which it is mostly relegated and takes on a dignity equal to that of the main body of the text by virtue of the manner in which it helps to determine its meaning. At a given point in the Postscript Freud interposes a blank line, as if to set off a portion of the text as a further postscript to the Postscript, as if to separate himself from what has gone before – just as, he writes, the analyst should 'separate himself from'[2] the transferences that have been 'stuck' on to him. In this part, amounting to a page and a half, his defence becomes performative. Freud *shows* that he has learnt the lesson in the relevant situation, with Dora and not alone reflecting on the matter as a fait accompli. For when Dora returns to him fifteen months after the treatment was broken off with the right-sided facial neuralgia that torments her night and day, he can no longer deceive himself, *and . . . he smiles*: 'I could not help smiling, for I was able to show her that exactly a fortnight earlier she had read a piece of news that concerned me in the newspaper. (This was in 1902.) And this she confirmed' (ibid., p. 121 f.). The news item related to his appointment as professor *extraordinarius* at Vienna University. Freud immediately recognizes that she is actually suffering from an 'alleged . . . neuralgia', because two weeks before, as Dora confesses at his precise request, she had read in the paper of his appointment, so that the neuralgia was manifestly caused by her sense of guilt at having 'boxed him on the ears' by breaking off the analysis.

In smiling, Freud absolves himself from the charges and forgives everyone – Dora, his critics and detractors and perhaps himself too – for having doubted the quality of his discoveries. He is in effect saying to them: 'Look, you offended me, but now I have become *Professor Extraordinarius* at Vienna University! . . . I forgive you.'

Freud is thus seen to present to us a Dora who adores him and regrets her ingratitude. He connects his triumph with Dora's self-punishment, as if she had finally acknowledged that she had been wrong about him. One readily discerns Freud showing off to the patient, who had wounded his narcissism. In other words, he is reassuring himself about the quality of his overall behaviour towards Dora, while concealing what is still weighing on his mind without his yet knowing what it is.

However, is this scene that occupies such a central position in the Postscript not the same as that of Dora with her mother (whom Freud incidentally describes as a foolish and uncultivated woman), that of Herr K with Dora, and that of Freud himself with his mother-as-Madonna/Martha? But I wish to consider this aspect in theoretical rather than biographical terms; as if, beyond the avowed purposes of the publication, *this* – the vital importance of mirroring in the construction of the subject – were its principal theme.

The same aspect constantly recurs, too, in the key moments of the text. For instance, in the fleeting pendant to the analysis Dora tells Freud what happened in the interim, before the onset of the new symptom. She had visited Herr K's family and calmly disclosed to his wife that she knew of her relationship with her father. The aphonia, her old symptom, had returned after she had witnessed an incredible scene (worthy of the talent of a gifted creative writer or film director): seeing her by chance in the street,[3] Herr K had 'stopped in front of her as though in bewilderment, and in his abstraction he had allowed himself to be knocked down by a carriage' (ibid., p. 121).

This instant, which could have been fatal to Herr K, like the off-the-cuff transference interpretation of the neuralgia, the scene of the Dresden gallery visit and Dora's being 'rapt in silent admiration',[4] places the moment of *agnition*, or recognition (Boitani, 2014; Rulli, 2015), at the very centre of *Dora*. In particular, the image of the *Sistine Madonn*a (which, as we have seen, is for Freud 'the nodal point in the network of her dream-thoughts') becomes the eye of the centripetal vortex that swallows up all the other aspects of the narration and causes them to converge on and be scattered in the person of Freud (as if the entire case of Dora were nothing but a dream of his) – a vortex already discernible in the author's important entry into the account as one of its protagonists. This is therefore the opposite of the centrifugal ('positivistic') movement that would characterize a neutral analyst or one concerned to act as a blank screen.

This reading is supported by a biographical – but not only biographical – detail that now in its own right forms part of the paratext of *Dora*. In his letter of 20 December 1883 to his bride, Freud tells her of *his* visit to the Zwinger in Dresden. The various pictures mentioned include two Madonnas, one by Holbein and the other by Raphael. It is interesting to see how Freud contrasts them in his letter. Holbein's Madonna annoys him because it also depicts some 'ordinary, ugly *human* faces', while not even the figure of the Madonna is really to his liking: 'the eyes protrude, the nose is long and narrow' (Freud, 1961, p. 81). However, as soon as he sits down to admire the *Sistine Madonn*a (Raphael's), the first thought that comes into his mind is of Martha ('Oh, if only you were with me!' – ibid., p. 97) – a remark we can interpret – especially if we re-write it leaving out 'with': 'Oh, if only you were . . . me!' as an impulse of total identification with an ideal object. Freud indeed writes that the figure 'emanates a magic beauty that is inescapable' (ibid.). His 'objection' to this painting concerns its sensuality:

> Raphael's Madonna, on the other hand, is a girl, say 16 years old; she gazes out on the world with such a fresh and innocent expression, half against my will she suggested to me a charming, sympathetic nursemaid, not from the celestial world but from ours.
>
> (ibid.)

In a nutshell, then, the one is too holy and the other too profane! Note also that Freud writes that the idea occurs to him 'half against his will'.

Furthermore, not a single one of the contributions I have read about *Dora* connects the other elements of this dream[5] – the father's death, the station and the late arrival for the funeral – with those of Freud's famous dream about the death of his own father, which also features a late arrival at a funeral and a railway station, where he sees a notice that reads 'You are requested to close the/an eye(s)' (Freud, 1900, p. 316 f.). This is in my view further significant evidence of Freud's presence as a person in this text. Considering that he originally intended the case of Dora as a supplement to *The Interpretation of Dreams*, one cannot but draw attention to the resemblance between the two dreams, which are so to speak accommodated in one and the same text.

The evidential paradigm versus the aesthetic paradigm

The image of Raphael's *Madonna* thus assumes, in the Postscript, the superluminous but enigmatic status of certain memories which, as Freud writes elsewhere, act as a screen concealing a trauma. In contrast to his interpretation in the body of the text (as a virgin-mother), in note 1 on page 104 he relates it to a fantasy of defloration as the other side of the coin of motherhood. In note 2 on the same page (which is presented as another of the various supplements to the text), the 'Madonna' is seen instead as the patient herself in the eyes of her 'adorers' – the young man who sent her the pictures and Herr K – another reason being that, although a 'girl', she has in effect had a child in consequence of the fantasy of giving birth.

Freud is thus seen to interpret the representational aspect of the Madonna principally in the paratexts of the note and of the Postscript, which accommodate the elements 'repressed' from the main part of the text – i.e. the text that lies more in the foreground. What then might this dazzling image point to? Putting together hypervisibility and repression, what hypothetical trauma might be involved? What is missing from the picture that we could add to *our* postscript? In their hyperbolic significance, the *two hours* spent contemplating a picture, however beautiful, could be seen as a symptom awaiting comprehension. While this extended period in front of the painting bears witness to Dora's emotion, it may be assumed to attest to Freud's too! After all, as he reports, he had visited the same gallery and gazed at the same picture. The duality of the Holbein and Raphael Madonnas in Freud's letter resonates with that of the Madonna and the nymph ('*nymphs* visible in the background of a *"thick wood"*' – Freud, 1905 (1901), p. 99) derived from Dora's material.

When we re-read this text today, what is blindingly obvious by its absence is not so much the analysis of the transference, as a detailed consideration of the effects, in the analytic relationship, of the person of the analyst – what we call analysis of the *countertransference*. The various clues in the subtext examined here and its most secret correspondences point in this direction. From this perspective, as stated, three aspects stand out because they are manifestly of greater importance than the others – the resemblance of Dora's dream to Freud's about the death of his father reported in *The Interpretation of Dreams*; the passage in the letters on the Raphael painting; and the quotation, again from *The Interpretation of Dreams*, about Freud's professorial appointment. All three point unambiguously towards the countertransference and lay the greatest possible stress on the role of the analyst's subjectivity in the treatment. All three are either overtly or cryptically self-quotations from the autobiographical novel of Freud's inner life that is the *Traumdeutung* – a self-quotation tantamount to summoning himself to appear before the court of his readers.

What then is the tendency of this analysis? If our reading makes sense, could the profusion of apologies made by Freud in *Dora* – all of which, however, are equally reproaches to those who do not understand him – be directed not so much to the reader or to Dora herself, as to his 'Madonna'? To his mother? Could the plethora of *excusationes* that pepper the text be expressions of guilt in response to his curiosity about his parents' intimacy? And might Dora's reproach to Herr K's wife be equivalent to his reproach to his mother for having preferred his father to him – to her son the 'Professor'? Had she not been wrong to behave in that way? But *now* he forgives her. Clearly, on this 'second occasion' his mother becomes the public.

In the *Standard Edition* the footnote reproduced below appears on the same page as the beginning of the final part of the Postscript, which is separated from the rest by a blank line. In it, the paratext becomes a protagonist in its own right. Freud writes:

> The longer the interval of time that separates me from the end of this analysis, the more probable it seems to me that the fault in my technique lay in this omission: I failed to discover in time and to inform the patient that her homosexual (gynaecophilic) love for Frau K. was the strongest unconscious current in her mental life.
>
> (Freud, 1905 (1901), p. 120)

Whether or not Freud's intuition is justified, what strikes one in the text of the footnote is that, for his part, he says he had been 'in complete perplexity' and 'brought to a standstill' (ibid.) in situations where he had not yet recognized the homosexual current in the neuroses. However, from the perspective of a creative re-reading, these phrases foreshadow those on the next page, on which Herr K is described as in 'bewilderment, 'knocked down' and in a state of 'abstraction' (ibid., p. 121). In this text, then, a dizzying sequence of psychic equivalences and/or metonymic effects are outlined, and cannot fail to make sense on a more or less subliminal level. Dora = K = Freud, all three caught up in the fateful moment of agnition, of 'divine' recognition. Was it not Freud who elucidated the mechanisms of displacement better than anyone else? Could he himself ever have avoided the effects of these unconscious processes?

The logic of the Postscript

Re-reading the *Dora* case history in an open and accepting spirit, we in turn are bewildered and transported into a state of abstraction by its beauty, its complexity, the refinement of its narrative construction and the efficacy of its theoretical introduction of the logic of the Postscript – that is, of *Nachträglichkeit*.

In the movement I have attempted to sketch out above, the text itself as it were evolves from a psychoanalysis of suspicion into one of relationship, as if the evidential paradigm were 'dreaming' its aesthetic counterpart. The image manifestly lies at the centre of the text, constructed as it is around two dreams and two paintings, that of the Madonna and that of the nymphs in the wood (the latter being, rather, an image of the street girl). The content of the Madonna picture evokes the earliest moments in the construction of the subject, as well as subsequent adulthood, with the still persisting need for positive mirroring – that is, for constant negotiation with the other of one's status as a 'person' (Esposito, 2014).

So could the case of Dora be read in the same way as note 4 of the 'Formulations on the two principles of mental functioning' – i.e. as Freud's (involuntary, implicit . . .) discovery of another (future) psychoanalysis in which the analyst is much more involved in the relationship than he thinks and perhaps hopes?

Clearly, both the non-analysis of the countertransference and the anticipatory 'allusion' to the intersubjective or relational developments of psychoanalysis can be identified only by acceptance of Freud's felicitous insight concerning the later attribution of new meaning to memory and indeed to any event, which he was to address in the celebrated notes added in 1918 to another famous case history, that of the 'Wolf Man'. Considered in these terms, the Postscript is an instance of *Nachträglichkeit* ahead of its time. However, the intrinsic reference to *Nachträglichkeit*, which is thus bound up with contemporary relativistic epistemology by way of the interplay of the postscript(s), is merely the third of the indirect but powerful effects exerted by the text.

The instances of *Nachträglichkeit* aroused by each fresh reading of the essay are equally legitimate. In the same way as an interpretation should operate, both a psychoanalytic text and its interpretation should not close off its meaning, but instead open a path to a plurality of creative readings. In so doing, it is not always necessary to avoid the explicit use of psychoanalytic concepts; indeed, a reading that, for example, ruled out taking the unconscious seriously would no longer be psychoanalytic. The difference between their use in reified form by imposing a preconstituted reading grid on the text, on the one hand, and an application intended to achieve a fruitful encounter with it, on the other, cannot depend on the instruments used, but has to do very much more with what Bion (1970) calls the 'vertex' adopted. The issue is whether the vertex genuinely expresses the courage to be receptive to the new or represents only the hallucinatory, reassuring need for confirmation. In other words, we can perfectly well play at being detectives if that then leads us into the area of recognition, of the essential game played in the aesthetic conflict, as is well represented in this splendid text by the central position of the Raphael painting. The value of a text – the extraordinary value of *Dora* – lies in its unceasing fascination, as well as in its generation of ever new readings that are felt to be 'true'. The most abstruse metapsychological language could be used either in order to encounter the other, and the other of the text, or, reduced to empty jargon, in order *not* to encounter it. What I feel to be most relevant today in *Dora*, an essay seemingly so 'unscientific' at its time, is, precisely, the internal movement of *Nachträglichkeit*. In this sense it is a gift ('Dora' means gift), not only from Dora to Freud, in terms of what she taught him or enabled him to learn, but also from Freud to us all. *Dora* could be said to demand another postscript – indeed, an infinite number of postscripts. Its ultimate, fundamental lesson arguably lies in reminding us again and again that, in Nietzsche's marvellous formulation, the world has once more become infinite.

Dora: its in/consistency with the *Zeitgeist*

Any contemporary re-reading of the *Dora* case history is bound to take account of our postmodern sensibility concerning the construction of texts, the pervasiveness of rhetorical truth and ideology, and what we have learnt from structuralism, deconstruction and narratology about the functioning of texts. Paradoxically, we today are more inclined to read the case history as a short story, but if so it is because we no longer deprecate narrativity as a factor of knowledge, even in the scientific sphere. After all, we are not so suspicious in the case of fiction. On the other hand, we have become such with regard to the suspiciousness of early-style Freud. Freud thus anticipates a possible objection that is the complete antithesis of that of being unscientific, to which he openly responds in his text: the objection this time would be that he failed to exploit the so-called neo-rhetorical tendency, whereas ultimately he was perfectly aware of the rhetorical nature of the evidential arguments he presents concerning the resolution of the case.

We are struck, for instance, by the role of a protagonist in which he casts himself in the text, which is very different from that of an ideal compiler of a neutral scientific report. Note that I am referring here not to Freud as therapist but to Freud as the narrator present as a character in his own narration. In this connection, two passages are particularly significant: the prefatory remark about the observance of professional secrecy, mentioned above; and, later, the defence (similar in tone) that an analyst who directly addresses delicate subjects even with young girls is behaving ethically. In these two passages, Freud defends himself against the more or less implicit charge of *abusing* his patients. The issue of 'publication' can in fact be apprehended in various ways, given that it is actually a kind of intersection of several different lines of sense. Might the forceful defence against the charge of violating patient confidentiality and professional secrecy be read as if it in fact concerned the rhetorical nature of his truths, as if he felt that he was betraying an ideal of scientific purity that he held dear?

In a passage which, like so many others, demonstrates the breadth of his vision, Freud tells us that he could have avoided quite a lot of annoyance had he only decided to take a more inclusive approach to dreams and not to reduce their nature to the key principle of the hallucinatory fulfilment of infantile wishes:

> I fancy my theory would have been more certain of general acceptance if I had contented myself with maintaining that every dream had a meaning, which could be discovered by means of a certain process of interpretation; and that when the interpretation had been completed the dream could be replaced by thoughts which would fall into place at an easily recognizable point in the waking mental life of the dreamer . . . Such a theory would no doubt have proved attractive from its very simplicity, and it might have been supported by a great many examples of dreams that had been satisfactorily interpreted, as for instance by the one which has been analysed in these pages.
>
> (Freud, 1905 (1901), p. 67 f.)

However, is this not the same as Bion's conception of dreams? Again, might the central importance assigned not only to two dreams, but also to the 'indirect method of representation' of the associations to a dream in the form of images, be a way of equating night dreams with those of the day?

Having regard to the foregoing, it is no longer possible to believe that the guilty party mentioned in the text is Herr K or Dora's father. In this case, the outcome of the search for the culprit is not so much (or not only) the establishment of Dora's incestuous passion for her father as the failure to take account of the transference, which in fact takes the stage only in the Postscript. Another culprit is the countertransference, which had not yet been conceptualized and was only to be identified some years later (Freud, 1910b). In accordance with our present-day sensibility, yet another guilty party might be Freud's surgical coldness, which is actually contradicted by his passion as a researcher and writer. His doubting formulation is in fact only a rhetorical manoeuvre: 'if I had . . . shown a warm personal interest in her – a course which, even allowing for my position as her physician, would have been tantamount to providing her with a substitute for the affection she longed for . . .' (Freud, 1905 (1901), p. 109). He ends as follows: 'I promised to forgive her for having deprived me of the satisfaction of affording her a far more radical cure for her troubles' (ibid., p. 122). This coldness must now manifestly be referred primarily to the theoretical level, where the concepts of neutrality and abstinence in classical psychoanalytic theory are at issue.

This reading of the case history of *Dora* could be summarized by stating that it presents itself as an account of an analysis, a *roman à clef* and a plea for the defence. These three levels are interwoven. The treatment as such proceeds like a detective's investigation. The obvious culprit – to be unmasked – would be the one who caused Dora's symptom in accordance with the trauma model of the aetiopathology of the neuroses. However, in reading and re-reading the text, one is struck by the fact that Freud proposes himself as the person accused of a variety of misdeeds. Why else would he do nothing else, throughout the text, than defend himself against one charge after another? Moreover, these charges are then reduced to a single, essential one: *that psychoanalysis does not enjoy the status of a strictly scientific discipline but instead constitutes a fictional narrative and – the other side of the coin – that the person of the analyst assumes an authorial role (that of a novelist) in it.* However, once again, what Freud is seeking to defend himself against is precisely an aspect, which could be summed up in the concept of the aesthetic paradigm, that we at present *particularly* value in psychoanalysis because it is perfectly consonant with our contemporary sensibility.

As a fascinating, complex textual vehicle, *Dora* commends itself to us today principally as an involuntary theorization of the role in the treatment of the analyst as a person and as the construction, always after the event (on the basis of *Nachträglichkeit*), of truth. The more Freud acts as a detached detective *à la* Sherlock Holmes or Auguste Dupin, the more he comes to resemble Philip Marlowe or Sam Spade. For as the narration progresses, more and more personal aspects take the stage: his appointment as professor by way of the quotation from his own *Interpretation of Dreams*; the visit to Dresden and the letter to his betrothed by way of the reference to the same picture as that contemplated by

Dora; the 'discovery' of the transference; the failure to discover the countertransference; and, the culminating point, the final near self-revelation and the mention of elements of style ('if I had . . . shown a warm personal interest in her'). In reality, the concept of the countertransference must be transcended because it still belongs, after all, in the context of a psychoanalysis of the isolated subject focused on the patient rather than on the relationship understood as the 'something that is created between' patient and analyst. The fact is that, as with all great texts whether literary or non-literary, each fresh reading adds yet another postscript to *Dora* and generates creative ideas that fuel both clinical work and theoretical reflection.

Notes

1 Translator's note: For convenience, the masculine form is used for both sexes throughout this translation.

2 Translator's note: That is the meaning of the word *distaccarsi* used in the Italian version of *Dora*; the *Standard Edition* has 'mastering'. The *SE*'s rendering more accurately conveys the sense of the German *Herr zu werden*.

3 This too is a detail whose possible meanings should not be overlooked: *Dora* as a 'street' girl and *Madonna* (as a woman who has given birth and become a mother).

4 The German original is *in träumender Bewunderung* (literally, 'in dreaming admiration').

5 '"Now he is dead, and if you like you can come." I then went to the station . . . The maidservant opened the door to me and replied that Mother and the others were already at the cemetery . . .' (Freud, 1905 (1901), p. 94).

Chapter 7

Where does the reality principle begin?

The work of margins in Freud's 'Formulations on the two principles of mental functioning'

The paratext

The text of 'Formulations' (hereinafter known as FTPMF) has a circular structure. At the end of the brief essay – in the very last line – requesting a good-natured disposition and an affectionate sympathy in the reader, Freud suggests that he or she pay attention to the performative aspect of the text, the plane in which enunciation and action coincide:

> The deficiencies of this short paper, which is preparatory rather than expository, will perhaps be excused only in small part if I plead that they are unavoidable. In these few remarks on the psychical consequences of adaptation to the reality principle I have been obliged to adumbrate views which I should have preferred for the present to withhold and whose justification will certainly require no small effort. But I hope *it will not escape the notice of the benevolent* reader how [*wo*, i.e., 'where'] in *these pages too the dominance of the reality principle is beginning.*
>
> (1911, p. 226, my italics)

This is a striking sentence. It gives us the feeling that something might have escaped us, and that what we have just passed through may have been written in code. So we are tempted to go through it again from the beginning. Freud's conclusion invites a re-reading of the text, but this time with the end already in mind. The game set up by this rhetorical gesture seems precisely intended to illustrate the psychoanalytic concept of 'posteriority' (*Nachträglichkeit*).

And that is what I am going to do. I shall play the same game in order to try and understand Freud's precise and obscure assertion. To underline how anything may acquire a new meaning in the light of what comes after, I shall proceed in my re-reading of FTPMF as in a film structured in a sequence of flashbacks. I shall begin from the end.

In fact, we see that if it is read attentively, Freud's statement that I quoted in italics unfolds in two principal motions. On the one hand it draws attention to a certain point (the 'where') to which Freud evidently attributes particular importance, while on the other hand he craves the reader's indulgence. He links the two things in this way: it will only be the 'benevolent' reader who discovers the 'where', and conversely, having discovered it, he will have to be 'benevolent' (*wohlwollend*) towards the author. The end of the sentence reverberates back on the beginning. So the thing that should not escape us is precisely something that will require our benevolence. But why should the ideal reader invoked by Freud be benevolent? *Who* should be benevolent? *What* would he have preferred to keep silent? And why? What 'psychical consequences' is he alluding to? For whom? FTPMF is certainly a text that seems to hold secrets and arouses the reader's curiosity.

So I shall adopt a second methodological principle to try and give an answer to these questions and to others that arise from them (the 'what' of the 'where', and the 'why' of the benevolence). By going through the text backwards, taking up the exhortation to be more perceptive, and starting with what can appear to be 'secondary' – for example, the sentence that closes the text – I shall above all highlight some of those textual elements that by definition stand *around* the text, and that, with respect to it, perform only the auxiliary role of influencing its reception. Doing this means receiving not only the explicit message contained in the close of the paper, but also the implicit one.

Therefore the title that I have given my re-reading of FTPMF is to be taken literally. I shall concern myself with Freud's paper from the *margins*, from that which acts as a frame for the text. In the *paratext* (Genette, 1982, 1987) and, as we shall see, in his final observation, Freud scatters various clues. And, as in the detective stories of Conan Doyle that he loved reading (Vitale, 2005) – and after all, the psychoanalytic paradigm, at least in classical psychoanalysis, *is* evidential (Ginzburg, 1979) – these often hide in insignificant details, so to speak in the margins of the text, in its paratextual components.

We consider as margins, paratext, or *parergon* (Derrida, 1978), all the elements that make up a supplement to the *ergon* or main text: blurb, preface, notes, epigraph, etc. But the letters from Freud's private correspondence – with Jung and Ferenczi – in which he speaks about FTPMF also rightfully come into this category, as well as the comments and critical notes edited by commentators: above all, once they have become canonical. More precisely these two series of productions are examples, respectively, of *epitext*[1] and *editorial paratext*.[2]

What I propose here, however, is to add to Genette's classification some elements of what we could define as the 'internal' *parergon* or paratext. I mean that which appears to be less relevant *in* the main text, but which nevertheless plays an important role there: a dream, for example, however paradoxical that may seem. A dream is indeed always 'only a dream' ('*Es ist ja nur ein Traum*', as Freud notes in the paper 'On Dreams', 1901b; GW, p. 694). But also, of course, the concluding sentence. It does not refer to the theoretical questions addressed in the text, but is purely interlocutory. Moreover, the last two lines have the structure of a revolving door. Placed at the threshold of the text, they usher the reader out and immediately make him plunge back in again. In their liminal position, in the metaleptic nature of the appeal that the intradiegetic author, 'stepping out of' the text, directs to the reader, and in the performative role it plays, we could say that while being part of the main text, the final lines play a paratextual role.

The epilogue

So I would like to accept Freud's invitation regarding the use of the text, and both propose a decoding of it and also suggest how, in my opinion, the process of understanding is acted out, even and *especially* in analysis. It is a process that addresses itself always to the past (the future too exists only as a memory of what was anticipated in the past). The analyst is an Orpheus who in every interpretation tries to resuscitate the meaning from the world of shades. Yet every time, in the very moment when it is offered – like Eurydice, the beloved who in the myth gives meaning to the life of the divine singer – it shines for a moment and then dissolves again.

But in the end what is Freud referring to? After years of structuralism and deconstruction we may have become more worldly-wise about the way texts work, but this does not make it any easier for us to intuit what he is pointing out. It is not at all clear where, in the here-and-now of the reading, Freud begins to abandon the pleasure principle for the dominance of the reality principle. Freud writes that, against his will, he feels constrained to enunciate things about which he would stay silent if he could. But what things? I do not believe there can be a single answer to this. Like any textual mechanism that never stops intriguing, FTPMF too is reluctant to show its hand.

However, we glimpse one card almost straightaway. As we have seen, the close of FTPMF closes nothing at all: instead it re-launches the endless game of interpretation; or rather, urges us to resume reading from the start and so on ad infinitum. A reading that is therefore inevitably a *new* reading every time, and one that uncovers tracks in the text that went unnoticed before, while seeing others in a different light. In this incessant retracing of his or her steps, the reader realizes that, in the ever-moving shadow of 'posteriority', interpretation never reaches a definitive point. Not only this, but it will become clearer to him step by step that he is also 'rewriting the text each time, and letting himself be read (Ogden, 2012), and therefore also written, by it.

But if this is how things are, then we have already found an initial answer to the question posed in the title of my commentary: Freud continually had to go further in renouncing the positivist dream (aroused in him by his own 'pleasure principle') of decoding the truth of the unconscious. In FTPMF Freud has come to a fully matured awareness that truth may be circular, rhetorical, a matter of perspective and affect, inasmuch as it is conditioned by the *manner* and the context in which one attains it – a manner and context shared with society and hence not arbitrary. Moreover, 1918 is also the year in which Freud published his book about the Wolf Man, the text in which he takes up the final challenge of the trauma theory of the aetiology of neuroses. The challenge that will close with the *non liquet* of the notes on *Nachträglichkeit* added a few years later; another splendid example of how, in an explosive overthrowing of perspective, the paratext assumes almost greater weight than the text.

The dream

Once we have identified this first re-*flection* of the text on itself, we make it easier for ourselves to bring some others to light and thereby confirm their intrinsic coherence. Two components with the function of *parergon* take on great prominence because of where they are placed: the dream about the death of the father (1911, pp. 225– 226) and note 4 on p. 219. (I further divide the text into sub-units in order to make clearer the metonymic game of retrospective significance through which each element acts first of all on the one that immediately precedes it. For example – from this point of view – the benevolence requested from the reader in the final sentence relates above all to the meaning of the dream.)

As we read this dream we cannot fail to apply an internal intertextuality (Genette, 1982; Kristeva, 1980) to Freud's work. I am referring to two of the most extraordinary dreams in *The Interpretation of Dreams* (1900). Although the situations of the two protagonists are different – in one case the father dies, in the other the son – they address the same Oedipal theme of relations between father and son. The first is Freud's famous dream on the day after his father's funeral, when he goes to a railway station and reads the notice, 'You are requested to close the eyes' (Freud, 1900, p. 317).

The second is the other way round. The son is dead, and the father who is holding a vigil for him in the next room does not realize that a candle has set alight the cloth draping the coffin. The father dreams that his son calls out, 'Father, don't you see I'm burning?' (p. 509). Leaving aside the different existential situation of the characters in the dream, *the plea for pity that the son makes to the father is just the same.*

However, the dream found in FTPMF tells us, with an obvious and inevitable *après-coup*[3] effect in relation to the two dreams I have just mentioned, that the father has not yet responded to the plea, he *has not* closed the eyes (he has not even closed *an* eye) and he has not ended the anguish of his son because inside him the son *is not* really dead. Instead, like a *revenant*, the father repeatedly comes back to pester him ('his father was alive once more and . . . talking to him in his usual way' (Freud, 1911, p. 225)). The dreamer *knows* that his father is dead and feels very sad about it. However, the father – he tells us – *does not know* that he is dead. It is as if something were stopping him. But we would think that the dreamer is himself by no means convinced that his father is really dead. If we consider that the son is the author who has put the father 'who does not know' into the dream-theatre, we can in fact attribute to the event the same structure of a dream within a dream: that is, a dream in which two different levels of awareness are present. In the end, the hallucinosis of the dream reveals something that is true, even if denied by the senses, both – if we accept this similarity – in waking and in the dream that acts as a frame.

Freud interprets the dream as having been provoked by the dreamer's repressed desire for his father to die. The phrase, 'his father had really died, only without knowing it' is ambiguous. To make it comprehensible, he completes it by adding the unconscious death wish directed by the dreamer towards his father. But – I repeat – the reader could also understand this to mean that the son too did not know that his father was dead, in the sense that he actually was not dead *in his internal world*. Otherwise his father's ghost would not have continued to torment him. Moreover, we could also apply this to Freud himself as composer of the text, and hypothesize that unconsciously he did not know what he was talking about. What prompts us to form this hypothesis is, among other things, the fact that at the beginning of this paragraph Freud notes the 'great self-discipline' that the investigator must have in order to recognize the influence of unconscious factors upon him.

So we have identified a second point at which the reality principle imposes its dominance. Freud tells us that if we truly want to be realists we must open our eyes also with respect to the most inadmissible desires inspired by the pleasure principle. As he writes elsewhere, the child desires to possess the mother entirely for himself and for this reason would like to kill the father. In other words, we think we have certain feelings and thoughts, but we deceive ourselves. We feign a reality for ourselves that is certainly not the one of common sense, and we do this not only when we represent the world to ourselves, but also with regard to our most intimate passions.

The note

It becomes clear immediately after this that Freud is subverting the naïve realism with which we look not only at the world and at internal life, but also at the truths of science. Another significant insertion in the margin of the text – we were saying – is note 4 on p. 219 (the fourth note of Freud's own, though because of editorial insertions, it is the eighth of the text. Hereafter I shall refer to it simply as note 4). The note is justly famous. In it Freud shows himself to be aware of the limits of the psychoanalytic model he has constructed, but nevertheless justifies it. The key word in the note is 'fiction'. Here too – and now for the third time – the dominance of the reality principle imposes itself in the moment when Freud is compelled to acknowledge that everything he has described and theorized is no more than a scientific myth after all.

As readers we detect all the bitterness and frustration that he must have felt before reaching this conclusion. Yet, here too, he wraps them in an exquisitely personal rhetoric and makes the best of a bad job. In essence, from the systematic acknowledgement of the Ego's limitedness, Freud derives an empowering of the Ego, similar to that which Kant derives from the feeling of the sublime inspired by the contemplation of nature's infinity.[4] In this way weakness is overturned and becomes strength. In the modern era this is the position of Freud's contemporary Nietzsche. The transvaluation of all traditional values by the Overman does not by any means generate 'a weakened subject (not in the sense of the exemption from metaphysical attributes), but one strengthened in the plurality of mortal souls and in the multiplicity of interpretative perspectives that establish a richer objectivity than that which can be ascertained by mere description' (Vozza, 2014, p. 10).

In any case, the fiction that the note addresses is that of an isolated psychic system that is 'able to satisfy even its nutritional requirements autistically' as if in 'a bird's egg with its food supply enclosed in its shell' (Freud, 1911, p. 220). And yet Freudian psychoanalysis rests to a large extent on this fiction. On the one hand Freud describes the development of an animal-infant and not a man-infant (i.e., affected *from the very outset* by the symbolic in language), and on the other hand confers upon him the status of an already established subjectivity, however immature: that is, he sees him as a solipsistic entity. The mother is assimilated as a presence that permits the child to live in this world without suffering too many of its assaults. She acts on behalf of the child to keep at a distance those external stimuli that would cause him an increase in unpleasure.

Note 4 is the return of what Freudian theory represses. The metaphor of the bird in the egg is the quintessential illustration of Freud's conception of man as an isolated subject endowed with consciousness: and, besides, it matches the psychological and philosophical dogma of his time. Although it is obviously a dogma to which psychoanalysis will itself contribute substantially to dissolving, there is in Freud no notion that from the outset the essence of being human consists in being transposed into the other.[5]

The fact is that there is a difference between animals, which are not 'world-forming' and are 'poor in world' (Heidegger, 1927), and men. For the latter to become human, maternal warmth and nourishment are not enough: they need someone to help them construct an unconscious, understood as the acquisition through language of the capacity to give existential meaning to experience.[6]

However, in the note Freud anticipates the idea expressed by Winnicott in a now famous formulation, that there is no such thing as a baby if viewed without the mother. The infant's apparently closed system is in reality constituted by the infant *plus* whoever is providing the care that is necessary for its survival. In fact, the subject is already a group. It is through having the mother's mind available – and not only when prompted by frustration – that the infant is not abandoned to its own world of hallucinatory images.

Therefore, we cannot fail to read the note also as a memory of the future, in that it anticipates and summarizes – 'remembers' – how psychoanalytic theory will evolve divergently from the classical model after the middle of the twentieth century specifically in order to remedy the effects of the fiction adopted by Freud. The limits that Freud honestly acknowledges, and that he places under the aegis of recognition of the reality principle while trying to pass beyond them, will be crossed by Bion; for example, with his concept of the protomental system.

We understand why it has been asserted that overall this brief text may be the one that most inspired the psychoanalysis of Bion. We have seen how strongly Freud relativizes the certainties of his time and how he lets us glimpse the seeds of a passage to a conception of intersubjectivity. So Freud, outlining a whole series of binary oppositions in this brief paper, lays down the premises by which they could begin to be transcended, something that Bion will bring to completion, starting with the overcoming of that very fiction that Freud speaks about in the note and that informs not only Bion's theory (Civitarese, 2008a), but perhaps to an even greater degree some of his later developments such as the psychology of the Ego.

Indeed, there are some other themes in FTPMF that can easily be recognized as leading to Bionian theory. For example, Bion takes up from FTPMF the idea of having to concentrate on psychic functions more than on their contents. We may note the recurrence in FTPMF of the term *function* as early as the fifth line, in relation to Janet, or the term *process*(*es*). We may also note the striking equivalence between the text and the way in which the Bionian design of the grid presents an analogous teleological development of the functions of the psyche on the philo- and ontogenetic planes simultaneously, from primitive emotions to concepts, and from concepts to moral action (Bion, 1977b, 1997; Civitarese, 2013a). In the end, both Freud and Bion delineate the life of man as a progressive acquisition of functions.

Then there is the significant passage in which Freud diminishes the opposition between the pleasure principle and the reality principle, writing that the latter only replaces the former so as to preserve it better. It is as if he were saying that every form of pleasure can only be a negative pleasure. We renounce something with a view to future compensation. The satisfaction of the pleasure stems from an initial moment of negation. In the following lines, Freud reduces the distance between neurosis and psychosis, making them a matter of quantity, of how large a part of reality the subject is able to tolerate, and immediately afterwards mentions the distinction between the neurotic and 'mankind in general'.

Lastly he presents the unconscious psychic processes as the most ancient, and above all, as closely bound to the pleasure principle. It would only be the disillusionment suffered by the hallucinatory satisfaction of desire that makes the recognition of external reality gradually emerge: 'the psychical apparatus *had to decide* to form a conception of the real circumstances in the external world and to *endeavour* to make a real alteration in them' (Freud, 1911, p. 219, my italics). It can clearly be seen how on the theoretical plane it may not be the introjection of the maternal alpha function that puts the baby more fully in contact with reality, but rather a kind of 'painful decision' by the baby himself, to accept his own deep 'situation of frustration' (p. 222).

Sleep brings us back every night to this primitive condition in which we know nothing of external reality, 'because a prerequisite of sleep is a deliberate rejection of reality (the wish to sleep)' (p. 219, n3). The dream is introduced as a residue of the hallucinatory route to the satisfaction of desire. Dream thinking would be at the service of the latent thoughts that express prohibited desires. Dreaming, for Freud, is equivalent to suspending the reality principle. He does not by any means believe, as Bion (1992) does, that dream thoughts are a rough draft of thought, that the dream designs maps for exploring the world and is not confined solely to the state of sleep. He gives no sign of dream's creative value, nor of the idea that it may be dreaming of the mother that initially acts as a complement to the condition of being 'all (and only) conscious' (Bion, 1967) of the baby at birth (Civitarese, 2011b). For Freud, reality knocks on the door because dreaming never works, because it fails as an investigation of reality and not, conversely, because it succeeds in giving a 'poetic' or integrated meaning to experience. Nor is the dream seen as an activity of digesting the real that also takes place in the waking state. For Freud, primary and secondary process are not a continuum, but separated by a clear caesura.

And yet, here too, if on the one hand Freud reaffirms the dichotomy of *C*/*Ucs*. and primary/secondary process, is he not at the same time eroding from within any metaphysical view of truth, and letting perception subtly and dangerously incline to the side of the hallucinatory? Do not dreaming, 'imagining', and 'pretending' end up almost superimposed on to each other? Is he not also clearly asserting that it would be a mistake to identify the dream solely with latent dream thoughts?

In a narrative crescendo worthy of Rossini, by which – I repeat – FTPMF anticipates the structure of the grid, we are present at the linear itinerary of the infant who from being immersed as he is in this hallucinatory world, step by step develops effective sensory channels, a consciousness, a memory and finally attention; an activity that instead of passively receiving sensory impressions, goes to meet them. All that is true. But there is more. When the psyche passes from the pleasure principle to the reality principle, writes Freud, a small part of it remains attached to the pleasure principle: the activity of fantasy, which is immediately located in children's play and in *dreaming with open eyes*. Here the Ego's drives are pulled away from the sexual ones, which remain much longer under the dominance of the pleasure principle. The neuroses find easy terrain in 'the delay in educating the sexual instincts' (1911, p. 223).[7] However, as soon as the two currents have diverged, in some ways they re-converge because the Ego takes account of reality in order to preserve better the achievement of pleasure. And here too a caesura begins to be broken little by little.[8] The reality principle is only the servant of the pleasure principle. The hallucinatory in dream begins to infiltrate perception. For example, if religions are able to bring about the complete renunciation of pleasure it is always with a view to a greater pleasure (in the afterlife), even if illusory. Even the pleasure offered by the sciences is a small matter, an intellectual pleasure with a view to a practical reward. Therefore, both religion and science are animated by dream, by a subterranean fantasy life, by the pleasure principle. But the point at which we can best pick up anticipations of the current vision of dreaming as an activity that characterizes waking life as well, and of the crisis in the opposition between primary and secondary processes, is in the Freudian theory of aesthetic experience.

In this text of Freud's, art is the *via regia* for reconciling the two principles. The artist, presented initially as in some way maladapted, is an artist because he does not renounce pleasure but addresses himself to reality 'by making use of special gifts to mould his phantasies into truths of a new kind, which are valued by men as precious reflections of reality' (p. 224). Then Freud adds an essential detail, which is that the artist 'can only achieve this because other men feel the same dissatisfaction as he does with the renunciation demanded by reality' (p. 224). So we see that in this text Freud on the one hand reaffirms a series of caesuras, but on the other does what he can to destabilize them.

In confessing in note 4 that he sees his theoretical construction as a model or framework for reaching the thing that in itself, however, remains unattainable, Freud admits that scientific truth is also a myth. Here his personal life coincides with his scientific vicissitudes. Indeed, *how* could Freud have wanted to 'kill' his father if not by annexing a continent new to science and hitherto unexplored? It is as if – we may speculate – Freud were telling us with the dream of FTPMF that his desire was to overcome the father and acquire a fame that he would demonstrate by means of an incontrovertible discovery. This discovery, the dominance of the reality principle imposes on him the need to recognize that *there had been no such discovery*: a 'rhetorical' or 'consensual' truth is only a pale reflection of it. In fact, Freud was thinking of himself as a 'true' scientist, not as the founder of a discipline that could only exist in a space half way between art and science – a *Zwitterart*, as Schiller said of himself and of the poet (Reitani, 2003, p. 124). This game does not merely happen in the background of FTPMF but, well hidden, is the principal game being played in the text.

So far we have seen how Freud's most intimate personal experiences are tightly interwoven in the text with his theoretical activity. The same thing occurs also in the final element of paratext that we shall take into consideration, the editorial introduction.

The introduction

Finally we come to the first crucial paratext in FTPMF, the preface by Cesare Musatti that acts as an introduction to the Italian edition of Freud's *Works*. It is of no importance that the preface was not written by Freud. Our reading could not now overlook it. It would be absurd to think we could gain access to the truth of a text in its original purity. We are not given a text without a context that determines its reception in some way. As has been said, just like the other paratextual elements inserted by the author, the introduction is an editorial *parergon* that acts as a frame and so engages in dialogue with the main text, contributing to the outlining of its meaning.

The most noteworthy element in the introduction refers to Jung's role in the conception of FTPMF (see also Blum, 2004). Introducing the figure of a parricidal Jung in Freud's eyes, the introduction merely anticipates what we encounter in the text's opening remarks, in the lines where Freud overtakes, and so 'kills' his father Janet, writing that the latter could not explain the reason for the lessening of reality function in neurotics.

But while the reference in the text to Janet is obvious, that to Jung is hidden, and in order to shed light on it we first need the introduction and then a reference to the Freud–Jung correspondence. In the letter of 19 June 1910 Freud praises a work by Jung (*Symbols of Transformation*) that will later flow into *Transformations and Symbols of the Libido*. Then he adds that he is taking up some of Jung's ideas for a paper, destined for the *Jahrbuch*, which will be called 'The two principles of psychic action and education'. This letter clearly shows that the two are now at loggerheads. Freud writes (Freud and Jung, 1974, pp. 330–332):

> Dear friend, I am really sorry to hear of all your overwork and irritation and thank you very much for your friendly explanations. You mustn't suppose that I ever 'lose patience' with you; I don't believe these words can apply to our relationship in any way. In all the difficulties that confront us in our work we must stand firmly together, and now and then you must listen to me, your older friend, even when you are disinclined to.

It is the tongue-lashing that a father would give a son who has disappointed him. Once we have read the rest of the letter our last doubts will vanish:

> You know how jealous they all are – here and elsewhere – over your privileged position with me . . . and I think I am justified in feeling that what people say against you as a result is being said against me.

Then Freud blames Adler, whom he describes as 'hypersensitive and deeply embittered' because he consistently rejects his theories. He comments that 'a secession were going to be attempted in Vienna' and mentions 'a step that implied calling the authority of the chairman into question', but he managed to avoid this. By and large 'The goings-on in Zürich' seem to him 'stupid' and the situation there 'untenable'. He wonders that Jung has not been able to develop sufficient authority. In the rest of the letter, if we read between the lines, we will be hit by expressions such as 'internal division', 'Swiss blockheads', and finally by the rhetorical but subtly provocative question directly addressed to his interlocutor 'Could you have given the impression that you were indifferent to them ['. . . to *me*'?!] as individuals?" '

Apparently at this point Freud intends a change of tone, adding that he would rather speak about pleasant things. Except that he continues unperturbed in a combative vein, albeit latent, when he refers to his 'plagiarism' (but by whom, we may ask, and from whom?) and to some pages of FTPMF still in progress. After praising Jung for the text, now lost in its original form, which came from the conference held at Herisau and was then included in *Symbols of Transformation*, he goes on:

> Don't be surprised if you recognize certain of your own statements in a paper of mine that I am hoping to revise in the first weeks of the holidays, and don't accuse me of plagiarism, though there may be some temptation to. The title will be: The Two Principles of Mental Action and Education. It is intended for the *Jahrbuch*. I conceived and wrote it two days before the arrival of your 'Symbolism'; It is of course a formulation of ideas that were long present in my mind.

As they say, *in cauda venenum*: who is plagiarizing whom? And that is not all, because Freud takes up with a phrase that is impossible not to understand even in a shrewd way: 'I identified your vulture only today', a sentence that can be translated as 'Only now I realize that you are a vulture.' Freud then again sets himself in open opposition: 'I am not inclined to let you have Count Zinzendorf for the *Jahrbuch*. Don't take it amiss', and lastly complains about health problems, 'a recurrence of the intestinal trouble . . . plain colitis', etc. But we can only understand the nature of these complaints by reading the list of no more than thirteen objections to Jung's text (another example of paratext!) with which Freud accompanies his missive. At the end of the letter he looks diplomatically ahead and tells Jung that he is aware that his criticisms will certainly not be received willingly, but that overall, in the end, he very much liked the work.

Jung's reply was not long in coming. A week later, 26 June, he replied to Freud in a conciliatory tone. Indeed, the *incipit* of the letter is significant in that respect: 'Today being a Sunday I am using it to go over your critique in peace' (p. 361). The polemical tone is evident in Jung's discourse. It is as if he were saying, 'Since it is Sunday, I am not responding in kind.' But that little word, 'peace', appears to have been placed there precisely to hint at the cold war that now seems to be under way, and that is reignited a few lines later when Jung firmly defends his position on sexuality, even though it had been attacked by Freud.

In the light of my observations so far, FTPMF appears as the 'dream' with which Freud tries to give meaning to the strong emotions (the 'psychic consequences') stirred up by Jung's rebellion. In his filicidal impulse, unconsciously denied, Freud finds yet another, stronger impulse for his parricidal drive, or rather cannot stop himself siding with Jung, except that now the father to be killed is . . . himself! Why do I say this? Essentially because the key to the three examined dreams – which, I repeat, I propose to consider similarly as paratextual elements – lies in the invocation to mercy that is always addressed by a son to the father *and never vice versa*!

In the dream about his father's death, Freud asks him to leave him in peace. The same thing happens in the other dream, not his, about the son who is burning. There too it is the son who asks the father to ease his torment. It is like this again in the dream of FTPMF and in the letter where Jung asks him to make peace. If in this incident with Jung, Freud finds himself objectively taking the other side (it is the father, Laius, who wants to kill the son who has been revealed as a danger to him by the prophecy), here he is burning above all with the suffering of Oedipus.

Perhaps this was more difficult for him to admit to himself than the impulse to kill his son (while accusing him of the reciprocal), as if unconsciously it was impossible for him not to identify – against himself – with the rebellious son. If my interpretation is plausible, the accusation against Jung is in reality a self-accusation.

The work of the margins

Do we now have to conclude that, paradoxically, it is in the introduction, in the editorial paratext (the text's unconscious?) that we find the 'where [*wo*]' – the thing that Freud would gladly have withheld, and on account of which he asks the reader to be benevolent towards him? As in *The Purloined Letter* of Poe, the meaning sought with such doggedness was always in plain sight.

The aspect of FTPMF that I have called performative, and to which Freud ambiguously calls our attention at the end of the text is of broad scope. It plays on a series of particular planes that intersect with each other. Not only the theoretical recognition of the fictional status of reality; nor only the admission by Freud that his too is nothing but a scientific fiction, not the real thing; nor yet the interpretation aimed at Jung of his desire to do away with him, nor the awareness of his own filicidal desire towards Jung: but perhaps, close to the core of the dream, the reappearance of the desire in Freud himself, this time unconsciously identified with Jung, to kill *his* father. Also in play here is the possibility that one achieves with greater or lesser success the 'complete psychical detachment from its [*sic*] parents' (1911, p. 220, n. 4) that signals the end of the pleasure principle. Even though, when we think of the *incipit*, with its 'elimination' of Janet and its invocations of the father in the two dreams and – in the letter to Jung – of the reader-as-judge-father, there can be no doubt about which passion prevails, what is still more important is the general principle: that one must accept we are no longer making use of a separating logic, of an absolute principle of non- contradiction.

The text's various planes follow one another in a centripetal direction, from the theoretical level to the most personal and vice versa, as if saying that, whichever way you look at reality, it is never how it appears, not even when viewed in the pure, disinterested manner of scientific research. FTPMF seems to reaffirm that at the bottom of any epistemophilic passion there is always a private nucleus of neurosis. With this text Freud is trying to treat himself. We also see, in the light of this, how effectively the oneiric participates in the construction of rational argument, and how the beginning of the reality principle consists simply in mourning our pretensions to knowledge. The dominion of the reality principle demands that we see everything in our inner or outer lives as fiction. But is this not the work of the margins? Is not the frame the component of a picture that takes on the job of marking out a space for fiction? Does not any frame warn us never to give in to the images' status as real? And is not the dream the threshold where one passes every time from internal to external and vice versa, but without our ever being able to do without either of the two termini lest we lose that which represents the quintessence of humanity? In FTPMF every time a paratextual element emphasizes or nuances something that has just been asserted, it reframes it, adjusts it. The reader is confronted on each occasion with a catastrophic change of perspective on various levels. What remains in essence is this very vertigo, which Nietzsche calls the world become infinite again.

We have seen at work repeatedly in the margins how they act to join together the internal and external. This is 'how' the reality principle begins, or rather where the fiction principle begins. FTPMF's discovery is that we are characterized more by the fiction principle than by the reality principle. The reality principle is merely a name we give to the occasional convergences that allow us to have a minimal common view of things.

In fact, to become human it is necessary to achieve the fiction which, in allowing us to tolerate the 'no' of the object's absence, simultaneously permits us the illusion that we attain it through its name. For this reason we can say that the only reality that concerns us – given that, strictly speaking, animals do not perceive objects but are merely immersed in a dynamic flow of automatic stimulus – responses – can only be a fictitious reality. The dominion of the reality principle lies in recognizing that the quality that makes us human lies in an essential principle of fiction and that every fiction has its beginning in the *no* of the name.

So where does the dominion of the reality principle begin? I would say, paradoxically, in the margins, from the start of the disappearance of the real in favour of reality. Reality is in the margins: or rather, only the frame makes a concept of reality available to us. The affirmation of the dominion of the reality principle means recognizing that reality is a fiction. This is the truth imposed upon us and that we struggle so hard to accept: that reality has the qualities of a dream. Acknowledging the dominion of reality means recognizing that we only possess reality by dreaming it. It means mourning our ability ever to possess the thing, the object, the truth. Dreaming is equivalent to representing, to transforming the real into a familiar and reassuring reality, to placing a desired but feared object at a safe distance that allows us the peace and quiet of thought.

Notes

1 See Genette (1987, p. 5):

> The distanced elements are all those messages that, at least originally, are located outside the book, generally with the help of the media (letters, conversations) or under cover of private communications (letters, diaries, and others). This second category is what, for lack of a better word, I call *epitext* . . . peritext and epitext completely and entirely share the spatial field of the paratext. In other words, for those who are keen on formulae, *paratext = peritext + epitext*.

2 See Genette (1987, p. 16): 'I give the name publisher's *peritext* to the whole zone of the peritext that is direct and principal (but not exclusive) responsibility of the publisher (or perhaps, to be more abstract but also more exact, of the *publishing house*).'

3 In this text I use the terms *après-coup*, *posteriority*, and *Nachträglichkeit* as equivalent.

4 See Civitarese (2014b). The passage which follows is extremely noteworthy:

> The place of repression, which excluded from cathexis as productive of unpleasure some of the emerging ideas, was taken by an *impartial passing of judgement*, which had to decide whether a given idea was true or false – that is, whether it was in agreement with reality or not – the decision being determined by making a comparison with the memory-traces of reality.
>
> (Freud, 1911, pp. 221)

Here it is the moral, Kantian man who comes into view. The Freudian rhetoric sparkles as it shows the necessity for the repression of pleasure, of sexuality felt as a danger for the order of meaning. It is moreover evident that Freud is here proposing a theory of knowledge. The moral man acts correctly in reality. ('A new function was now allotted to motor discharge, which, under the dominance of the pleasure principle, had served as a means of unburdening the mental apparatus of accretions of stimuli . . . Motor discharge was now employed in the appropriate alteration of reality; it was converted into *action.*' We may note here too, the coincidence with key terms from Bion's vocabulary.)

5 Cfr. Heidegger, 1983, p. 206: philosophy has propounded:

> the dogma that the individual human being exists for him or herself as an individual and that it is the individual Ego with its Ego-sphere which is initially and primarily given to itself as what is most certain. This has merely given philosophical sanction to the view that some kind of being with one other must first be produced out of this solipsistic isolation.

See also Brown (2011) who has shown in Freud's work the presence of a 'proto-intersubjectivity'.

6 The contemporary psychoanalysis that draws most on metapsychology has identified in the paradigm of the *Nebenmensch* one possible way to highlight the presence even in Freud of a form of proto-intersubjectivity.

7 Before subverting the laws of civilized life, a sexuality not regulated by a paternal/third function would subvert the very establishment of symbolic order, because it would tend to wipe out the space between subject and object from which all difference arises. The dominance of the reality principle begins with the introjection of the father's *no*. The father as third function prevents incest between infant and mother and allows the symbol to arise from the space thus created, but at the same time the symbol arises from the fact of keeping a link between subject and object and thence de facto transgressing the paternal interdiction. Moreover, thanks to the desire to which it always gives rise, sexuality also acts as a safeguard against the risk that this distance becomes infinite. Pleasure and unpleasure are thus both consubstantial with the capacity for symbolization.

8 On the concept of 'caesura' see Civitarese (2008a).

Chapter 8

Truth as immediacy and unison: a new common ground in psychoanalysis?

Commentary on essays addressing 'Is truth relevant?'

First of all, I would like to thank Jay Greenberg for having asked me to comment on this group of essays by extremely well-respected authors who were invited to write about the topic of the relevance of the concept of truth in psychoanalysis. I find this discourse to be of great importance, not at all an abstract or philosophical one, and I feel that it has definite consequences on both theoretical and technical levels. In discussing the various papers – which I have very much appreciated for what they say, and perhaps even more for the questions that they raise – I will follow a path leading approximately from the more traditional positions towards the more innovative ones, in order to highlight an emerging paradigm in psychoanalysis. Here and there and in the concluding section, I will also express my own opinions on the topic.

I will try to identify in the various papers a kind of red thread in which the connections between *truth* and *immediacy* (Blass, 2011) and between *truth* and *unison* are interwoven in various ways, both explicitly and implicitly. To my mind, in assigning value to these connections, we can begin to construct a new common ground in psychoanalysis. The differences among the various papers must not be silenced, nor must the conflicts they reflect, but just as important is the attempt to discover their points of convergence.

The history of psychoanalysis can be re-read as the attempt to come up with ever more effective tools[1] with which to establish the truth of emotionally lived experienced in the here and now in analysis, even when the objective could seem to be a different one – for example, when analysis is aimed more at the recovery of the repressed – in order to identify the ultimate basis of personal truth within the emotional unison. *Personal* truth, but also – I would add in the light of contemporary epistemology – *social* truth. In this perspective, truth is seen as the food that nourishes the psyche in that it creates order; that is, starting from the meeting of minds, it simultaneously generates proto-experiences of 'unity and multiplicity' (a scholastic definition of *concept*; see Heidegger, 1977, p. 155). Initially of an emotional or sensorial type, these proto-concepts are gradually developed to the point of actual concepts. In this way, self-awareness is established and the subject can fully enter into the symbolic.

My theoretical frame of reference is Bionian psychoanalysis and the mother–infant relationship as the model of the mind's growth. In his attempt to formalize psychoanalysis – or rather to start out again from its earliest principles in order to formulate concepts of concepts (an example of which is *unison*) – Bion could have had much greater success than I myself would have been prepared to credit him with until a short time ago. That is, restarting from the basic elements of psychoanalysis, he could have formulated theoretical systems of a more abstract type to encompass various tools that are analogous but come from different models. Bion's phenomenological effort – think of the keywords of the titles of his most noteworthy books and some of his minor writings, and of their clear inspiration from Husserl: *elements*, *attention*, *experience*, *transformations*, *evidence* – opened our eyes to other models that have tried to, and continue to try to, carry out their own 'return to the things themselves'.[2]

The capacity to love

I will begin with Rachel B. Blass's paper because it most closely reflects the classical conception of psychoanalysis and can thus serve as a touchstone for the other papers. Blass (2016) recognizes that what counts in analysis, in the end, is that the patient reaches an openness to truth and a capacity to know more than the recognition of specific repressed contents, even though she sees the two things as joined together. What surfaces in the transference, Blass explains, are not so much factual truths, but mental attitudes – ways of thinking, libidinal impulses – not only contents but forms of contents. In this way, she makes it clear, if it is truth that one is dealing with, this cannot be reduced merely to its informative or biographical quotient. More than remembering in and of itself, what becomes fundamental in the analytic process is the working through.

The incapacity to know depends on the desire not to know, resulting from the struggle between hate and love, life and death instincts. If the capacity to know depends on the *capacity to love*, in the therapeutic relationship, it becomes important to develop this capacity; the only way to do so is obviously to endow the relationship with a particular quality. But Blass professes to be convinced that there is nothing new under the sun: 'I see this as a stance that has always lain at the very foundation of psychoanalysis' (p. 306).

Blass argues clearly and convincingly for the importance of the search for truth ('the alpha and omega of psychoanalysis', p. 306), both in Freudian theory and in the Kleinian approach. Towards that end, she cites Freud's pointing a finger at the patient and reminding him of his responsibility: 'The blame . . . lies with yourself' (p. 308). By definition, 'one perverts [one of the most recurrent verbs in the paper] reality' (p. 328). But the truth that the neurotic denies, destroys, and conceals is something he knew and still unconsciously knows, as is seen by the fact that it reappears symbolically in symptoms. This is why, in the return of the repressed, Blass recognizes the patient's wish/passion (epistemophilia/search instinct, *Wissbegierde*) to know the truth and not only to avoid it.

All this notwithstanding, Freud's evolution from the *thing* of the memory to the *how* of psychic functioning as the consequence of a given capacity to know/to love, and from the memory-as-a-content to remembering as a *process* of the recording of reality, remains incomplete. '[Freud's] notion of mental attitudes, as well as that of the patient's search for truth, are not sufficiently articulated or grounded in the rest of his thinking' (p. 317), Blass writes. Freud's position on love is ambiguous; on the one hand, he sees it as a denial of reality, while on the other, as the expression of a powerful desire for knowledge and an openness to reality. That uncertainty is reflected in the suspiciousness of classical psychoanalysis towards transference love, seen as 'false' in comparison to its more genuine or 'true' version. Equally vague and not sufficiently defined would be the principles of translating the unconscious into consciousness and bringing the Id under the control of the Ego.

Klein would have shed some light on these opaque points of Freudian theory, according to Blass: '[Klein's] way of thinking . . . *resolves* many of the basic difficulties that Freud encountered as he brought together ideas on memory, libidinal trends, and mental attitudes' (p. 318, emphasis added).[3] But in what way does Klein 'resolve' the problems encountered in Freud's theory? Mainly by introducing the concept of unconscious fantasy, not thoughts on something/someone, even if influential, but 'building blocks', 'the material of the Ego and of the mind itself' (ibid.). Both the self and the object with which one is in a relationship in unconscious fantasy are parts of the self. Attacking an object is equivalent to attacking/damaging part of one's own mind. 'Content' (fantasied action) and 'form' (the process of psychic functioning) are thus reunited in a convincing way, from one theoretical viewpoint: the 'instinctual trend' (the erotic or aggressive quality of the fantasy) and the mental attitude (the internal vision of the state of the object) and 'the way one actually thinks'.

Focusing the analysis on the interpretation of unconscious fantasy would resolve the Freudian indecision about remembering versus repeating: '[Klein's] notion of phantasy helps make sense of the idea that there is no distinction between coming to know split-off and denied truths of the mind and developing the capacity to think' (p. 322).[4] The *thing/how* dichotomy would actually be erased. Recovering denied or split-off aspects of the self would coincide with the development of the capacity to think.

In then discussing a paper by Segal, Blass provides us with a clarifying example of the passage from Freud to Klein, showing how a possible interpretation of a patient's material in an Oedipal key[5] (of a *thing*) might be transformed into an interpretation of an operative unconscious fantasy (of a *how*), read in the key of Oedipal sexuality between the minds of analyst and patient in the here and now. The fantasy of penetrating the mother comes to be understood as the fantasy of penetrating the analyst's mind with projective identification. In addition, Blass quotes Segal, who wrote perceptively: 'What should be an awareness of his thoughts is experienced as an external fact – something happening in mother's body' (Segal quoted by Blass, p. 325). To my ears, these statements sound very much in tune with post-Bionian field models, which also concentrate on the detailed analysis of the here and now, as well as on a transformation of past events and the external world, in the 'oneiric' account of what happens between patient and analyst.

Now I will mention some problematic points that in my opinion are yet to be clarified. In the first place, in this perspective, there is at least a part of the patient that is seen as an enemy: the part that does not want to know and has no desire for sturdier truths, or in which the death instinct predominates (those who do not accept that notion will find themselves discomfited with respect to this point). My suspicion is that it can easily happen that this (hostile) part may come to be unconsciously identified with the whole, with the result that we sometimes witness the establishment of subtly moralistic and paranoid attitudes in the analyst. It is true that any model can be 'perverted' in this same way, but in my opinion some have more antibodies than others to defend against this risk – to be precise, those models that favour more systematically raising questions about the role played by the analyst's subjectivity.

In the second place, the question of the analyst's authority remains unaddressed. As we know, this is precisely the point that other psychoanalytic models – for example, relational ones – have incisively criticized. Let us now examine this factor in greater detail, and it is a factor that closely correlates with the question of truth in psychoanalysis. As we have seen, for Freud, analysis is a struggle in which the analyst must conquer the patient's resistances to knowing. For him, a fundamental idea is that it is the patient who misunderstands and distorts the truth of a given emotional experience. Hence there is a risk of imposing one's own truth on the patient through a pedagogical–educative demand, and this risk was anticipated and dramatically experienced by Freud in the crisis of his 'neurotica', as Blass reminds us. In short, the patient is certainly not seen as the 'analyst's best colleague' – the one who, in the event of necessity, 'treats' his therapist and continually points out to him how he is functioning via derivatives of unconscious thinking. Here we are fully immersed in what Ricoeur (1965) defined as the *hermeneutics of suspicion*.

The same is true, and perhaps even more so, for Kleinian interpretations.[6] Since there will always be an unconscious part of the patient's mind that receives them, one abstains from making use of other parameters in order to have an idea of the effect produced by them. Profound, fearless, indifferent to the degree of tolerance on the patient's part or to the psychic pain that may be engendered ('without fear of causing psychic pain or out of more theoretical concerns such as "timing,"' – Segal and Meltzer quoted by Blass, p. 329), and aimed at the unconscious (which would 'automatically' recognize their goodness): this is how Kleinian interpretations are characterized. The analyst is portrayed as though he is 'naturally' capable of 'understanding' what happens in the transference relationship. But how can one know whether an interpretation is 'well founded on the presenting material' (ibid.)? And on what criteria for truth is this conviction based?

Blass herself expresses the concern that 'in the eyes of contemporary culture, this approach to authority and responsibility belittles the patient, blames him for his predicament, and makes him vulnerable to abuse by authoritative figures' (p. 333). In contrast, she hopes to have presented a portrait that is different from the usual Freudian–Kleinian approach, one that does not belittle the patient. In part, this is true. If, however, the central tenets remain the concepts of distortion/misunderstanding/perversion of transference, and of destructiveness tied to the death drive, of an 'enemy' to be defeated, then *how* does the capacity to love, the royal road to knowledge and thus actually *identified with truth*, become a theoretical-technical parameter?

Blass allows us to glimpse a possible line of thinking to support her point, which will appear clear in the perspective of some of the contributions that I will address after this one, and in Bionian theory, through the connection between truth and *the capacity to love* and *an offer of truth* and an *act of love*. But this part, in my opinion, is still presented in a way that is not sufficiently developed on a theoretical level. A strongly content-focused tone is still prominent here: the analytic encounter is indeed a 'lived encounter' (p. 306), but how can one make Eros win? What is the value of truth that is intrinsic to emotional unison, just as, in Freud's terms, a great knowledge of the object is intrinsic to the love for it? The impression is substantially that – even though some notable new perspectives are offered – we are still in the neighbourhood of the evidentiary paradigm (Ginzburg, 1979).

Not by chance, the end of Blass's article is polemic, with approaches that aim more at grasping the inevitably emotional-aesthetic truth of the encounter. That seems to be symptomatic of what the author's theory works hard to integrate, which I would say is all that is not on the order of psychic representation, and not only from the standpoint of pathology and of trauma (not necessarily in relation to a deficit), but also from that of the aesthetic/corporeal/material/semiotic quotient of human signification. Not for nothing did Bion restore emotion to the centre of psychoanalysis (and not for nothing did he introduce the idea of a *truth drive*). When, furthermore, in following up on a quotation from Freud, Bion asks himself about the vestiges of foetal life, is he abandoning the idea of truth?

The truth, Blass laments, may be seen by some as only the 'detached, objective concern of scientists that does not encompass relational needs. *People . . . do not need understanding, but to feel understood, loved, appreciated, and validated*; their capacities – often viewed as stunted because of environmental limitations – need to be developed' (p. 334, my emphasis). Certainly, scientific truth, too, has been brought into the discussion by contemporary epistemology, and furthermore, we understand that truth can be based only on a process of mutual validation (with the other, an 'integrated' form of comprehension). I would not say, however, that the idea of truth has gone out of fashion. Blass stigmatizes the crisis of a 'neutral, truth-seeking stance' (p. 332n), as though this concept of neutrality might still be predominant. I would not confuse a metaphysical vision of truth with the crisis of this vision itself or the search (painful as well) for alternative methods.

Nor would I say that the analyst avoids taking responsibility for his knowledge; on the contrary, it seems to me that the one who assumes more responsibility is the analyst who takes into greater account, based on the instruments he has at his disposal, his own subjectivity.

Certainly, nowadays the search for Truth with a capital *T* is believed to be an illusion, though not that of a 'human' truth, the only possible one. The fact is that Blass seems to take for granted the concept of truth. She does not much deal with issues that might contribute to formulating a more *general* definition that pertains to *how* we reach a consensus – for example, on the interpretation of unconscious distortions. In the same way, the criterion of 'immediate accessibility' as the royal road to what truly happens – a method common to all modern philosophy and all psychoanalytic models – is extremely useful, but not enough. If it is not bound to other concepts (for example, those of unison and consensual validation), it could itself actually embody a para-metaphysical principle of presence as perfect transparency of the subject to himself.

Blass alludes to other approaches that are not well identified except through the description that Greenberg gives in presenting this virtual symposium on the relevance of truth in psychoanalysis. She denies that they can add anything to Freudian and Kleinian approaches: 'from the perspective of the traditional approach, addition of other approaches is not possible' (p. 332n), and she negates even the possibility that these other approaches could be integrated with traditional analysis, because they start off from a viewpoint too distant and 'incongruent'. She wonders, then, what justifies looking at these radical new developments of theory as 'psychoanalytic' (p. 332) – if indeed they even merit that designation.

To some, this could appear to be a drastic way of settling her question at the beginning of the paper on the problem of competition among theories. The terms of the matter could actually be reversed. One could legitimately ask whether models still merit being called psychoanalytic when they adhere faithfully to its past iterations, by now canonized, or whether those that, for example, do not take into serious consideration the findings of the neurosciences or of infant research can be called psychoanalytic. Although not the case with this author, how many times in our discussions have we heard an authoritative principle invoked as a guarantee of a certain vision of things?

Therefore, with respect to the opinion expressed by Blass, I would personally not support the idea that taking into consideration the way in which proto-experiences that have not been memorialized as representations – either because they occurred too early in life or were the result of trauma – and that might be symbolized 'in some way' through transcription/inter-semiotic translation/transduction, etc., would make the reference to truth in psychoanalysis irrelevant. One would not understand how all that belongs to the dimension of feelings, and not to that of meanings, would end up. For us as human beings, all that pertains to sense (as different from denotation) is equally true, if not *more* true, and I cannot think of it as foreign to the dimension of language or culture, or to what defines us as human.

All in all, on the one hand, I do not think it is possible any longer to continue to cling to a psychoanalysis based on the 'empire of representation', as it was for Freud. And on the other hand, I do not see why one cannot think that, even though in infancy an Ego is not yet established, the mother can transmit conflicts tied to the culture and inscribe them in the infant's body. At a later time, these conflicts would also find a psychic transcription. This could be a way to rethink the deficit/conflict dichotomy. Is it possible to think that a kind of originary repression may be produced in the infant through maternal manipulation and non-verbal communication, and that a transmission of cognitive patterns may therefore occur, patterns that are fully determined by culture and by its demands?

Blass brilliantly lays out the two versions of the classical vision, but skips over the problem of internal congruence between the two models and what passing from one to the other might mean from an epistemological point of view. (If it were this easily accomplished and were not debatable at all, no one would still be working according to the Freudian model.) Instead, Blass presents the Kleinian innovation as a natural and self-evident development of Freudian theories (and what, then, do we make of the Controversial Discussions?). But as we know, the two models remain quite different from each other, from both theoretical and technical points of view. For example, they involve different conceptions of the unconscious. It would be interesting to ask what Klein's 'addition' to Freud, and then those of Winnicott, Fairbairn, and Ferenczi, produces. Isn't it true that all these authors introduced new conceptual vocabularies and new lexicons and elaborated new metapsychologies? Not under discussion here, of course, is the possibility, which always exists, of identifying elements of continuity among them, or of development and integration between parts of them, but rather how the shift from one to the other is theorized.

The inconsistency among models that the author regrets could perhaps be seen simply in terms of the concept of incommensurability among different paradigms, of which Kuhn (1962) speaks – a concept that is useful in taking stock of differences, but without thereby denying that any paradigm (nor any of the various models that mark the transition from one to the other) legitimately belongs to the same disciplinary realm, and one that can thus be used as a lens for understanding even what happens in the passage from Freud to Klein.

The ironic road to truth

Through a brilliant analysis of Ibsen's *The Wild Duck* and Sophocles's *Oedipus the King* as models of what is true in analysis, John Steiner brings the aesthetic experience into our discussion. In these plays, he highlights the role of tragic irony, an expression referring to an omen of catastrophe that seems to be contained in the words uttered by a character who apparently does not intend them to have that effect. By analogy, analysis becomes a game (as I myself have defined it in one of my papers) of immersion and interactivity (Civitarese, 2008b). Like the spectator at a play (and the same could be said in relation to any of the arts), the analyst must both identify with the patient as he participates in the staging of his dramas in the analytic setting, and also maintain a minimal sense of distance and critical capacity. Since it is difficult, however, to dwell in both these attitudes at once, this will be more of a continuous oscillation between different levels of participation. The awareness of this disparity that the double role of spectator and actor engenders in the analyst is the source from which a feeling arises that can be defined as *irony*.

The contradiction underlying the concept of irony – as if it were a fiction that expresses a complex position that is both ethical and epistemic – is located between the thought and the word, between the idea and its 'publication', between the 'true' sentiment and its antiphrastic (ironically opposite) expression. In speaking, one says the opposite of what one thinks. The practice of irony is therefore a form of honest pretence. But irony is also the exercise of a certain type of violence that, according to the situation, can be sweet (bearable) or bitter (traumatic – the subject does not have a space in which to receive and contain it). In the end, irony is always the appraisal of a victorious outcome: of one's own triumph and defeat of another, and also of another within the self; the analyst cannot help but doubt himself and see even himself reflected in the mirror of irony.

Steiner is well aware of this violent side of irony, and indeed of the difference of irony from sarcasm and derision: 'In true irony, the smile is always tinged with pain' (Steiner, 2016, p. 444). And he correctly points to the concept of the *tolerability* of truth, and asks whether truth must always be 'gentle' or whether it can also be cruel. After having analyzed Ibsen's drama according to this perspective (a commentary that I do not have the space to recapitulate here), he brings in an apt quotation from EM Forster, with which one cannot disagree: 'Truth is not truth in that exacting land unless there go with it kindness and more kindness and kindness again' (Forster quoted by Steiner, p. 434). Steiner notes that, for Forster, 'kindness is as important as truth – not only to mitigate the harshness of truth, but also to make it more true' (p. 434).

This is an important point. It is not just a matter of avoiding useless injury and of being merciful, but rather that 'kindness' also points out what is (more or less) 'true'. It is not only a critical factor in the cure, but also a key technical factor by which to understand what is meant by truth. Steiner comments: 'Forster's point is not simply that truth without kindness can be cruel, but that *truth without kindness is not fully true*' (p. 434, emphasis added). In fact, the word *kind* links back etymologically to 'the feeling of relatives for each other', and is synonymous with *compassionate*. *Compassion* means 'sympathy, pity', from the Latin *compati* – that is, 'to feel pity, from *com* (together) and *pati* (to suffer), thus 'participating in the other's suffering'. Steiner does not venture beyond this theme, but if we think of Bion, it will be easy to do so in our turn. For Bion, what is born only in the analyst's mind is not true for the patient. It can be true with respect to a consensus between the analyst and the members of other ideal communities of human beings, but will certainly not be useful to the patient, and will even risk damaging him.

Steiner therefore criticizes analysts for having too often forgotten that the truth must be *bearable* for the other, or else it is not truth – something that can easily happen if a rationalistic attitude predominates. We can add that, in effect, to idealize truth for its own sake, without having sufficient consideration for he who must accept it, is at times nothing more than a fig leaf pulled over the analyst's striving for power, the shadowy appearance of a denied ideological stance. The Freud of the hermeneutics of suspicion, of the evidentiary paradigm, often gives us the impression of wanting to force patients to accept supposed truths; to convince ourselves of that, we need only re-read the case of Dora (Civitarese, 2015). But today we no longer have the alibi of positivism.

In regard to the temptation towards authoritarianism, in Steiner's eyes, irony and self-irony (remember that this, too, is an element of postmodernism) represent effective safeguard systems. In Bion, they become the use of systematic doubt. I myself prefer (with Barthes, 2015) to speak of a (benign (in Italian, 'dolce')) scepticism that loses its punch in the sense of translating itself into an offer of acceptance. After all, a principle of scepticism is part of the foundation of modern philosophical reflection – from Descartes onward, through Nietzsche, Husserl, Heidegger, Merleau-Ponty, and Wittgenstein – that appears to be aimed with increasing radicalism at placing between parentheses what has already been noted. For Steiner, the ironic vision of analytic work involves an exercise of tolerating the paradox of many perspectives on reality, each of which can be valid if taken by itself.

It would be beyond the scope of this paper to discuss, then, how the effect of tragic irony may contribute to the aesthetic experience, to the greatest pleasure (Freud, 1920) that tragedy produces in the spectator and that I consider has to do with, at bottom, the negative pleasure of the representation as inevitably influenced by the object's absence. Steiner touches only lightly on this point, but I think that the discussion could be deepened in the light of the aesthetics of the sublime.

In any case, Steiner's contribution is an elegant and useful one to the definition of truth (with the important 'apocryphal' concepts of *kindness*, *tolerance*, and *irony*) and supports its ongoing relevance in psychoanalysis. More generally, Steiner portrays the change in psychoanalysis, in process today, from the evidentiary paradigm to the aesthetic one. The type of truth that we can obtain in our field, and that we must pursue, is the same as the aesthetic experience. I would add: this is because it is a somato-psychic truth, an integrated one that is not split. But Steiner suggests his own reason why, perhaps more implicitly than explicitly: *kindness* refers us back to the notion of unison and consensuality, and *irony* to the feeling of what is real (as a sense of the antagonistic solidarity that ties together different viewpoints;[7] etymologically, *irony* can be traced back to the verbs *to ask* and *to interrogate oneself*; Chantraine, 1999), to transitionality and poetic ambiguity.

Truth or psychic reality?

Among all the contributions, perhaps Fred Busch's paper explores in greatest depth the topic of the change in paradigm and the emergence of a new common ground in psychoanalysis – not only in general terms, but also against the backdrop of a personal evolution. Thus, it, too, is a paper that helps frame all the others. For Busch, what does the change of paradigm consist of?

- More than offering insight to the patient, the analyst aims at creating the conditions so that insight may be possible.
- The focus of the session is on what emerges in the here and now.
- What counts is the development of a way of knowing *how* one knows, more than directly knowing *what* dwells in the patient's mind.
- The historical reconstruction paves the way to the construction of representations that are gradually more complex.
- The patient contributes to the exploration and is not simply the passive receptacle of the analyst's discoveries.
- The concept of transformation takes the place of dissolving repression.
- What 'truly' happened cannot be known in an unequivocal way.
- The search for factual truth instead of psychic truths (in the plural, at various levels and according to many perspectives) can be misleading.
- The investigation in and of itself and the acquisition of a relevant method are more curative than the revelation of presumed truths, which are by nature unstable.
- The patient's narratives are the royal road not to the historical past, but to knowledge of his internal world.
- Some of these narratives are expressed in non-representational, non-linguistically codified forms and as vague sensations and affective states, and are disguised as actions.
- It is better to adopt the technique of not asking the patient about his past history because this could portray a stereotypical idea of analytic work, and operating on this level could take on a defensive nature.
- The aim of analysis seems to be more in the investigation itself than in the conclusions reached through it.
- The acquisition of the method of successfully thinking more freely about the self is the goal of analysis.

What, then, is the truth? Is it *One, No One, and One Hundred Thousand* (Pirandello, 1926)? Is the truth that there is no truth? With Alex, the patient in the vivid clinical vignette that Busch presents, was the analyst too tough – 'hard on him' – or not? The answer remains (felicitously) ambiguous. We are left with some possibilities. As in a remake of the film *Rashomon* (Kurosawa, 1950), the analyst allows the patient 'the freedom to consider other possibilities about what had happened in the previous session (Busch, 2016, p. 352). The analyst leaves open to himself as well the possibility of thinking that he was really hard on the patient, but also that he was not so hard.

In short, here we have an analyst who, like Steiner, is disenchanted and sceptical in the more noble sense of the words. It remains to be better understood, however, why the truth would be intrinsically therapeutic. In the emphasis that he places on the process (the *how*) in relation to the content of truth (the *thing*), Busch comes close to giving a convincing answer, but without yet reaching a clear position, at least in my reading, on a more abstract but still necessary level.

A possible criticism I might make is that, to my ear, this position appears to indicate a certain indefinite quality in the concept of truth and to raise a question about consistency between the chosen theoretical system and the clinical practice derived from it. The reader might wonder, in addition, whether the problem of truth does not end up being evaded in some way. Why? Because if the truth is levelled to the patient's subjective experience, to what is true *for the patient*, there would be no need to bring up the concept of truth. By the way, in adopting this attitude, the analyst positively allows room for the patient's point of view and is less likely to give abusive interpretations – which is far from, for example, the Kleinian 'indifference' that Blass mentions.

The truth for Busch would lie in tolerating the dizzying array of all the possible meanings. This is something that can be shared, but *how* does one arrive at sharing with the other the idea of the existence of this multiplicity of perspectives? If the patient's truth were *already given*, so to speak, and it is that which the patient avows/sees, then there would be no need to go on to explore something true, obviously *more* true. But Busch himself maintains the importance of understanding whether the patient's truth corresponds to the reality of things.

The essentially unconscious nature of our psychic processes – it is true that one does not need to consider *only* unconscious truth, but in order to know more about how and where to meet the patient, one must consider *especially* unconscious truth – calls for a recourse to interpretation. And then we are again referred back to our basic queries on the reliability of interpretation, made explicit or not made explicit as they may be. I understand that, by *reality* here, Busch means 'something that really happened in the past', but I question the usefulness of applying the name of psychic truth – even with the qualifying adjective *subjective* – to what we have always indicated as psychic *reality*. The impression is that one falls back into the problem that one wanted to resolve in avoiding the use of the term *reality*, apparently already confused with *objective reality*, replacing it with psychic truth.

At any rate, beyond questions of terminology, what remains a key factor is the dramatic re-dimensioning of the analyst's authority and consequently of our faith in what he can authentically know. I appreciate Busch's portrayal of a certain sceptical sensitivity that comes to embody a 'respectful' style of working – a point that is important in understanding what the change of paradigm actually consists of, and what can hopefully be a new common ground for psychoanalytic models. One takes the patient's point of view seriously, letting go of the 'suspicious' attitude of the classical tradition. This availability is typical of relational approaches in the broad sense.

Within this vast galaxy, the differences among models can be very broad, with extremely diverse theoretical systems being utilized – for example, among interpersonalists and the so-called post-Bionians. The type of listening, for example, can be very different: whether the analyst gives precedence (it is not, then, a matter of all or nothing) to the conscious experience, and the unconscious dimension is in some way restricted to the interpretation of enactments, or whether he tries to be fully receptive, at 360 degrees, to the unconscious dimension of the dialogue and thinks of it as virtually always active.

Dancing with truth

Jody Messler Davies (2016) begins her paper by offering us the clinical vignette of Jake, a 'compulsive liar', perhaps 'sociopathic' (2016, pp. 362, 363). In the beginning, the analyst tends towards a certain suspiciousness and doubts about whether or not to take him into treatment. The 'characters' of two previous analysts who 'angrily dismissed' him (p. 362) and a thought/sensation that can be summed up as 'Stay away!' (p. 363) warned her to keep her distance and to ignore the siren song of therapeutic omnipotence. One could say that, through projective identification, the patient immediately makes the analyst play the part of an object that abandons him, and at this point we understand that the real problem is whether or not *he* can believe in *her* (in general, in the other), and that, due to some of her mental reservations, the one who is 'lying' is the analyst.

The author describes the case at length with a literary eloquence that is truly admirable, worthy of novelist Philip Roth:

> Jake's mother was blonde and fair skinned, the un-Jew, New England WASP-girl, painted in soft pastels, pink cashmere sweaters and pearls, having attended debutante balls in her youth, balls to which she defiantly brought her darkly handsome Jewish boyfriend to mingle among the Ivy League chosen – he of the deep, penetrating, black-silk, smiling-sad eyes.
>
> (p. 364)

This same eloquence, she writes, is also displayed by the patient: another detail of the intense identification taking place between the two of them – which, moreover, is not devoid of intellectual overtones and is intensely self-aware. (Can these two other elements be seen in this context as signs of an emotional distancing that must still be bridged in order for them to meet up with each other?)

Now, on the one hand, Davies refers to the Winnicottian notion of a transitional area, according to which it would not make sense to ask whether something is true or not ('The question is not to be formulated', Winnicott quoted by Davies, p. 367), and on the other hand, suffering the dilemma of the Cretan liar,[8] she returns to asking herself what she will think if the patient is deliberately lying. For the second time, she uses the word *sociopathic*, this time together with *diagnostically*. On this second occasion, it is even more apparent that the problem arises if we forget that the paradigm of the session is the dream, and if we again assume an 'objectifying' perspective on the patient, like that of psychiatric semiotics would be. But the 'objectifying' perspective that creeps in here could again symbolize an excessive emotional distance (from 'lightyears away', pp. 362, 363) between patient and analyst.

There seems to be a certain friction, then, between the different positions adopted towards the patient. In fact, the author writes: 'But I would really like to ask Winnicott: what of a patient who openly makes these distinctions for himself and tells us forthrightly that much of what he will relay is untrue?' (p. 367). We play this game; 'I invite the reader to play with ideas about these issues' (p. 362), Davies authorizes the reader at the beginning of the paper, and we try to respond. Perhaps Winnicott would get himself out of this by saying, first of all, that the transitional area (to refer to the quotation in the text) 'is a matter of *agreement* between us and the baby' (Winnicott quoted by Davies, p. 367, italics added). I emphasize *agreement* to indicate that, for Winnicott, the establishment of the transitional area follows from an agreement/unison between the parts – an agreement that is not at all extraneous to the problem of truth, but instead illuminates its intimate nature. If, then, the transitional area is based on something true that comes to be shared, transitionality cannot really represent a simple solution to the question of whether or not to take into account the fact that the patient tends to lie. The problem is again simply pushed back upstream to what lies at the basis of anything that is heard as true.

So the solution must be sought at another level (at the level, I would suggest, of receptivity to unconscious communication as the compass with which to emotionally meet the other). In fact, perhaps Winnicott (1989) would explain that, just as children play with toys, adolescents (and adults, we would add) play with the things of the world, and so we would always be dealing with 'play'. It is the same question that immediately comes up after Davies quotes Ferenczi in relation to Jake: whether this, too, is not about seeing the therapy as 'child's play'. But as we know, play, like literary fiction, involves the willing suspension of disbelief.

We see this in the text, which is a kind of mandala in which the microcosm of the analysis is reproduced to perfection if it is listened to according to the perspective of the analyst's dream about the analysis. Davies 'mimes' the continual movements of approaching and distancing that have characterized her relationship with Jake over the years. At a certain point, the essential question becomes 'lying or playing?', and whether transitionality, understood as a refusal to question the truth or falsehood of the patient's statements, cannot represent a defence against *actual* truth. Obviously, the answer would differ according to the chosen theoretical perspective and the role assigned to 'truth' factors, the past and material reality. It would represent a defence if it had the meaning of a sleight-of-hand manoeuvre, but it would not do so if it were the compass used to contain the patient's anxieties.

After some early hesitation, the analyst chooses the path of transitionality as constructive of the analytic scene and as the only way – just as with children – to gain access to the goal of a shared truth. What Davies presents as a tailor-made strategy for Jake would not be anything other than the golden rule according to other models of psychoanalysis, however: 'I could believe in the unconscious reality of certain "lies"' (p. 370), a kind of 'emotional truth' (p. 371). For example, one thinks of the Bionian concept of the *waking dream thought* and of the technical consequences that it involves in relation to the analyst's listening.

My tendency would be to see what Davies defines as 'this oddly constructed transitional space' (p. 372) as the norm, even though I myself would prefer to speak of the *field* to make use of the entire constellation of concepts of which this metaphor forms a part. Again taking up the question that Jake poses to the analyst ('True or not true – it doesn't matter?'; '"No," I tell him', p. 371), I would add that, from another point of view, we would certainly take this into consideration, but there, too, strictly speaking, we would have to use analytic listening and ask ourselves: now what is this patient saying from the unconscious point of view in revealing to me that he has lied/that he lies? Who is lying to whom? What is the character/hologram 'lie' talking about? In fact, the analyst succeeds in ceasing to worry (or at least sufficiently ceasing to worry) about factual reality and about being manipulated, and this opens a space of authenticity for the analysis.

I will conclude my discussion of this impassioning clinical vignette at this point and go on to develop some further theoretical reflections brought to mind by this paper. At the beginning, Davies questions herself about therapeutic factors and wonders (translated into my preferred form of jargon): 'insight or unison?' It is true that psychoanalysis cannot simply base its therapeutic action on implicit or nonspecific relational processes. The challenge, however, is not one of putting these processes between parentheses in order to concentrate on rationalistic psychoanalysis, but to theorize them, in turn, as accurately as is possible with the tools that we have – with new conceptual equipment, new lexicons,[9] and new models, without fear that 'this is no longer psychoanalysis'.

Would it be useful to take from the 'play therapy' – or from the fiction of the analysis – the 'father', the 'mother', the 'compulsive lying', the 'Holocaust', the 'Ivy League', 'the abusive father', and so forth, and interpret them as characters of the analyst's (or of the couple's) 'internal' dream about this analysis, and not only in their referential meanings? What would happen, then, if we were to drag what is created in the act of writing and reading this paper into the new transitional space?

Davies asks whether the 'precondition' (a kind of 'parameter') that she devised in order to treat Jake – of making parenthetical the veracity of facts reported by him, and of explicitly asking him to avoid the true/false distinction – might not have had a sadistic connotation ('I stuck to my psychoanalytic guns', p. 373). Certainly, an alternative way of resolving the problem would have been to agree to fully participate in the game proposed by the patient, without the necessity of explicating to him the technique adopted to resolve the problem of intentional lying. Moreover, insistence on not wanting to consider the issue of reality in the patient's discourse reveals, conversely, an enormous concern precisely around this same issue. Refusing to judge whether or not what Jake says is true means confirming how important all this is.

Declaring to the patient, furthermore, that for the analyst everything is true could sound mystifying and belittling in relation to the patient's statements. (In Jake's words, the analyst defined truth in a 'crazy, "internal" sense' (p. 375) as though, if he is such a liar, he is no longer even taken into account.) In addition, it could have an overly intellectual flavour, at the cost of the emotions that the true/false game – if one agrees to play it – could mobilize. (Here a comment of Bion's comes to mind, to the effect that, when the child needs milk, he does not need to be indoctrinated in the anatomy and physiology of the digestive system.) After all, as Steiner maintains in his paper, shouldn't the emotional attitude of a kind of 'tragic irony' be the rule in analysis?

One could also ask whether the technical artifice introduced by Davies really cleared the way for her to move away from feelings of humiliation and rage at having felt herself deceived, and from triumph in the patient for having successfully lied to her, and whether what the patient experienced as an imposition could really have established an authentic potential space.

Jake's response does not leave us in the dark. At a certain point, he loses patience and says to the analyst, 'God damn it, you really *are* such a pain in the ass!' (p. 378). But, we might say that to the pure man, all things are pure (*omnia munda mundis*), and the analyst, too, needs to protect herself – by using the right pot holders to take the pan off the fire without burning her fingers: 'I needed to survive the patient's attempts at negation and destruction' (p. 374). Furthermore, it seems that the 'precondition' permitted her to keep open the possibility of maintaining an intense investment in the patient without too much fear of being manipulated or destroyed. In the end, it seems that the analyst succeeded in silencing her inner 'sneaking suspicion' (a feeling that often has both a subtly persecutory and a moralizing implication), carrying out a true transformation in O.

As with Blass's paper, here, too, the text ends polemically and in some ways touches on the same points. Davies stigmatizes the naive idea that one might be able to cure by behaving as a good object substitute. She reaffirms the necessity of focusing on listening to the unconscious in order to avoid gross errors. However, I would object that, if one manages to transmit new relational patterns to the patient and to promote the development of his mind without making gross errors and without avoiding conflict, even to the point of setting aside some more common, 'obligatory' contents of the analysis (as in child analysis), I do not see why this would not be sufficient to positively influence the analytic relationship and the patient's relationships outside the analysis. The dichotomy that the author sets up between more relational moments and more cognitive ones no longer needs to exist if one acts according to a principle of bearable truth guided by careful listening to unconscious communication.

If, then, she criticizes the classical formulation of conceptualizing interpretation from the standpoint of 'one-person authoritarianism' (p. 382), Davies also worries that psychoanalysis may totally lose a cognitive point of view, and she finds that the empathy/confrontation opposition may have become too dichotomous. I would be in agreement if *empathizing* has to mean using only the patient's conscious experience, without paying attention to what is revealed through unconscious communication – a criticism that we ourselves have made of the interpersonalist trend (Ferro and Civitarese, 2013). Like the author, I do not trust a romanticizing conception of empathy, and at any rate I rarely use this term, preferring the Bionian one *unison* (or *at-one-ment*), which seems to me both more precise and more versatile.

To my mind, the problem is that terms such as *empathy*, *unison*, *attunement* are at times understood in too vague a way and are not translated into precise clinical instruments. I would say that the cognitive contribution of analysis is not in question, but rather what we mean by *cognitive contribution*. If, for example, we discover that a transference interpretation in reality carries a defensive aspect belonging to the analyst, where would the cognitive value (in the broad sense) lie for the patient?

Wouldn't it reside, rather, in the transformation by which the analyst eventually becomes capable of returning to his greatest level of receptivity after having been in a situation of emotional closure? Aren't two tango dancers who dance in unison sharing the 'truth' of their movements in harmony? Why must truth be wholly equated with representational content?

What might be helpful in conceptualizing the overcoming of the empathy/confrontation dichotomy is the concept, well illustrated by Steiner, of *kindness* as a dimension of truth. Davies touches lightly on this point as well when she refers to the analyst's 'tact and poetic capacity' (p. 383). In the field theory perspective, the problem of confrontation somehow disappears (Ferro and Civitarese, 2015, 2017). Unison can be both a quality of the encounter and a confrontation. There are useful and bearable confrontations, and there are others that are not useful and are actually disruptive. Unison can be achieved at a non-verbal level, or even in pondering together the phenomenological interpretation of Kant's *First Critique* (1781). Being on the same purely emotional wavelength is what I see as the first step towards the acquisition of a first 'concept', and I view the concept itself as the result of fine tuning, first bipersonal and then collective.

For Davies, the truth is 'interpersonally negotiated' and has to do with the 'consensual validation of an external world' (p. 381). I agree with the necessity of external validation, but only if we take into account that validation is reached also through unconscious processes, and not exclusively conscious and rational ones. Furthermore, I am not inclined to so clearly differentiate the internal from the external, and I prefer instead to speak of a concept of continuity.

The social nature of truth

The standpoint from which Elizabeth Allison and Peter Fonagy start out is that of the theory – which they themselves formulated – of psychopathology as a deficit of *mentalization*, with the latter defined as: 'the ability to interpret both our own and other people's behaviour in terms of underlying thoughts, feelings, and wishes . . . a multidimensional capacity that is acquired in the context of attachment relationships' (Allison and Fonagy, 2016, p. 285). They also refer to the therapy based on this concept: *mentalization-based treatment*, or MBT.

Perhaps because of a common Bionian root ('our . . . indebtedness to Bion', p. 280), I found myself substantially in agreement with some of these authors' points regarding the problem of truth in psychoanalysis. I believe that this is one of the papers most in line with my proposal of locating a new common ground, of trying to work out a theory that might tie together the concepts of truth, unison, and immediacy within a broader epistemological theory.

Bion (1959) speaks of attacks on linking between thoughts – that is, attacks on the capacity to think more than attacks on single ideas or representations. Ferro (2002) writes that there are at least two principal areas of pathology: the first is at the point at which the transformation of beta elements into alpha elements occurs, from proto-sensations to proto-emotions in images that can be utilized for thinking, and the second is at the level of articulation of alpha elements among these usable images. Ogden (2003) speaks of patients who have never managed to dream and of others who have started to have nightmares. Like all these authors, Allison and Fonagy establish a clear pathway leading from *thing* to *how*. In studying seriously disturbed patients, they have arrived at the same conclusion – that patients do not suffer so much from memories (as Freud would have said), but from the defensive inhibition of the capacity to think.

Therefore, the truth we deal with in analysis does not pertain as much to mental representations as to interactive patterns stored as implicit memories. And not even those truths that emerge in the transference can restore the purity of what truly happened in the past. The eventual recovery of memories is an epiphenomenon, defined by Meltzer (1984) as a by-product; it is the consequence and not the cause of psychic change. Allison and Fonagy see the objective of the analytic encounter less in terms of contents ('the recovery of threatening ideas and feelings', p. 280) and more in terms of psychic processes: 'to gradually reactivate the inhibited mental process by elaborating the patient's preconscious mental content and giving him opportunities to explore the analyst's mental states in the context of transference' (pp. 280–281).

More precisely, they aim for 'validating, clarifying, sometimes challenging, and elaborating on the mental state perspectives adopted by the patient (p. 285). In their model, the analyst confers a collaborative stamp on the work and respects the patient's sense of agency, recognizing and valuing his perspective on things. The analyst is prepared to learn from the patient, demonstrates curiosity and mental openness, and does not hide his own ignorance or his own doubts; he is motivated to understand the meaning of what happens.

Central in Allison and Fonagy's essay is the theory of *epistemic trust* and of *ostensive cues* in caregiving and treatment relationships. They write:

> The key signals that allow this kind of learning to take place are the communicator's *ostensive cues* . . . signals used by an agent to alert the addressee that the agent intends to communicate relevant pieces of cultural knowledge.

> Ostensive cues for infants include eye contact, turn-taking contingent reactivity, and the use of a special vocal tone ('motherese') – all of which appear to trigger a special mode of learning in the infant. Ostensive communicative cues, such as being called by name, trigger the *pedagogic stance* . . . By using ostensive cues – both in childhood and in adulthood – the communicator explicitly recognizes the listener as a person with intentionality.
>
> (p. 289)

It is not enough for something to be true in order for it to be assimilated by the infant or by the patient; it must be *personally true*. When it is present within a relationship of secure attachment, *ostensive cueing* guarantees a non-split, integrated, and therefore 'true' communication.[10] In this situation, thoughts and affects say the same thing; they express a somato-psychic truth, the same truth that the analyst pursues in using gradually more sophisticated techniques of *immediacy*. The result is that the subject to whom the communication is directed lives an experience of agency and acquires the 'faith' necessary for learning from the other.

Following Bion, one could say that *epistemic trust* is the favourable resolution of what Meltzer calls the aesthetic conflict in the mother–child interaction (but also in any meaningful relationship – see Civitarese, 2011a). 'What I see is equal or similar to what I hear; and when what I hear is equal/similar to what I see, I notice an emerging sensation, that of becoming true and real' – this is what *aesthetic truth* means. When the environment fails to engender a basic faith in the child, a state of hyper-vigilance is set up, of suspicion, mistrust and rigidity, that makes it difficult to learn from the experience or from the other.

From time to time, the mentalization approach has been criticized 'from the right' for not being able to arrive at historical truth, which would be necessary to modify psychic conflicts in a positive way and which impedes falling into a sort of *folie à deux*. It is clear that this risk always exists, but the corrective is found in the fact that the couple is simultaneously operating within several other areas of consensuality, which partially overlap each other to varying degrees. So this problem does not arise much because, sooner or later, the couple's delusional truths would be disconfirmed by the wider community. Patient and analyst are never truly alone; the space that they share is always public.

The mentalization approach has also been criticized 'from the left' for failing to grasp the psychic truth of active unconscious conflicts, due to the emphasis given to the role of environmental deficits and trauma and the marginalization of insight. Accusations of superficiality have also been launched, of providing only corrective experiences. We should keep in mind, however, that for Alexander (1950), the point was not the corrective experience in itself – how could it not be in some way 'corrective'? – but the active manipulation of the setting as a means of reaching it. At any rate, in response to these criticisms from 'left' and 'right', Allison and Fonagy appeal to the impact of infant research and to the centrality of the mother–child relationship.

Now we come closer to the topic of truth in the therapeutic relationship, and, more in general, as an epistemological problem. In Allison and Fonagy's language, what Bion calls *psychic growth* becomes *mentalization*, and mentalization becomes the truth: 'Truth, if relevant, rests in the reality of perceiving the object (self or other) as fully mentally functioning' (Allison and Fonagy, p. 281). Truth would coincide with the (intersubjective) experience of 'presence, vitality, and at oneness' (p. 286) that patients undergo in mentalizing. Contained in frequent references to attachment theory, and implied in the idea of *vitalization*, is, at the most basic level, the equation of truth with unison. In fact, the authors highlight the contributions of the Boston Change Process Study Group and the theory of *moments of meeting*, which, as we know, are called by various names here and in the literature (*now moments*, *moments of truth*, *kairos*, *unison*, *mutual sharing of mental states*, *co-consciousness*, *oneness*, *dyadic connection*, *socialization*, etc.). But in Allison and Fonagy's paper, the identification of truth with unison is never clearly expressed in these terms, or at least not in the explicit terms that I am putting forward here in attempting to interweave truth, unison, immediacy, and language into the same realm.

Furthermore, the experience of truth would serve only the purpose of learning, and therefore which truth we are talking about remains open. A point that is not clear to me is Allison and Fonagy's vision of the experience of truth as relevant not in itself, but only because it represents an *ostensive cue* that, in arousing an experience of 'felt truth' in the patient, fosters acceptance and usage – both within and outside the consulting room – of the knowledge they offer. Mentalization would not be of use in better understanding the self or others, but only in better negotiating one's own relationships; here I find the distinction to be so subtle that it is difficult to grasp.

That the topic of truth is a thorny one is in fact evidenced by this paper Why? Because, in tilting the truth towards the aesthetic (the *how*), it seems that one loses contact with the truth as knowledge (the *thing*, the transmitted 'relevant knowledge', p. 289), and a problematic dichotomy is revived: truth – in this case, emotional or 'felt truth' – versus 'social knowledge'. And what if the ostensive cue serves to transmit false truths in perfect good faith? Who guarantees that what is communicated is true? Instead, I suggest that we view 'felt truth' and 'social knowledge' as two sides of the same coin or, alternatively, as in continuity with each other and by gradual degrees subjected – virtually infinitely – to other and ever more extensive intersubjective 'verifications'.

Allison and Fonagy find it necessary to broaden the area of discourse to more general considerations. In the light of what they have observed clinically – that is, the presence of epistemic hyper-vigilance in borderline patients – the authors interpret within a wider frame the tendency of some to cling to the idea of an absolute truth, and of others to that of an absolute relativism. The two attitudes would be, respectively, an expression of *non-mentalizing* conditions, or of *pre-mentalizing* conditions, in particular of *psychic equivalence* and *pretend mode*. But between the Scylla and Charybdis of the two extremes of the debate on the issue of today's concept of truth, here, too, it is not clear what the authors' position is. The solution to the question of truth cannot reside simply in a neither-this-nor-that.

The epistemological background of the discourse remains vague. One could object that this is the stuff of philosophers, but I believe, by contrast, that the thing pertains directly to us – because to question ourselves on this level of the concept of truth is useful in refining our tools, to rid the field of useless conflicts, and to identify felicitous and even unexpected areas of convergence, as well as to legitimize psychoanalysis in the field of science.

I share the criticism of absolute relativism. I consider absolute relativism, however, more of a phantom than a cultural position that really exists; and even if it really existed, i.e., if it were sustained by a respected author, it would not be anything other than the affirmation of a sort of 'negative' absolute truth: it would be merely the reverse side of a metaphysical position. What is less consensual, however – because it could be exactly the opposite – is the idea that 'the relativization of truth can similarly [to the hyper-vigilance that is observed in certain clinical contexts] serve as a protection against learning and the conferment of "better ideas"' (p. 277). Would forms of fundamentalism facilitate the development of this capacity? I see individual hyper-vigilance – collective hyper-vigilance, as well – as associated with paranoid positions that are not relativistic in relation to truth; there the truth is one truth and only one, and all the rest is heresy. Relativism, if it is authentically understood, cannot be associated with a form of repression or cynicism, but rather with *hospitality* (Civitarese, 2007a; Derrida and Defourmantelle, 1997), as long as it does not itself become a form of dogmatic thinking.

In contrast, when Allison and Fonagy make reference to philosophy, they quote Hume. But even if, at bottom, one is dealing with eternal themes, I would rather seek illumination in the philosophy of the last century, because there a closer reflection of our own sensibilities can be found. If one turned one's gaze in that direction, it would not be possible to say that 'to the philosopher, truth cannot be guaranteed if it is learned from others' (p. 296), because it is precisely that which in some way contemporary philosophers have supported and are supporting, at least if by *learning* here, we are referring to the intersubjective constitution of the individual.

Moreover, the current sceptical tendency in psychoanalysis (according to Eco's (2002) formula, a kind of *minimal realism* or *negative realism*) is presented as a reaction to the dogmatism and authoritarianism of more orthodox North American psychology (to the 'intellectual reign of terror' that it set in motion). But this is only a small part of the story, because what has changed enormously is the overall world in which psychoanalysis lives, and in particular epistemology – the very same reaction we have in relation to the arena of science (e.g., Kuhn, 1962).

Allison and Fonagy are more convincing when they offer a sociobiological picture. Their proposal in that regard would be difficult to disagree with. Evolution is not determined only by genetics, but also by the genetics of ideas and by the transmission of knowledge that has already been accumulated by humanity. The truth would lie at the heart of the interpersonal transmission of knowledge. As we know, ontogeny models phylogeny; it arranges things so that phylogeny continues to evolve and move forward. While of course the life of the individual is limited, phylogeny, by definition, will not be interrupted until the human species disappears.

I fully agree with the emphasis that the authors place on the aspect of socialization. They appropriately refer to Freud's famous statement that brings together individual and social psychology: 'From the very first individual psychology . . . is at the same time social psychology' (Freud, 1921, p. 69).

In a passage from their paper (which I can refer to only briefly here due to space constraints), Allison and Fonagy touch on the same critical point alluded to by Blass and by Davies. In the role attributed to everything of the non-representational type (the implicit, and non-verbal communication), they foresee the risk of losing sight of the moment of knowledge (insight, and verbal communication). To this reservation, Allison and Fonagy respond by reaffirming the traditional psychoanalytic hierarchy that assigns primacy to the word ('the backbone of the therapeutic encounter', p. 284). If this did not happen, they maintain, one would have an imprecise theorization.

As already mentioned, I would be more in favour of the idea of transcending the caesura of cognitive/not-cognitive: of seeing as well the cognitive value that is intrinsic to what is not stated semantically. From another point of view, I would radicalize the importance of language, and I would say that it must be maintained also at another level – in the sense that nothing happens beyond language, not even when there is a non-verbal, paralinguistic communication in the foreground. The explicitness of the word always transmits the implicit as well, and the implicit is never outside the laws of language.

To conclude my comments about Allison and Fonagy's paper, nuances and particular points aside, I think that these authors – though without specifically saying so – are approaching the point of placing the 'aesthetic' of the mother–child or analyst–patient encounter at the centre of the therapeutic relationship. In fact, I think that, overall, every contributor to this special issue of the *Quarterly* on truth is prioritizing, in different ways, the presence of this aesthetic in the therapeutic relationship. For Allison and Fonagy, too, the goal of therapy is to provide the patient with tools for negotiating present and future relationships with maximal success. This is very similar to the idea of the analytic field, according to which whatever is said is always aimed at negotiating the relational 'closest/farthest' in the here and now.

I would not want to stretch these authors' convictions, but it seems to me – notwithstanding some uncertainties and perhaps inconsistencies – that what emerges from their argument may be a *social* theory, and thus one that is relativistic in relation to the truth. But again, it is certainly not so in the sense of a presumed absolute relativism – or, caricature-like, not in the sense of the notorious *anything goes*. The intersubjective, negotiated, inter-human nature of truth could not be stated in clearer terms.

The process of mentalization is clearly interpreted as tied to the experience/feeling of truth, but here, too, what is missing is the link I propose – and that seems to me more precise – with the idea that what is created is a sort of proto-concept. For this reason, the direction of the process moves towards self-consciousness and 'vitalization'. That this proto-concept of a sensorial–emotional type is always important, together with actual concepts, is evident in clinical work, as the authors observe from forms of pseudo or hyper-mentalization. I would call both of these, perhaps, *depersonalization* (Civitarese, 2013c), in which language is present but split off from affect, and therefore it does not lead to genuine experiences of truth.

Forms of content

In his outstanding contribution, Thomas H Ogden puts forward a 'traumatic' theory of truth that presents in analysis, relative to unprocessed, painful events of childhood – not thought, not actually experienced, nor ever put into words. These aspects can finally be contacted when they are relived *with the analyst* in sessions. *To relive* here means to succeed in giving personal meaning to the experience. Analysis privileges the means of language, but the author observes that truth is multidimensional, and in a given moment, it can be represented by the manifest content of a statement, but in another by the tone of voice or by silence. The form of the content (the material body of language and its syntactic organization) is as related to what is heard as true as the content itself is. And not only that – at times it is precisely when this semiotic aspect of language comes to light that, for the first time, the possibility arises of successfully giving meaning to what was set aside, not claimed, and not experienced.

In Ogden's view, this is a way of emphasizing the importance of style. Style – not only content, but also the manner of speaking – is a person's signature, the most authentic expression of the patient's and the analyst's subjectivity. It is style that transmits affective aspects – perhaps more than the content of the discourse, which is primarily indebted to the speaker's rational side. (Notice the resonance here with Allison and Fonagy's *ostensive cues*.)

It seems to me that, in placing the formal aspects of language at the centre of his discourse, Ogden, in approaching the problem of the relevance of truth in psychoanalysis, is also using a criterion of the aesthetic or 'poetic' type. In contrast to a rationalistic vision of truth, the 'aesthetic' criterion of truth is a way of overcoming the mind–body split, and of leaving behind the dry terrain of a technical-scientific objectivization of the facts of analysis that would be disastrous for its very goals. Using such a criterion is a way of claiming the emotional aspect of truth and the role that emotions play both in analysis and in life – the 'sensitive' or 'musical' aspects, so to speak.

Something that sounds true is always complete, somato-psychic, not split. On the one hand, what Ogden describes is easily comprehensible; we think about how true we find the voice of John Fante in the novel *Ask the Dust* (1939), that of

Ralph Ellison in *The Invisible Man* (1952), or of Philip Roth in *Indignation* (2008). But on the other hand, as we know from the vicissitudes of criticism, to say why and how one might reach that degree of authenticity is completely another matter. The method of psychoanalysis is to avail itself of the poetry of the dream (in its negative form as well – that is, at times, being aware of its absence). The dream-thought is the type of thinking in which this reconnection can take place. This is why so much importance is attached to the types of analytic dialogue that make it possible to approach the thought-dream and the multiplicity of perspectives that it can offer us.

Ogden examines three types of discourse (*discourse* here is used as synonymous with *dialogue* or *conversation*). These specific, formal organizations of discourse promoted the appearance in analysis of elements of truth with three of his patients, and each patient used one of these forms to successfully find his own voice, to express the most complete range of his being. Ogden's admirable development of clear and distinct ideas – which one might call Cartesian – is something we consistently see in his writing; his descriptions of the three forms of discourse, which he calls *direct discourse*, *tangential discourse*, and *discourse in non sequiturs*, are no exception.

These three types (which of course do not represent all the possible forms of discourse that can be utilized) can ideally be placed along a gradient that goes from secondary process to primary process. One can consider them, that is, as expressive forms that are gradually more effective in allowing unconscious truths to surface. The gradient actually expresses a growing level of destructuralization of conscious discourse.

In each of the three clinical cases described, the particular formal organization of the discourse, and not the story being told, is the starting point of an interaction that lands on something true. The vehicle or medium of truth therefore becomes the 'symptomatic' articulations of the discourse – moments of disjunction between expectations and actual realizations, occasions of apparent mis-attunement in the manifest dialogue or of idiosyncratic use of the lexicon. In the first case (that of *direct discourse*), the outline of the discourse is too literal, too 'consistent'. In the subsequent cases (*tangential discourse* and *discourse in non sequiturs*), unravellings are revealed through which something new but also something threatening is glimpsed; the discourse is less 'consistent'. These ruptures in communication produce anxiety and disorientation, but they can be the doors through which something unexpected and surprising glimmers.

I have described similar moments with the concept of *transformation in hallucinosis* (Civitarese, 2014c). These are moments that derive, however, from the reawakening of micro-delusions and micro-'hallucinations'. A misattunement/disjunction is first introduced unconsciously into the discourse, and then, when it is eventually noted, often a true impression about what is happening is produced (Civitarese, 2015). In the same way that Ogden describes in relation to the three forms of discourse, however, it is not enough to realize the 'error'; one must carry out particular psychological work in order for it to become truly meaningful.

But how can we know when something truthful is happening? Why is it necessarily *more true* than the manifest discourse? Here we can only invoke a principle referenced by Ogden at the beginning of his paper: that the unconscious speaks with an accent of truth that is missing from the conscious experience. Why? Because, we might speculate, the unconscious actually uses a more well-rounded and complete way, not a divided one, of expressing the two sides of the truth-coin of the experience of life that human beings can draw from – the emotional and the rational – and its truth is more profound precisely because of this 'aesthetic' and inevitably ambiguous/'poetic' character.

If we wanted to express the thing in linguistic terms (for Lacan, the unconscious is structured *as* a language, as we know), we could say that, as we are not only speakers of a language but are also spoken by it and since the language is created by virtually all its terms operating in a reciprocal dialectical relationship,[11] it is not surprising that new impressions of meaning escape our control. And when these new meanings become manifest, they bring with them an increased knowledge that is not of the individual but of the language – or rather, of the community and of the culture.

In that sense, one could reformulate the concept of the unconscious as the not (yet) thought, but as existing in the virtual state of language, in the game of signifiers, in the body itself as a signifier. Furthermore, this vision corresponds to Bion's idea of the unconscious, which is that it is not endowed at birth, but is gradually transmitted from the mother to the infant as a system of symbolization. It is also understood that, as Ogden writes, this unconscious is not by definition truly comprehensible or graspable; the most we can achieve is at times to intuit its presence and action through felicitous metaphors.

Ogden's attention to disjunctions of the discourse make us think of the method of deconstruction adopted by Derrida in his very close re-readings of classical philosophical texts (see, for example, Derrida, 1990), which are obviously an investigation of their truth quotient and performatively on the nature of truth. Derrida positions himself similarly in listening to these texts, and he takes them apart in order to bring them to the level of a thought-dream. (In relation to Ogden's formula of *talking-as-dreaming*, one could say that Derrida *writes-as-dreaming*.) This is the same way in which every poem and some literary canonical texts function in relation to themselves (creatively self-deconstructing) – for example, *Finnegans Wake* (Joyce, 1939), but also Bion's *A Memoir of the Future* (1975). Is it so, once again, that truth shines through in these circumstances? I would say that the truth of our *social* essence does. Through being spoken by language, we rediscover that we are not masters of ourselves, because new and surprising perspectives are shown to us, and from this knowledge we can progress towards greater integration.

Ogden's paper helps us get a glimpse of what today might be a unified, liveable theory of truth for all of us – a consensual agreement within the couple, that is, but also in language and through language (not understood only in its semantic value, however, but also semiotically) in the wider community. This is why the disturbing experience must be 'dreamed' by patient and analyst, individually and together. (Ogden writes 'collectively' (p. 414), which on first reading I connected not only to the couple, but also to their being inserted into the broader human community, and so it is as though every individual dream cannot really be other than a collective dream.) In fact, patient and analyst, as protocommunity or intersubjective unity, are the metonymic representatives of the entire ideal community of speakers.

It is not enough, however, to avail ourselves of the forms of meaning that have already been deposited, so to speak, into language. In order to progress towards subjectivization, consensual validation is also necessary – validation, that is, of the experience lived out in the here and now. A shared thought is already a 'sublimated' or abstracted thought; a third thought that is born of two single thoughts as the germination of a principle of unity in multiplicity opens the way to a concept (to the growth of the capacity to think).

What I am here trying to call attention to is the double articulation between the 'unconscious' discourse of language and the individual appropriation of this discourse that can only happen in the context of a meeting between minds. Language puts an infinite virtual repertoire of meaningful impressions at our disposal, but these can come to life only if they are 'claimed' in the immediacy of the shared emotional experience. Perhaps something of the sort is expressed in existential philosophy (Heidegger, 1927) in the theory of the movement from 'they' (*das Man*) – that is, from the horizon of shared meaning among all human beings as an already given, preliminary form of understanding the world – to the individual's achievement of an authentic life: one of responsibility, choice, and acceptance of the finite nature of life.

Truth as linguistic play

Howard B. Levine moves within a Bionian paradigm (Levine and Civitarese, 2015). He emphasizes the intersubjective dimension of truth and the priority assigned to the procedural and the inter-psychic over the content-related and the intrapsychic. In treatment, repressed memories are no longer as sought after, but instead the development of the psychic container is pursued. According to Bion, truth is the food of the mind, and the subject is guided by a truth drive (Civitarese, 2013a). But the truth that interests us from a psychoanalytic standpoint cannot be directly grasped by the senses but only by educated intuition. It has to do with the psychic qualities that characterize the emotional experience at hand. Bion goes so far as to assert that their somatic correlates, too, can block comprehension.

It would be different and much simpler if psychoanalytic knowledge pertained to objects situated in a concrete spatio-temporal dimension. But beyond whether or how we can grasp it, the question remains of the *nature* of this truth: 'What *is* "truth" in psychoanalysis, and is there a "psychoanalytic truth" that is different from what we mean by *truth* in its ordinary social sense?', Levine asks (2016, p. 396).

Stimulated by Levine's question, I would respond that the nature of an act of cognition, whether it pertains to concrete objects or to psychic qualities, is not in essence any different. Therefore, I would say that one can respond positively to this question on one side and negatively on the other, invoking the concept not of a clear dichotomy between emotional truth and logical truth, but rather that of a continuum, with both truths anchored in the linguistic root that forms the basis of self-consciousness and thus of humanity.

The truth of emotional unison, of *at-one-ment*, is achieved when the felicitous recognition between mother and child springs forth, creating a 'primordial concept'[12] – a sensitive/musical idea that is not, however, extraneous to the world of concepts and self-consciousness, represented by the adult couple (by definition, an element of unity among various terms is identified), and that is still pre-verbal (even though not a-cultural). It gives order to chaos, nevertheless, and at bottom it is the basis of every human truth, even those of the sciences.

The distinguishing characteristic of psychoanalytic truth would be, rather, that it locate itself at the most basic level, where what counts is to promote the processes of the mind's growth at the molecular level. It is not enough, however, to get out of a fix, as Bion does, by saying that what counts is whether or not a certain intervention by the analyst promotes growth, because we are then brought back to the problem of deciding whether or not this is true growth.

But why is truth so important for psychic growth? This is not at all trivial. I would say that it is so important because Psyche dwells in the house of Love: what we call *truth* is none other than a process of *at-one-ment*, of unison. This dimension is closely tied to pleasure; see Allison and Fonagy's paper: 'An upshot of fitting together is vitalization, experienced by both partners, which in turn leads to a greater feeling of liking each other' (Boston Change Process Study Group quoted by Allison and Fonagy, p. 283). Through the process of unison, the mind is developed, step by step, in the presence of another mind.

One should use the word *truth* less often as though it pertained only to content, and more as expressive of a process, one of becoming real. That is to say, one can state that being true – or rather, meeting the other – coincides with the very process of subjectivization. Self-consciousness is identifiable with language, even though it cannot be limited to semantic language. The subject's processes of verification are carried out according to a model that it would be appropriate to view as fractal. Social agreement, which does not need to be ingenuously restricted to verbal agreement, nor even less to be based only on verbal meaning, represents at bottom the realm of *all* knowledge.

Levine writes:

> Ogden (2016) refers to 'multiple coexisting, discordant realities, all of which are true' (p. 300). If there are 'multiple coexisting discordant realities', are there also multiple coexisting discordant truths? In the everyday world of external reality, truth tends to *feel* singular and never discordant: a shirt is

> blue or not blue. It might be blue and white, but its white stripes do not nullify the fact that it is also partly blue; its blueness is not in question.
>
> (p. 396)

One could respond that, certainly, *blueness* is not in question, but only if one accepts reasoning based on the ingenuous realism with which we move in practical life – but which in the modern era, at least from the time of Kant onward, we have had to mourn the loss of.

For Kant, knowledge is not the passive apprehension of the object as it truly is, but rather a modification of the knowing subject. What is under discussion can never be the object of perception in itself (this expresses the notion of a *thing-in-itself*, or of O in Bion), but rather inter-human agreement in making an interpretation of it. This vision could also be defined as *postmodern*, even though it may have been elaborated with the contribution of psychoanalysis long before Lyotard (1979) coined this term as a sort of master key. And in relation to postmodernism and relativism, see the recent monograph issue of *Psychoanalytic Inquiry* devoted to postmodernism and psychoanalysis (Civitarese, Katz and Tubert-Oklander, 2015); I find totally incomprehensible how, as Eco (2007) says, the spectre of relativism has come to be built up as a standard ideology, 'the canker of contemporary civilization' (p. 36). Indeed, I would not be able to find any serious author in the psychoanalytic literature or on the broader cultural scene who has truly maintained or maintains a gnoseological or moral absolute relativism. This is very far from Nietzsche's assertion that facts do not exist, but only interpretations, or Derrida's that there is nothing outside the text. These affirmations, in my opinion, are to be interpreted as a way to strongly emphasize the inevitable role of linguistic mediation that renders us human and capable of self-reflection, but that obviously cannot place us directly in contact with Kant's *thing-in-itself*. The authentic markers of postmodernism are, rather, the end of the great narrations, the ironic revisit to the past and the crisis of a transcendental concept of truth.

What some object to in a vision such as Kant's, mentioned earlier (that knowledge is not the passive apprehension of the object as it truly is, but rather a modification of the knowing subject), is that then anything could be considered true. Such a position – which is certainly not Levine's – expresses only the difficulty of letting go of a fundamentalist or metaphysical vision of truth, of accepting the relativist *but not antifundamentalist* vision (because that itself would be absolute) of the bottomless abyss underlying every principle. It would also be the reassertion, through invoking the opposite, of a new fundamentalism, in the same way that an atheist is none other than a 'negative' believer.

The concept of *adequatio rei et intellectus* – that is, of a strict correlation between words and things – has not been current in philosophy for centuries now. In fact, we might correctly state that blueness *is* in question (see Braver, 2014). What is less in question is the socially shared rule, entirely contained within the system of language, of calling *blue* or *red* a certain condensation of pigments on a surface. Without a similar reference to the *third* represented by society, we would again fall into a metaphysical vision of perception and truth. More than one truth, for example, can exist within a logic that does not obey the *principle of non-contradiction*, a dialectical logic – or rather one of correlatives – in which 'A' is at the same time both 'A' and 'not-A'. So the logic that we employ also changes according to the situation. Bion's explanation of how representation is born, for example, certainly does not obey a logic of non-contradiction.

In the same way, isn't the logic of psychoanalysis really one of non-identity or difference? The dialectic, the process on which Hegel based subjectivization, describes a relationship in which 'A' can be 'A' only if in relation to 'not-A', and not simply if present together with a second property, 'B'. The two terms reciprocally define each other. Without 'not-A', 'A' would not exist as such and vice versa. Now, what I am pressed to reaffirm is that neither the logic of non-contradiction nor dialectical logic (or a logic of non-identity) can aspire to a privileged foundation. All these – the same concepts that I am discussing here in order to frame the problem of truth – are expressions of linguistic games.

In his paper, Levine emphasizes the Bionian principle of systematic doubt. Bion seems almost to make us think of a form of absolute scepticism, while on the other hand, he assigns the maximal possible importance to the concept of truth within a psychoanalytic theory, with almost mystical overtones. I think there is no contradiction here; Bion is not invoking a special mandate for the emotional truths of analysis, but is simply practising the phenomenological principle of transcendental reduction (also known as *epoché* or 'suspension')[13] – the philosophical but also the psychoanalytic one – of starting up again from a criterion/postulate of immediacy: the truth that is before our eyes (it is more probable that it is true), or that we experience with all of ourselves in the here and now, after having put between parentheses, as much as possible, the knowledge already acquired. (It is clear from a certain point of view that this is a paradox, because nothing would be knowable if we had not already constructed a trustworthy system of knowledge.)

It would not make sense to give contradictory definitions of truth. If Bion takes from Kant the concept of *thing-in-itself* and calls it O, it is to force us to be suspicious of our senses and to carry out an operation similar to Kant's – that is, to shift the problem of truth from the thing to the subject that knows it, or, better yet, to their relationship, and certainly not to allude to a mystical type of truth. If Bion opposes O to K (knowledge), it is to remind us that no truth/meaning is ever disembodied. The word, which is by definition *effabilis* (expressable), is at the same time ineffable, but it would not make sense to think of splitting one part from the other.

Thus, emotional truth, psychoanalytic truth, even though it is no longer identified with 'the thing that really happened' in regard to rational truth, is none other than the other side of the coin. It expresses an emotional consensuality that is equally important as the rational in giving meaning to life and also in knowing how to manage affective relationships. We can perhaps do without this aspect of practical goals, but not every time that the meaning of existence is at stake. Emotion has an obvious and powerful cognitive value. But it is important to understand that, to paraphrase Winnicott, a pure emotion does not exist in itself as isolated. For human beings, even in the infant before he can speak, nothing can exist that has not already been brought into the network of the symbolic; nothing exists that cannot be seen as the result of a process of becoming 'educated' to feel, the outcome of a process of a gradual acquisition of 'somatic/emotional categories'.

Emotions are our bodily thoughts, the other half of truth. Why must the mind nurture itself with truth? I repeat: this is not at all self-evident. It is so because, if truth is the manifestation of our capacity for consensuality or for cooperative intentionality (Tomasello, 2014), then truth *is* the mind and the mind *is* truth. A mind is composed of language, and language is exactly what results from this innate human capacity, which, however, also needs exposure to culture in every instance. Saying that truth nourishes the mind because it puts us in contact with reality is true, but it is not specific, and it does not encompass all the implications of this statement. So when we speak of aesthetic truth and of an aesthetic paradigm, it would have to be clear that the reference is very precise and pertains to the truth of ideas *and* of emotions (or of the body).

Another dichotomy that should be re-examined, in my opinion, is that between what is discovered and what is created and produced for the first time. Discovering repressed truth is often contrasted with 'making unconscious', 'unconscious-ing' (Civitarese, 2011b), to contribute to the *emergent* or *unformulated* unconscious. In reality, this contrast, which is reflected in different treatment techniques, emanates from two different conceptions of the unconscious – the first from Freud's unconscious as a prison, and the second from Bion's unconscious as a psychoanalytic function of the personality. In Bion's conception of the unconscious, the dichotomy can be overcome. If the capacity to think grows, it is easier for the patient to arrive at having a more consistent version of his history with fewer gaps; but the opposite is not always true, because the search for repressed content is not said to occur in regard to the patient's ability to bear emotion, and thus it does not necessarily lead to a better integration.

The change in paradigm inheres in this: the reintegration in psychoanalysis of the meaning of affects and the development of a true theory of affects. Nothing is discovered to be as it was, apart from how much one agrees or disagrees on its reality quotient – just as nothing is created from nothing. Otherwise one could fall into differentiating among the contents, while the activity of transformation of minds and contact between them should be in the foreground. Every discovery is also an emergent truth, and every emergent truth is also a discovery. This is not the point, but rather, discovered or created as it may be, whether the truth in question is or is not the product of unison. If I discover a repressed memory, something new is born; if I transmit a new ability, it will also be easier to remember (contain) things that had been distanced.

A discourse of this type must highlight another relevant aspect of Levine's paper – and here it is as though he were responding to Blass: his attention to non-represented states of mind and to what is not along the lines of repression or what is hidden, but rather to the non-formulated. He affirms, and I cannot fail to agree, that all this belongs with full rights to the field of psychoanalysis. Otherwise, I would add, Bion would not have written, following Freud, that one must make the caesura between foetal life and post-foetal life permeable, and he would not have spoken metaphorically of 'thalamic' or 'subthalamic' fears.

Truth-as-unison

One must never forget that, although he operated within a positivist frame, Freud was one of those who brilliantly eroded the foundations of positivism. For example, in addition to the concept of the unconscious, with that of *Nachträglichkeit*, he posed the unavoidable question regarding the topic of which truth one might come to in psychoanalysis. If the memory of things is continually subjected to rearrangement and rewriting, for the subject, obviously, the past can truly change.

If we imagine, instead, an external observer, he would have a different text of the same subject's past. Neither of the two would have the truth of what was, but from their hypothetical dialogue, a shared version of reality would emerge. As is evident, a theory of the role of the observer in the knowledge of things is intrinsic to the definition of what is true and of what is not true, and has always been especially the property of psychoanalysis.

After Freud, Bion is the author who has most investigated the topic of truth and the lie, and, finding himself halfway between the foundation of a bipersonal psychology and the residues of a psychology of the isolated subject, at times he did so with a subtly judgmental tone. It is enough to look at the terms in which he expresses himself regarding column 2 of the grid, for example, and at how brilliantly Grotstein (2007), by contrast, renamed it the column of the dream, no longer that of the 'lie'. In this way, Grotstein brought Bion's 'Kantian' revolution to completion, writing along the axis of 'I think I lie I dream . . . therefore, I am.' We recall that *mind* and *lie* have the same etymological root, and that *person* means *mask*.[14] Far from being discouraged by the weak constitution of the concept of truth in psychoanalysis – the equivalent of Hume's *philosophical melancholy and delirium*, to which Allison and Fonagy allude – we could make this weakness into a strength if we use it as a measuring device to demonstrate the material of which *any* truth is composed, including truths in the objective sciences, and then construct a new paradigm drawing on the idea of emotional unison as the original foundation of truth. Psychoanalysis is not a science in the same way that physics and chemistry are because it has to do not with the material world, but with the world of meaning. It is not that the truths of the hard sciences have more solid bases of consensuality; simply put, they pertain to less complex objects, and so for them it is easier to arrive at a consensus. (Within these sciences, however, there are and always will be conflicted and incompatible theories.)

The weakness of psychoanalysis is an unrecognized strength for analysts because, as human beings, they would like to delude themselves about having certainties on which to base their conduct (and with which to nurture – as is justifiable – their own narcissism). When, for example, we speak of *co-created narrative* and we fear losing the link to history, reality and the subject, we are actually neglecting the enormous weight that the prefix *co-* brings with it: it connotes *interhuman* agreement (virtually generalizable to the entire community of speakers, in the same way that a single word takes meaning from all of language, and indeed from all language*s* in the plural). The freedom that we gain in ridding ourselves (or, according to tastes, in mourning this loss) of the idea of an ultimate and absolute truth is strongly linked – and to my mind in a revitalizing way – to the concept of *consensuality*.

In the papers that we are examining here, the various authors have each illustrated the linguistic game that they consider the most effective within the broader linguistic game of psychoanalysis, and within the even broader linguistic game of culture in its totality.[15] None of them can claim that his or her views have a more sound basis than those of the others. But the reader will immediately experience differing reactions in reading each essay. Some of them will seem more persuasive, others less so. Some are moving; others appeal primarily to the rational side. It is in this way that, without particular disturbance and yet inevitably, not only a rational but also an 'aesthetic competition' is played out among alternative theories. We might note that this competition is an integrated one in that both symbolic and pre-symbolic factors are incorporated, but always within the realm of language.

Furthermore, in considering: (1) the eclectic idea of a non-antagonistic, pure difference among models, without the criterion of greater or less adequacy (an acritical relativism); (2) an authoritarian, dogmatic, or ecclesiastical position (which implies only one and absolute truth); and (3) the human, 'intermediate' conception that I am advocating here – each of these can be seen as nothing else than a legitimate rhetorical tool in this competition.

Truth in psychoanalysis has always been relevant and remains so. I maintain that it is not useful to complain about the excessive number of models, as though one could establish a central authority to regulate what is in the official canon and what is not – a sort of Congregation for the Doctrine of Faith of the Catholic Church.[16] The competition among different psychoanalytic theories is always in process, has already been happening; it *is* happening now, here, through the dialogue offered by *The Psychoanalytic Quarterly* on the topic of truth in psychoanalysis. If one allows time to do its work, gradually, the new paradigm will be clearly delineated.

I repeat: if we try to carefully consider and think out our truths, to consider how we reach them in various areas of our experience of life, we see that the only secure basis lies in *socialization*.[17] Through socialization, we learn to *be* in a certain way, to reason in a certain way, to use specific principles of logic. Above and below this ground level endowed by our own life forms, and preliminary to any prescientific and scientific understanding of things, there is nothing more secure unless one wants to trust in metaphysical solutions. The truth cannot all be said because, at least in part, it is the same as living. We live our truth, and this truth can 'become', but not be said or said only in part. Our more sophisticated and higher-level truths submerge their obscure origins in criteria of the self-organizing livability of biological systems.

Truth, so to speak, coincides with *being*. Ideas are a part of this being, but not only ideas. As analysts, even if we are concerned with truths manifested in the body, with truths that are transmitted by emotions, it is as though we have a nostalgic wish to translate everything into perfectly logical linguistic formulas. But for us, the sense and not only the meaning is important. Wittgenstein's (1984, p. 36) exhortation 'let us be human' is an invitation to accept our finite nature and to give up wanting to have a divine point of view on things.

When all is said and done, what we do has meaning only within a certain context of norms shared by a larger or smaller social group. We cannot move beyond our linguistic games. Psychoanalysis is one of these games (Bion (1965) referred to *a psychoanalytic game*), but one can say the same of a physics experiment or of a *Lectura Dantis*.[18] However, there is nothing like an *Ur*-game that excuses us from the rules of various other games. It happens that there is no attainable ultimate truth from which to derive all the principles of our rationality, just as it is not at all true that our way of being permits us to play any game, as would be affirmed by those who fear absolute relativism. We follow these rules almost (but not entirely) *blindly*. We can play infinite games, but not *all* games, and we really do not know why. There are limits to what we can know, and one of the consequences is that we can only live with truths based on a *groundless ground* and not on a *grounded ground* (Braver, 2014). We cannot enter into the world if not through language, but we cannot use language to surpass language.

A new common ground

If we embrace the point of view expressed here, we benefit on many fronts: on the one hand, there is a significant reduction of tension both between the two terms of the hermeneutic/scientific dichotomy, to the point of making it appear false, and among different models. On the other, in drawing on modern principles of epistemology and finding in various models some shared elements along the immediacy–truth and truth-as-unison axes, we gain the possibility of identifying what might be a new common ground for psychoanalysis.

In regard to the first point – that is, relationships with the other sciences – even if psychoanalysis remains amphibious, a hybrid, both artistic and scientific, an art in the middle zone (Civitarese, 2012c), it should not be seen as in the middle between science and non-science. One could say, however, that it lies between a knowledge of simple objects and a knowledge of hyper-complex objects (of course, in practical matters we would retain more pragmatic distinctions[19]).

By contrast, in regard to the relationships between theory and different psychoanalytic models, it would follow that recognizing there is no 'transcendental' method for deciding if one psychoanalytic theory is better than another, and thus a renouncement of any dogmatism, there is no renouncement of competition in the area of the treatment of psychic suffering. Each theory plays a different linguistic game, but not all psychoanalytic games are equally effective. Each of them struggles with the others to proclaim itself the most valid. How a model develops and comes to prevail over another cannot be fully thematized – that is, it cannot be expressed in words, because factors other than those of semantic communication (emotional, aesthetic, cultural, etc.) enter into the game. The criterion of truth becomes in some way aesthetic, which does not at all mean *arbitrary*, but simply that it takes account of the existence of aspects that are not translatable into words.[20]

A third point is that we would have a theory that permits us to respond more easily to queries such as that posed by Levine about the . . . paradox of (ill-)timing and *après-coup* – that a factually correct intervention may interrupt analytic process and psychic growth, while a well-meaning but incorrect (false) interpretation may lead to a new experience or new thought that opens the mind to true discovery (p. 402).

What can we say about this? That perhaps the intervention was correct on the level of content, but not on the 'aesthetic' one in the first case, and vice versa in the second. Also, perhaps the 'aesthetic' correctness predominates over that of the content. Truth is relevant in psychoanalysis because at this point it appears to us as another name for unison/*at-one-ment*/meeting of minds/dyadic expansion of consciousness (Stern *et al.*, 1998; Morgan *et al.*, 1998) – that is, because it assumes an intensely *social* flavour. It is no longer limited to some contents of truth, but begins from an agreement of minds that gradually interweaves liveable contents. In addition, and more readily, we would include within psychoanalysis the approaches that explore what Bion defined as the *inaccessible unconscious* (Civitarese, 2013d).

In coming now to the topic of the common ground, we have arrived at the point that the paradigm of psychoanalysis can be either evidentiary (the search for the *thing*) or aesthetic (the development of the *how*). In the second case, the truth in question can be defined as emotional or aesthetic. Bion is the author who most clearly theorized and carried out the passage from *thing* to *how*. But what we have seen is that this passage is evident in all the papers in this issue of *The Psychoanalytic Quarterly*, and in Blass's reading of the Freudian–Kleinian model, it is interesting to see that the tendency had already begun with Freud.

From truth-as-content, one moves to the process of arriving at feeling oneself to be real and *true*. It is not as important to recuperate certain contents relative to the past, but to develop a new ability to think – in short, to proceed in step with the other. If it is true that the investigation of contents and the development of the capacity to think are not at all in opposition, it is also true that, hierarchically, we have ended up prioritizing the former, and the theoretical challenge is now to arrive at a clarification of how much of the cognitive resides in the semiotic or non-verbal, and how one can develop the mind by beginning from the music of the relationship, *before* words.

What we need is a well-articulated theory that, as I have tried to outline here, succeeds in locating some essential points in relation to each other:

- A certain idea of truth as the name that we give to what intrinsically develops the psyche in that it corresponds to unison (intersubjective agreement), which at birth (or in analysis with respect to still unborn and regressed parts of the mind in the immediacy of the here and now) transforms the disorder into order and the multiplicity into the abstract – which generates, that is, not only logical concepts or ideas, but also non-verbal/emotional 'concepts'. This idea of truth involves transcending an overly rigid caesura between the representational and the non-representational.
- The possibility of tracing a continuum between this truth-as-unison and the human truth as consensual truth and linguistic game – that is, a theory of emotional truth that can also bear up to a close epistemological examination.
- A strong conception of language as that which forms the basis of the subject and so of the unconscious not as something given at birth, but rather that is acquired from the object (from sociality). In reading the various essays, more than by their differences, I was struck by some common elements, in fact, and in particular by the structuralization of progressively more effective tools in making *immediacy* a key parameter with which to arrive at something true. I was also impressed by the emphasis on the *process* in all the papers, and by the 'skeptical' dimension in relation to the idea of an absolute truth. In this respect, both philosophy and psychoanalysis, in a parallel and ever more radical way, have followed the path of returning to the things themselves. Even in the exact sciences, one could say that technological progress has allowed researchers to embrace the phenomena that were earlier too distant or infinitely small, in a way that makes it possible to observe them while leaving all the rest between parentheses.

In fact, the interpretation of transference is indeed directed towards reconstructing the past and revealing contents, but it also *indirectly* establishes a criterion of immediacy because, with the rhetorical arrangement of the metalepsis, it powerfully draws our attention to the here and now (Civitarese, 2007b). The same is true of systematic interpretation of unconscious fantasy in the Kleinian model and of enactment in the interpersonalist one. The most recent version of psychoanalytic *epoché* can be found in the post-Bionian model of the analytic field and the session viewed as a dream, in which we really try to bring in a totally new view of the facts of the analysis and to carry out the most extreme exercise of hermeneutic phenomenology of the unconscious that I know of. In particular, the field model embraces a criterion of radical immanence because it places between parentheses the question of how things really happened and how they happen outside, in order to increase the chance of truly intuiting what is going on in the here and now on a deep emotional level.

But this is nothing other than the more rigorous result that the application of the principle of the philosophical method, of linking truth with immediacy, is having in psychoanalysis. It is obvious that, on these premises, if the truth–immediacy and truth–unison connections become the abscissa and the ordinate with which to frame the various approaches in the discipline of psychoanalysis, it would be a great deal easier to identify the minimum common denominator of the various psychoanalytic models, and one could not only start out from infinite and abstract discussions about truth, but these would also come to be grounded in a fertile theoretical and technical conception in clinical work.

It is also true that we need to acknowledge Bion for having had this fundamental intuition of wanting to reform the basis of psychoanalysis by starting from a rigorous phenomenological principle, which he then translated into formulas such as *transcending the caesura*, *the truth drive*, and *without memory, desire, and understanding*, etc. Perhaps only with Bion are we truly able to descend from the abstraction of the concept of truth (even when we intend it as the obvious handmaiden of reality), to that of emotional truth as a proto-concept and the foundation of the individual mind, starting from the meeting with another mind. Thanks to his contribution to thinking, contemporary psychoanalysis is not only in perfect harmony with the state of the art of modern epistemology; it can also contribute to epistemology itself in an essential way, making available its *own* theoretical–clinical method of research with which to clarify how the prescientific understanding of the world is formed on the collective level – the same level on which even the scientific understanding of things cannot fail to be built.

Notes

1 First, for example, is the tool of transference interpretations, and then that of unconscious fantasy, of enactment, the metaphors of the intersubjective third and of the analytic field, and so on. See Davies's comment in her paper: 'The very statement implicit in any moving interpretation, that "I think I understand something about you that you may not yet understand or see in yourself", is penetrating in that it puts the analyst at the core of the patient's most hidden selves' (p. 383).

2 See Husserl: 'We want to go back to the "things themselves"' (1900, p. 168).

3 In passing, it seems important to share an implicit aspect of this point of view: that one must attempt, in an atmosphere of mutual respect, to discuss which theory or which technique permits us to better frame our problems and seems to us to be *more effective* in treating psychic suffering. It seems banal to repeat it, but not everyone would accept such a 'truth', perhaps because they are too worried about sinking back into the climate of 'theological' disputes that have marked the history of psychoanalysis. This would indeed be a position of absolute relativism: admitting the difference, but considering the comparison unwarranted.

4 See the distinction made by Allison and Fonagy (2016) between pathologies of representation and pathologies of psychic processes.

5 Consider Bion's comment: 'Thus, if the content is Oedipal material, I do not concern myself with this, but with the transformation it has undergone, the stage of growth it reveals, and the use to which its communication is being put' (1965, p. 35).

6 This in contrast is the typical position of the Lacanian analyst, who on the one hand denies identifying himself as the subject who is supposed to know, and on the other remains the absolute master of the situation.

7 Blass expresses something similar when she speaks of two unconscious tendencies that coexist and come to know each other, so to speak; they become integrated and are overall beyond awareness.

8 *Translator's Note:* 'Epimenides was a Cretan who made one immortal statement: "All Cretans are liars." A paradox of self-reference arises when one considers whether it is possible for Epimenides to have spoken the truth' (https://en.wikipedia.org/wiki/Epimenides_paradox).

9 For example, in Davies's paper, we find the terms *faith, play therapy, transitional space, characters* and *field*.

10 Allison and Fonagy see *ostensive cues* as the offer of clear communicative signals. Framed in this way, the concept seems cold and mechanical, but later on the authors allow the idea to slip out that this is a 'loving and caring' (p. 291) attitude.

11 The word *table*, for example, means nothing in itself if it is not in opposition to all the other words and terms that a language is composed of.

12 'Every word immediately becomes a concept, draining away with its pallid universality the differences between fundamentally unequal things' (Eco, 2002).

13 'In phenomenological research, *epoché* is described as a process involved in blocking biases and assumptions in order to explain a phenomenon in terms of its own inherent system of meaning. One actual technique is known as bracketing. This involves systematic steps to "set aside" various assumptions and beliefs about a phenomenon in order to examine how the phenomenon presents itself in the world of the participant' (https://en.wikipedia.org/wiki/Epoché).

14 *Translator's Note:* In Italian, both *mente* (mind) and *menzogna* (lie) derive from the late Latin *mens*, meaning 'mind, reason, intellect'. *Persona* (person) derives from the Etruscan word *phersu*, meaning 'mask'.

15 Wittgenstein (1984) wrote that what belongs to a language game is a whole culture.

16 *Translator's Note:* As many readers will know, this is the body responsible for promulgating and defending Catholic doctrine.

17 'We never explicitly learned our world-view but swallowed it down in the process of socialization . . . This is not a choice but a matter of finding oneself magnetically oriented towards asking certain kinds of questions and accepting certain kinds of answers, which is why Heidegger defines thinking as responding . . . Wittgenstein speaks of "conversion," "persuasion," or "combat" among language-games' (Braver, 2014, pp. 199, 203).

18 *Translator's Note:* The Latin expression *Lectura Dantis* is used in Italian to refer to the reading out loud or public recitation of the works of Dante, and in particular of the verses of his *Divine Comedy* (Dante Alighieri, 1320).

19 One thinks of the field of economics and of the equal level of uncertainty about its scientific nature, even though, alone among the social sciences, it has the privilege of the award of the Nobel Prize.

20 Bion (1965) gave two different versions of a clinical report. The first was more factual, verbally exact, almost a mechanical recording, but the second, which was very detailed – and, we might say, artificial – sounded much more 'true'.

References

Abraham K (1924). A short study of the development of the libido, viewed in the light of mental disorders. In *Selected papers on psycho-analysis*, transl. D Bryan and A Strachey. London: Hogarth Press/Institute of Psychoanalysis, 1973, pp. 418–501.

Agamben G (1994). *L'uomo senza contenuto*. Macerata, Italy: Quodlibet.

Agamben G (2014). *Il fuoco e il racconto*. Rome: Nottetempo.

Aho KA (2009). *Heidegger's neglect of the body*. New York: State University of New York Press.

Alexander F (1950). Analysis of the therapeutic factors in psychoanalytic treatment. *Psychoanalytic Quarterly*, 19: 482–500.

Allison E and Fonagy P (2016). When is truth relevant? *Psychoanalytic Quarterly*, 85: 275–303.

Amoroso L (2014). *Schiller e la parabola dell'estetica*. Pisa, Italy: ETS.

André J (2005). Les sublimations, finalités sans fin. *Revue française de psychanalyse*, 69: 1475–1483.

Arensberg M, (ed.) (1986). *The American sublime*. New York: SUNY Press.

Aulagnier P (1975). *The violence of interpretation: from pictogram to statement*, transl. A Sheridan. Hove, UK: Brunner-Routledge, 2001.

Baldacci JL (2005). 'Dès le debut' . . . la sublimation? *Revue française de psychanalyse*, 69: 1405–1474.

Barile E (2013). *Pensare Damasio. Due o tre cose che so di lui*. Milan, Italy: FrancoAngeli.

Barthes R (2007). *Il discorso amoroso: Seminario a l'École Pratique des Hautes Études 1974–1776, seguito da Frammenti di un discorso amoroso (inediti)*. Milan-Udine, Italy: Mimesis.

Barthes R (2015). *Le Neutre: Cours et séminaires au Collège de France (1977–1978)*. Paris: Seuil.

Berger H (2000). *Fictions of the pose: Rembrandt against the Italian renaissance*. Stanford, CA: Stanford University Press.

Berliner B (1958). The role of object relations in moral masochism. *Psychoanalytic Quarterly*, 27: 38–56.

Bion WR (1959). Attacks on linking. *International Journal of Psychoanalysis*, 40: 308–315.

Bion WR (1962). *Learning from experience*. London: Tavistock.

Bion WR (1965). *Transformations: change from learning to growth*. London: Heinemann.

Bion WR (1967). *Second thoughts: selected papers of psychoanalysis*. London: Heinemann.

Bion WR (1970). *Attention and interpretation*. London: Tavistock.

Bion WR (1975). *A memoir of the future*. London/New York: Karnac, 1991.

Bion WR (1977a). The past presented. In *A memoir of the future*, London: Karnac, 1991, pp. 219–426.

Bion WR (1977b). Caesura. In *Two papers: the grid and caesura*. London: Karnac, pp. 35–56, 1989.

Bion WR (1992). *Cogitations*. London: Karnac.

Bion WR (1997). *Taming wild thoughts*. London: Karnac.

Blass RB (2011). On the immediacy of unconscious truth: understanding Betty Joseph's 'here and now' through comparison with alternative views of it outside of and within Kleinian thinking. *International Journal of Psychoanalysis*, 92: 1137–1157.

Blass RB (2016). The quest for truth as the foundation of psychoanalytic practice: a traditional Freudian–Kleinian perspective. *Psychoanalytic Quarterly*, 85: 305–337.

Bléandonu G (1990). *Wilfred R. Bion: his life and works (1897–1979)*. London: Free Association, 1994.

Bloom H (1982). Freud and the sublime: a catastrophe theory of creativity. In *Agon: towards a theory of revisionism*, New York: Oxford University Press, pp. 91–118.

Blum HP (2004). Beneath and beyond the 'Formulations on the two principles of mental functioning'. *Psychoanalytic Study of the Child*, 59: 240–257.

Bodei R (2008). *Paesaggi sublimi. Gli uomini davanti alla natura selvaggia*. Milan, Italy: Bompiani.

Boitani P (2014). *Riconoscere è un dio. Scene e temi del riconoscimento nella letteratura*. Turin, Italy: Einaudi.

Botella C and Botella S (2001). *The work of pshychic figurability: mental states without representation*. London: Routledge.

Bottiroli G (2015). La possibilità di non-coincidere con se stessi: una lettura di Heidegger come pensatore modale. *Rivista di psicoanalisi*, 61: 963–983.

Braver L (2014). *Groundless grounds: a study of Wittgenstein and Heidegger*. Cambridge, MA: The MIT Press.

Brown LJ (2011). *Intersubjective processes and the unconscious: an integration of Freudian, Kleinian and Bionian perspective*. London: Routledge.

Burke E (1756a). *A philosophical enquiry into the origin of our ideas of the sublime and beautiful*. London: Penguin, 1998.

Burke E (1756b). *On the sublime and beautiful*. (Vol. XXIV, Part 2.) P.F. Collier and Son, 1909–14; Bartleby.com, 2001. New York: The Harvard Classics.

Busch F (2016). The search for psychic truths. *Psychoanalytic Quarterly*, 85: 339–360.

Calvino I (1998). *Our ancestors: the cloven viscount, the baron in the trees, the nonexistent knight*, transl. A Colquhoun. London: Vintage.

Carbone M (2008). *Proust et les idées sensibles*. Paris: Vrin.

Carbone M (2011). *Amore e musica. Tema e variazioni*. Milan, Italy: Mimesis.

Celenza A (2013). Maternal erotic transference and merger wishes. *Rivista di Psicoanalisi*, 59: 821–838.

Chantraine P (1999). *Dictionnaire étymologique de la langue grecque: histoire des mots*. Paris: Klincksieck.

Chasseguet-Smirgel J (1993). Auto-sadism, eating disorders and femininity: reflections based on case studies of adult women who experienced eating disorders as adolescents. In *Essential papers on masochism*. MA Fitzpatrick Hanly (ed.). New York: NYU Press, 1995, pp. 453–470.

Chemama R and Vandermersch B (1998). *Dizionario di psicoanalisi*. Rome: Gremese, 2004.

Chetrit-Vatine V (2012). *The ethical seduction of the analytic situation: the feminine-maternal origins of responsibility for the other*, transl. A Weller. London: Karnac, 2014.

Cimatti F (2015). *Perché l'essere umano non può essere come un lombrico? Wilfred Bion e il transindividuale*. Available at http://riviste.unimi.it/index.php/noema/article/viewFile/4683/4883.

Civitarese G (2004). Simbiotic bond and the setting. *Rivista di Psicoanalisi*, 51: 1117–1147; and in *The intimate room: theory and technique of the analytic field*. London: Routledge, 2010, pp. 22–49.

Civitarese G (2007a). More affects . . . more eyes: on postmodern issues and deconstruction(s) in psychoanalysis. In *The intimate room: theory and technique of the analytic field*. London: Routledge, 2010, pp. 155–179.

Civitarese G (2007b). Metalepsis or the rhetoric of transference interpretation. *Rivista di Psicoanalisi*. 53: 5–28.

Civitarese G (2008a). 'Caesura' as Bion's discourse on method. *International Journal of Psychoanalysis*, 89: 1123–1143.

Civitarese G (2008b). Immersion versus interactivity and analytic field. *International Journal of Psychoanalysis*, 89: 279–298.

Civitarese G (2010). *The intimate room: theory and technique of the analytic field*. London: Routledge.

Civitarese G (2011a). Aesthetic conflict and the alpha function. In *The violence of emotions: Bion and post-Bionian psychoanalysis*. London: Routledge, 2013.

Civitarese G (2011b). Exploring core concepts: sexuality, dreams and the unconscious. *International Journal of Psychoanalysis*, 92: 277–280.

Civitarese G (2012a). *Losing your head: abjection, aesthetic conflict and psychoanalytic criticism*. Lanham, MD: Rowman & Littlefield, 2015.

Civitarese G (2012b). L'argent di Robert Bresson e la redenzione dello stile. Available at http://stateofmind.it/2012/07/largent-di-robert-bresson-la-redenzione-dello-stile/.

Civitarese G (2012c). Intermediarity as an epistemological paradigm in psychoanalysis. In *Truth and the unconscious in psychoanalysis*. London: Routledge, 2016, pp. 174–191.

Civitarese G (2013a). The grid and the truth drive. *Italian Psychoanalytic Annual*, 7: 91–114.

Civitarese G (2013b). L'envers de penser: Bion et la théorie des psychoses. *Psychanalyse et Psychose*, 13: 109–120.

Civitarese G (2013c). Poésie du rêve et depersonnalisation. *Revue françcise de psychanalyse*, 77: 1066–1081.

Civitarese G (2013d). The inaccessible unconscious and reverie as a path of figurability. In *Unrepresented states and the construction of meaning: clinical and theoretical contributions*. HB Levine, D Scarfone and GS Reed (eds), London: Karnac, pp. 220–239.

Civitarese G (2014a). *Truth and the unconscious in psychoanalysis*. London: Routledge, 2016.

Civitarese G (2014b). Bion and the sublime: the origins of an aesthetic paradigm. *International Journal of Psychoanalysis*, 95: 1059–1086.

Civitarese G (2014c). Transformations in hallucinosis and the receptivity of the analyst. *International Journal of Psychoanalysis*, 96: 1091–1116.

Civitarese G (2015). Transformations in hallucinosis and the receptivity of the analyst. *International Journal of Psychoanalysis*, 96: 1091–1116.

Civitarese, G (2016a). Truth as immediacy and unison: a new 'common ground' in psychoanalysis? Commentary on essays addressing 'Is truth relevant?' *Psychoanalytic Quarterly*, 85: 449–501.

Civitarese G (2016b). On sublimation. *International Journal of Psychoanalysis*, 97: 1369–1392.

Civitarese G, (ed.) (2017a). *Bion and contemporary psychoanalysis: reading 'A memoir of the future'*. London: Routledge.

Civitarese G (2017b). *Trasposizioni. Glossarietto di psicoanalisi.* Milan–Udine, Italy: Mimesis.

Civitarese G, Marinelli S and Hinshelwood RD (eds) (2014). A memoir of the future. Funzionegamma.it 33. Available at http://funzionegamma.it/category/issues/number33/.

Civitarese G, Katz M and Tubert-Oklander J, (eds) (2015). Postmodernism and psychoanalysis. *Psychoanalytic Inquiry*, 35: 559–662.

Coleridge ST (1817). *Biographia literaria, or, biographical sketches of my literary life and opinions*, Princeton. NJ: Princeton University Press, 1984.

Conrotto F (2004). La sublimazione nella cura e nella teoria. *Rivista di Psicoanalisi*, 50: 1027–1048.

Cuaron A, (Producer and Director) (2013). *Gravity* [Motion Picture]. Hollywood, CA: Warner Bros.

Dante Alighieri (1320). *La divina commedia*. Milan, Italy: Edizioni San Paolo, 1985.

Davies JM (2016). The man who would be everything (to everyone): the unconscious realities and fantasies of psychic truth and change. *Psychoanalytic Quarterly*, 85: 361–389.

De Mijolla A (2005). *International dictionary of psychoanalysis: G–Pr* (Vol. 2). London: Macmillan Reference Library.

Derrida J (1978). *The truth in painting*. Chicago, IL: University of Chicago Press, 1987.

Derrida J (1980). *The post card, from Socrates to Freud and beyond*, transl. A Bass. Chicago, IL: University of Chicago Press, 1987.

Derrida J (1990). *Who's afraid of philosophy? Right to philosophy* (Vol. 1), transl. J Plug. Stanford, CA: Stanford University Press, 2002.

Derrida J (1994). *The politics of friendship*. London: Verso, 2005.

Derrida J and Defourmantelle A (1997). *Of hospitality*, transl. R Bowlby. Stanford, CA: Stanford University Press, 2000.

Eco U (2002). Some remarks on a new realism. Paper presented at Twenty-Third World Congress of Philosophy, August 2013, Athens.

Eco U (2007). *Inventing the enemy*, transl. R Dixon. Boston, MA/New York: Houghton Mifflin Harcourt, 2012.

Ellison R (1952). *The invisible man*. New York: Random House, 1980.

Esposito R (2014). *Le persone e le cose* [*Persons and things*]. Turin, Italy: Einaudi.

Falzeder E and Brabant E (eds) (1996). *The correspondence of Sigmund Freud and Sándor Ferenczi, 2: 1914–1919*. Cambridge, MA: Harvard University Press.

Fante J (1939). *Ask the dust*. New York: Harper Perennial Modern Classics, 2006.

Ferenczi S (1915). The ontogenesis of symbols. *Psychoanalytic Review*, 2: 106.

Ferro A (2002). *Seeds of illness, seeds of recovery: the genesis of suffering and the role of psychoanalysis*, transl. P Slotkin. Hove, UK/New York: Brunner Routledge, 2004.

Ferro A and Civitarese G (2013). Analyst in search of an author: Voltaire or Artemisia Gentileschi? Commentary on 'Field theory in psychoanalysis, part II: Bionian field theory and contemporary interpersonal/relational psychoanalysis', by DB Stern. *Psychoanalytic Dialogues*, 23: 646–653.

Ferro A and Civitarese G (2015). *The analytic field and its transformations*. London: Karnac.

Ferro A and Civitarese G (2017). *Un invito alla psicoanalisi*. Rome: Carocci.

Fornari F (1977). I processi di simbolizzazione tra mondo interno e mondo esterno. *Rivista di Psicoanalisi*, 23: 44–62.
Fornaro M (1990). *Psiconalisi tra scienza e mistica, L'opera di Wilfred R. Bion*. Rome: Studium.
Foucault M (1963). *The birth of the clinic*. London: Tavistock, 1973.
Freud EL (ed.) (1961). *Letters of Sigmund Freud 1873–1939*, transl. TJ Stern. London: Hogarth.
Freud S (1895). Project for a scientific psychology. *SE*, 1: 281–391.
Freud S (1900). The interpretation of dreams. *SE*, 4–5.
Freud S (1901a). Fragment of an analysis of a case of hysteria (*Dora*). *SE*, 7: 1–122.
Freud S (1901b). On dreams. *SE* 5:629–686
Freud S (1905). Three essays on the theory of sexuality. *SE*, 7: 125–248.
Freud S (1910a). Five lectures on psycho-analysis. *SE*, 10: 1–56.
Freud S (1910b). The future prospects of psycho-analytic therapy. *SE*, 11: 139–152.
Freud S (1911). Formulations on the two principles of mental functioning. *SE*, 12: 213–226.
Freud S (1914). On narcissism: an introduction. *SE*, 14: 73–102.
Freud S (1917). A metapsychological supplement to the theory of dreams. *SE*, 14: 217–236.
Freud S (1918). From the history of an infantile neurosis. *SE*, 17: 1–123.
Freud S (1919a). The 'uncanny'. *SE*, 17: 217–256.
Freud S (1919b). 'A child is being beaten': a contribution to the study of the origin of sexual perversions. *SE*, 17: 179–204.
Freud S (1920). Beyond the pleasure principle. *SE*, 18: 1–64.
Freud S (1921). Group psychology and the analysis of the ego. *SE*, 18: 65–144.
Freud S (1923). The ego and the id. *SE*, 19: 12–66.
Freud S (1924). The economic problem of masochism. *SE*, 19: 159–170.
Freud S (1930). Civilization and its discontents. *SE*, 21: 57–146.
Freud S (1985). Letter from Freud to Fliess, 2nd May, 1897. In *The complete letters of Sigmund Freud to Wilhelm Fliess, 1887–1904*, JM Masson (ed.). Cambridge, MA: The Belknap Press of Harvard University Press, pp. 207–214.
Freud S and Andreas-Salomé L (1966). *Letters*, E Pfeiffer (ed.). W Robson-Scott, transl. E Robson-Scott, London: Hogarth, 1972.
Freud S and Jung CG (1974). *The Freud/Jung letters: the correspondence between Sigmund Freud and C. G. Jung*. W McGuire (ed.). Princeton, NJ: Princeton University Press.
Gaddini E (1982). Early defensive fantasies and the psychoanalytical process. *International Journal of Psychoanalysis*, 63: 379–388.
Gaetano R (2002). *Giacomo Leopardi e il sublime. Archeologia e percorsi di una idea estetica*. Soveria Mannelli, Italy: Rubbettino.
Genette G (1982). *Palimpsests: literature in the second degree*, transl. C Newman and C Doubinsky. Lincoln, NE: University of Nebraska Press, 1997.
Genette G (1987). *Paratexts: thresholds of interpretation*. Cambridge, UK: Cambridge University Press, 1997.
Genovese C (1995). Presentazione di cosa e forme autoprodotte nella situazione analitica. *Rivista di Psicoanalisi*, 41: 45–64.
Ginzburg C (1979). Morelli, Freud and Sherlock Holmes: clues and scientific method. In *The sign of three: Dupin, Holmes, Peirce*, U Eco and T Sebeok (eds). Bloomington, IN: Indiana University Press, pp. 81–118, 1988.
Girard M (2010). Winnicott's foundation for the basic concepts of Freud's metapsychology? *International Journal of Psychoanalysis*, 91: 305–324.

Glick RA and Meyers DI (2013). *Masochism: current psychoanalytic perspectives*. London: Routledge.

Grotstein J S (2007). *A beam of intense darkness: Wilfred Bion's legacy to psychoanalysis*. London: Karnac.

Grotstein J (2008). The play's the thing wherein I'll catch the conscience of the king! Psychoanalysis as a passion play. In *The analytic field: a clinical concept*. A Ferro and R Basile (eds). London: Karnac.

Grube GMA (1957). *Longinus: on great writing (on the sublime)*. New York: Liberal Arts Press.

Guidorizzi G (1991). Introduzione. In *Anonimo, Il sublime*. Milan: Mondadori. pp. 5–25.

Harris Williams M (2010a). *The aesthetic development: the poetic spirit of psychoanalysis: essays on Bion, Meltzer, Keats*. London: Karnac.

Harris Williams M (2010b). *Bion's dream: a reading of the autobiographies*. London: Karnac.

Heidegger M (1927). *Being and time*. Albany: SUNY Press, 2010.

Heidegger M (1977). *Phenomenological interpretation of Kant's critique of pure reason*. Bloomington, IN: Indiana University Press, 1997.

Heidegger M (1983). *The fundamental concepts of metaphysics: world, finitude, solitude*. Bloomington, IN: Indiana University Press.

Heidegger M (2009). *Pensieri–guida: Sulla nascita della metafisica, della scienza contemporanea e della tecnica moderna*, transl. T Scappini. Milan, Italy: Bompiani, 2014.

Hertz N (1985). *The end of the line*. Aurora, CO: Davies Group.

Holtzman D and Kulish N (2012). *The clinical problem of masochism*. Lanham, MD: Aronson.

Husserl E (1900). *Logical investigations*, transl. N Findlay. London: Routledge, 2001.

Joyce J (1939). *Finnegan's wake*. London: Penguin, 1992.

Kant I (1763–1764). *Observations on the feeling of the beautiful and the sublime*. Oakland, CA: University of California, 1960.

Kant I (1781). *The critique of pure reason*, transl. JME Meiklejohn. Seattle, WA: Pacific Publishing Studio, 2011.

Kant I (1790). *The critique of judgement*. Radford, VA: Wilder Books, 2008.

Kirby V (1997). *Telling flesh: the substance of the corporeal*. London: Routledge.

Klein M (1930). The importance of symbol-formation in the development of the ego. *International Journal of Psychoanalysis*, 11: 24–39.

Kristeva J (1974). *Revolution in poetic language*. New York: Columbia University Press, 1984.

Kristeva J (1980). *Desire in language: a semiotic approach to literature and art*. New York: Columbia University Press.

Kristeva J (1982). *Powers of horror* (Vol. 98). New York: Columbia University Press.

Kristeva J (2005). L'impudence d'énoncer: la langue maternelle. *Revue française de psychanalyse*, 69: 1655–1667.

Kuhn TS (1962). *The structure of scientific revolutions*. Chicago, IL: University of Chicago Press, 1996.

Kurosawa A (director) (1950). *Rashomon* [Motion Picture]. Japan: Daiei Film.

Lacan J (1966). *Écrits: the first complete edition in English*, transl. B Fink. New York: Norton, 2006.

Lanfredini R (ed.) (2011). *Divenire di Merleau-Ponty. Filosofia di un soggetto incarnato*. Milan, Italy: Guerini e Associati.

Laplanche J (1980). *Problematiche III - La Sublimazione*. Bari–Rome, Italy: La Biblioteca, 2001.

Laplanche J (2004). Tre accezioni del termine 'inconscio' nella cornice della Teoria della Seduzione Generalizzata. *Rivista di Psicoanalyisi*, 50: 11–26.

Laplanche J and Pontalis JB (1980). *The language of psychoanalysis*. London: Karnac.

Le Guen C (2008). *Dictionnaire Freudien*. Paris: PUF.

Lemma A (2013). Whose skin is it anyway? Some reflections on the psychic function of necrophilic fantasies. *Rivista di Psicoanalisi*, 59: 283–304.

Leopardi G (2013[1898–1900]). *Zibaldone: the notebooks of Leopardi*. London: Penguin.

Levine HB (2016). Psychoanalysis and the problem of truth. *Psychoanalytic Quarterly*, 85: 391–409.

Levine HB and Civitarese G (2015). *The W. R. Bion tradition*. London: Karnac.

Loewald HW (1988). *Sublimation: inquiries into theoretical psychoanalysis*. New Haven, CT: Yale University Press.

Loewenstein RM (1957). A contribution to a psychoanalytic theory of masochism. In *Essential papers on masochism*. MA Fitzpatrick Hanly (ed.). New York: NYU Press, pp. 35–61, 1995.

Lombardi R (2012). Il corpo nella teoria della mente di Wilfred R. Bion. Available at: http://consecutio.org/2012/02/il-corpo-nella-teoria-della-mente-di-wilfred-r-bion/.

Longhurst R (2001). *Bodies: exploring fluid boundaries*. London: Routledge.

Longinus D (2008). *On the sublime*. Alcester, UK: Read Books.

Lyotard J-F (1979). *The postmodern condition: a report on knowledge*. Minneapolis, MN: University of Minnesota Press, 1984.

Lyotard J-F (1984). L'istante. In B Newman, *Il sublime, adesso*, Milan, Italy: Abscondita, pp. 47–62, 2010.

Lyotard J-F (1991). *Lessons on the analytic of the sublime*. Stanford, CA: Stanford University Press, 1994.

Markman, H (2012). Varieties of masochistic experience: modes of analytic relating. In *The clinical problem of masochism*, D Holtzman and N Kulish (eds). Lanham, MD: Aronson, pp. 129–144.

Meltzer D (1973). *The apprehension of beauty*. Strathtay, Scotland: Clunie Press, 1988.

Meltzer D (1984). *Dream-life: a re-examination of the psycho-analytical theory and technique*. Strathtay, Scotland: Clunie Press.

Meltzer D and Harris Williams M (1988). *Amore e timore della bellezza. Il ruolo del conflitto estetico nello sviluppo, nell'arte e nella violenza*. Rome: Borla, 1989.

Merleau-Ponty M (1945). *Phenomenology of perception*. London: Routledge, 2002.

Merleau-Ponty M (1960). *Signs*. Evanston, IL: Northwestern University Press, 1964.

Micotti S (2013). Personal communication.

Moore B and Fine DB (1990). *Psychoanalytic terms and concepts*. New Haven, CT: Yale University Press.

Moravia A (1998). L'Argent. In *Robert Bresson*, J Quandt (ed.). Toronto, Canada: Cinematheque Ontario Monographs, pp. 407–408.

Morgan AC, Bruschweiler-Stern N and Tronick EZ (1998). Noninterpretive mechanisms in psychoanalytic therapy: the 'something more' than interpretation. *International Journal of Psychoanalysis*, 79: 903–921.

Nancy J-L (2002). *Listening*. Milan, Italy: Raffaello Cortina, 2004.

Nietzsche F (2001). *The gay science*. Cambridge, UK: Cambridge University Press.

Ogden TH (1989). On the concept of an autistic-contiguous position. *International Journal of Psychoanalysis*, 70: 127–140.
Ogden TH (1994). The concept of interpretive action. *Psychoanalytic Quarterly*, 63: 219–245.
Ogden TH (1996). The perverse subject of analysis. *Journal of the American Psychoanalytic Association*, 44: 1121–1146.
Ogden TH (2003). On not being able to dream. *International Journal of Psychoanalysis*, 84: 17–30.
Ogden TH (2012). *Creative readings: essays on seminal analytic works*. London: Routledge.
Ogden TH (2014). Fear of breakdown and the unlived life. *International Journal of Psychoanalysis*, 95: 205–223.
Ogden TH (2016). On language and truth in psychoanalysis. *Psychoanalytic Quarterly*, 85: 411–426.
Oppo A (2011). 'Fancy' e 'imagination' in Coleridge. Una distinzione inattuale? Theologica & Historica. *Annali della Pontificia Facolta Teologica della Sardegna*, 20: 253–267.
Panella G (2012). *Storia del sublime*. Dallo Pseudo-Longino alle poetiche della modernità. Florence, Italy: Clinamen.
Pirandello L (1926). *One, no one and one hundred thousand*, transl. W Weaver. New York: Marsilio Publishers, 1992.
Proust M (2006). *The remembrance of things past* (Vol. II). Hertfordshire, UK: Wordsworth Editions.
Reitani L (2003). *Poetiche della caducità*. Afterword to Schiller, F (1793). SE, Milan, Italy: Del sublime, pp. 109–139.
Ricoeur P (1965). *Freud and philosophy: an essay on interpretation*, transl. D Savage. New Haven, CT: Yale University Press, 1977.
Rilke RM (1995). *Poesie II (1908–1926)*. Torino, Italy: Einaudi.
Rilke RM, (2005). *Duino elegies and the sonnets to Orpheus*, transl. A Poulin Jr. Boston, MA: Houghton Mifflin Harcourt.
Rimbaud A (1871). *A season in hell and illuminations*, transl. B Mathieu. Rochester, NY: Boa Editions, 1991.
Roth P (2008). *Indignation*. New York: Houghton Mifflin.
Roussillon R (2001). *Le plaisir et la répétition: théorie du processus psychique*. Paris: Dunod.
Roussillon R (2005). Le processus et la capacité sublimatoire. *Revue française de psychanalyse*, 69: 1565–1573.
Rulli R (2015). Intelligenza del sogno. In *Le parole e i sogni*, G De Giorgio and G Civitarese (eds). Rome: Alpes.
Sartre J-P (1965). *Being and nothingness*. New York: Open Road, 2011.
Schiller F (1793a). *The essays on the sublime*. CreativeSpace, 2013.
Schiller F (1793b). *Of the sublime toward the further elaboration of some Kantian ideas*, transl. D Platt. Washington DC: Schiller Institute, 2001. Available at www.schiller institute.org/transl/trans_essay.html#sublime.
Schiller F (1794). *The correspondence between Schiller and Goethe from 1794–1805*. London: Putnam, 1845; New York: Wiley.
Schiller F (1799). Nänie [Lament]. In *The Penguin Book of German Verse* (*German edn*), L Forster (ed.). London: Penguin Books, p. 242, 1959.
Sechaud E (2005). Perdre, sublimer. *Revue francise de psychanalyse*, 69: 1309–1379.

Sertoli G (2002). Introduzione. In E Burke (1796). *Inchiesta sul bello e il sublime.* G Miglietta and G Sertoli (eds). Palermo, Italy: Aesthetica edizioni, pp. 9–42.
Souter KM (2009). The war memoirs: some origins of the thought of W.R. Bion. *International Journal of Psychoanalysis*, 90: 795–808.
Steiner G (1978). *Martin Heidegger.* Chicago: University of Chicago Press, 1991.
Steiner J (2016). Illusion, disillusion and irony in psychoanalysis. *Psychoanalytic Quarterly*, 85: 427–447.
Stern DN *et al.* (1998). Dyadically expanded states of consciousness and the process of therapeutic change. *Enfant Mental Journal* 19: 290–299.
Szanto T and Moran D (2015). *The phenomenology of sociality: discovering the 'we'.* London: Routledge.
Szondi P (2007). *La poetica di Hegel.* Torino, Italy: Einaudi.
Terman DM (2014). Self psychology as a shift away from the paranoid strain in classical analytic theory. *Journal of the American Psychoanalytic Association*, 62: 1005–1024.
Tomasello M (2014). *Unicamente umano. Storia naturale del pensiero.* Bologna, Italy: Il Mulino.
Torres N and Hinshelwood RD (eds) (2013). *Bion's sources.* London: Routledge.
Tustin F (1972). *Autism and childhood psychosis.* London: Karnac.
Valenstein AF (1973). On attachment to painful feelings and the negative therapeutic reaction. *Psychoanalytic Study of the Child*, 28: 365–392.
Vitale S (2005). *La dimora della lontananza. Saggi sull'esperienza dello spazio intermedio.* Brescia, Italy: Moretti & Vitali.
Vozza M (2014). *Il nuovo infinito di Nietzsche. La futura obiettività tra arte e scienza.* Rome: Castelvecchi.
White K (2010). Notes on 'Bemächtigungstrieb' and Strachey's translation as 'instinct for mastery'. *International Journal of Psychoanalysis*, 91: 811–820.
Winnicott DW (1949). Birth memories, birth trauma and anxiety. In *Through paediatrics to psycho-analysis.* New York: Basic Books, pp. 174–193, 1975.
Winnicott DW (1955). Metapsychological and clinical aspects of regression within the psycho-analytical set-up. In *Through paediatrics to psycho-analysis.* New York: Basic Books, pp. 278–294, 1975.
Winnicott DW (1964). *The child, the family and the outside world.* London: Penguin.
Winnicott DW (1965). *The maturational processes and the facilitating environment: studies in the theory of emotional development.* London: Hogarth Press.
Winnicott DW (1989). Notes on play. In *Psychoanalytic explorations,* C Winnicott, R Shepherd and M Davis (eds). Cambridge, MA: Harvard University Press, pp. 59–63, 1992.
Wittgenstein L (1969). *On certainty.* New York: Harper & Row, 1972
Wittgenstein L (1984). *Culture and value*, transl. P Winch. Malden, MA: Wiley Blackwell, 1998.
Žižek S (1989). *The sublime object of ideology.* New York: Verso, 2009.
Žižek S (2000). *Il trash sublime.* Milan-Udine, Italy: Mimesis, 2013.

Index